The Economic Approach

The Economic Approach

Unpublished Writings of Gary S. Becker

Edited by
JULIO J. ELIAS, CASEY B. MULLIGAN,
AND KEVIN M. MURPHY

THE UNIVERSITY OF CHICAGO PRESS
CHICAGO AND LONDON

The University of Chicago Press, Chicago 60637
The University of Chicago Press, Ltd., London
© 2023 by The University of Chicago
Published 2023
Printed in the United States of America

32 31 30 29 28 27 26 25 24 23   2 3 4 5

ISBN-13: 978-0-226-82720-9 (cloth)
ISBN-13: 978-0-226-82721-6 (e-book)
DOI: https://doi.org/10.7208/chicago/9780226827216.001.0001

Library of Congress Cataloging-in-Publication Data
Names: Becker, Gary S. (Gary Stanley), 1930–2014, author. | Elias, Julio J.,
    (Economist), editor. | Mulligan, Casey B., editor. | Murphy, Kevin M., editor.
Title: The economic approach : unpublished writings of Gary S. Becker / edited by
    Julio J. Elias, Casey B. Mulligan, and Kevin M. Murphy.
Description: Chicago : The University of Chicago Press, 2023. | Includes
    bibliographical references and index.
Identifiers: LCCN 2022053757 | ISBN 9780226827209 (cloth) | ISBN 9780226827216
    (ebook)
Subjects: LCSH: Economics.
Classification: LCC HB171 .B335 2023 | DDC 330—dc23/eng/20230127
LC record available at https://lccn.loc.gov/2022053757

♾ This paper meets the requirements of ANSI/NISO Z39.48-1992 (Permanence of Paper).

Contents

Foreword by Edward Glaeser   *vii*

1. JUST THE BEGINNING   *1*

   Acceptance Speech at Bradley Award Ceremony, June 4, 2008   *5*

   The Spirit of the University of Chicago, September 14, 2010   *8*

2. ACCOUNTING FOR TASTES   *11*

   Preference Formation within Families, June 1992   *15*

   Rational Indoctrination and Persuasion, March 2001   *32*

   Some Notes on Drugs, Addiction, Families, and Public Policy,
   May 2000   *43*

   Promotion Tournaments, Power, Earnings, and Gambling,
   July 1991   *48*

3. HOUSEHOLD PRODUCTION AND
   HUMAN CAPITAL   *55*

   Should the Military Pay for Training of Skilled Personnel?
   August 15, 1957   *61*

   Further Reflections on the Allocation of Time, February 2014   *69*

   The Insurance of Market and Nonmarket Human Capital,
   November 1980   *73*

   On Whether Intergenerational Mobility Has Declined in US
   While Inequality Has Increased, March 2012   *80*

   Derivation of Relation Between Schooling of Parents and
   Children and Inequality, April 2012   *85*

4. INCOME INEQUALITY AND THE PUBLIC
   SECTOR   *91*

   A Positive Theory of the Redistribution of Income, April 1978   *95*

   A Note on Optimal First Best Taxation and the Optimal
   Distribution of Utilities, 1982   *123*

5. FAMILY ECONOMICS   *127*

   Economics and the Family, September 21, 1999   *129*

CHRONOLOGICAL ACADEMIC LIFE OF
GARY S. BECKER   *137*

   Selected Writings about Gary S. Becker   *157*

   Bibliography of Gary S. Becker   *159*

   Dissertations Chaired by Gary S. Becker at Columbia University
   and the University of Chicago   *165*

Acknowledgments   *171*

Notes   *173*

Index   *179*

Foreword

EDWARD GLAESER

Gary Becker was a dazzling economist. His presence brought intellectual light to every room that he entered. His work transformed economics. His teaching and advising shaped countless lives, including my own.

This volume contains a fascinating collection of Becker's unpublished writing. Some of these works are polished, such as the two speeches contained in part 1. Others give us Becker unvarnished, such as his "Some Notes on Drugs, Addiction, Families, and Public Policy," which is contained in part 2. The raw pieces may be more valuable for many readers, because they provide a clearer view of Becker's thinking process. They are the closest that the written word can come to duplicating the experience of listening to Becker in a workshop, where his responses to research papers taught generations of Chicago PhD students how to think.

Gary Becker was the most important intellectual influence on my life. His course on price theory taught beginning graduate students how to craft their own economic models, rather than simply consuming models produced by others. The problem sets, which gave verbal queries but required mathematical formalism in response, forced incoming PhD students to create their own algebraic representations of the messy world around us. I have spent the past twenty years at Harvard doing my best to provide a similar experience for our first-year PhD students and for a modest number of our most intellectually ambitious undergraduates. That path was set for me at the University of Chicago in 1988 by Gary Becker.

Becker's price theory class was so exhilarating because it empowered us to create our own models, but also because it broke down all subject barriers that could limit our imagination. One final exam question asked whether parental transfers to children should be expected to rise or fall after a divorce. Becker has been called a conquistador among economists, colonizing other fields, and George Stigler himself used Becker's work to illustrate his claim that economics was "an imperial science."

But Becker is better seen as a liberator, who broke down the barriers that had limited economists' imaginations. Becker was no Cortez leaving havoc in his wake. His work has done no harm to sociology, political science, or anthropology, which continue to move along using their own methods, borrowing what they see fit from economics. All social science benefits when members of different fields look for links across disciplines.

In this foreword, I will do my best to provide a sense of Becker's significance, by situating Becker in two very special trinities of economists. One of these triads had a distinct policy orientation, and also includes his advisor, Milton Friedman, and his friend and coauthor George Stigler. This Chicago School threesome collectively made the case for rethinking the embrace of public interventions in the economy that had been endorsed by both Keynesians, such as Paul Samuelson and Alvin Hansen, and earlier progressive economists, such as John Bates Clark and Richard Ely. The second triad is defined by the great methodological innovators of the postwar decades, and it also includes Kenneth Arrow and Paul Samuelson. This group transformed economics into a discipline that spoke using the language of mathematics and that applied that language to virtually all aspects of human existence.

This preface will attempt to do three things. First, I will attempt to explain Becker's place in the pantheon of methodological innovators in economics. Second, I will discuss the policy perspectives implied by his work. Finally, I will give my own reactions to the fascinating essays contained in this volume.

Becker as Methodological Innovator

Paul Samuelson's 1941 PhD dissertation, published in 1947 as *Foundations of Economic Analysis*, gave economics a mathematical coherence that the field has embraced ever since. No single work and no other economist had changed the field's basic methods more completely. Before Samuelson, economists took a plethora of approaches to describing markets. The meaning of Keynes's *General Theory of Employment, Interest, and Money*, published in 1936, has been debated ever since, partially because its author preferred a literary rather than a formal presentation of his ideas. After Samuelson, the field inexorably moved to mathematics, complete with ubiquitous comparative statics and widespread use of optimization tools. It became increasingly expected that when economists chose to present ideas with words rather than algebra, the presenter would know how to translate the ideas into the language of formal symbols.

I have chosen to include Kenneth Arrow in these trios of methodological heroes. The citation for Arrow's 1972 Nobel Prize emphasized his role as one of the two parents of general equilibrium theory and his formulation of the associated welfare theorems. These are indeed indispensable tools for economists, especially for modern macroeconomists who try to grasp how economic or policy shocks ripple through the entire system. Economics has no comparative advantage in understanding the actions of any lone individual. Our field's strength lies in understanding the system as a whole, and Arrow took the building blocks provided by Samuelson and derived their implications for a complete economy.

Arrow also deserves credit as one of the innovators who brought informational questions into economics. In the 1960s, he introduced what is now called "Arrow's Information Paradox," which describes settings in which describing an idea to a prospective buyer requires disclosing the critical elements of the idea. In the 1970s, along with Edmund Phelps, he introduced the idea of statistical discrimination, which suggests that race or class may be used as a signal for unobserved individual attributes. He also supervised Michael Spence's PhD dissertation on labor market signaling, which was itself a signal event in the study of asymmetric information. Arrow's own breathtakingly brilliant PhD dissertation describes the difficulty of translating individual preferences into community-wide rankings. This Impossibility Theorem can be seen both as a reflection on the difficulties of aggregation and as an early foray of economists into the study of politics.

Becker did not introduce formal optimization techniques into economics, and he did not develop new mathematical tools. His methodological contribution was nonetheless field-defining. He scrapped any attempt to limit economics to a finite set of topics or questions. In the first paragraphs of the introduction to *The Economic Approach to Human Behavior*, which is something of a manifesto for the Beckerian revolution, he rejects definitions of the discipline such as "the allocation of material goods to satisfy material wants," or "the market sector," or "the allocation of scarce means to satisfy competing ends." Instead, he writes that "the combined assumptions of maximizing behavior, market equilibrium, and stable preferences, used relentlessly and unflinchingly, form the heart of the economic approach as I see it" (Becker 1976, 5).

Those assumptions can be used to understand financial markets, but they can also be used to make sense of divorce or homicide or racial discrimination. In the decades since Becker wrote those words, economists have indeed wandered happily across different topics. Eli Berman and Laurence Iannaccone, among others, have explored religious sects and signaling one's devotion to the deity. Steven Levitt has looked at cheating among Sumo wrestlers and Chicago teachers. When economists study nontraditional topics, such as suicide, addiction, riots, warfare, charity, and identity, they are all ultimately following the path that Gary Becker blazed.

In a sense, Becker has two clear antecedents: Paul Samuelson and Milton Friedman. Becker's debt to Samuelson should be clear from his emphasis on "maximizing behavior" and "market equilibrium." Samuelson's *Foundations* enshrined the mathematics of optimization at the heart of economic theory, and maximizing behavior became intrinsic to almost all post-Samuelson economic theory. Samuelson also worked through the economics of market equilibrium, and Arrow took this even further.

But Becker had a more empirical side to his work than either Samuelson or Arrow, and this connects more closely to Milton Friedman. Friedman was the central figure in Becker's formation as an economist, and Becker was Friedman's greatest student. In 1953, while Becker was in the midst of his graduate school career, Friedman published "The Methodology of Positive Economics," which serves as his own methodological manifesto, comparable to Becker's introduction to *The Economic Approach to Human Behavior*. At the end of this essay, Friedman (1953) concludes that "economics as a positive science is a body of tentatively accepted generalizations about economic phenomena that can be used to predict the consequences of changes in circumstances" and that "progress in positive economics will require not only the testing and elaboration of existing hypotheses but also the construction of new hypotheses" (39).

Here Friedman seems to be channeling the ideas of Karl Popper's *Logic of Scientific Discovery*, which taught that all science proceeded through the formulation and rejection of hypotheses. Friedman would later tell an interviewer, "one of the major benefits that I personally derived from the first meeting of the Mont Pelerin Society in 1947 was meeting Karl Popper and having an opportunity for some long discussions with him, not on economic policy at all, but on methodology in the social sciences and in the physical sciences," and "that conversation played a not negligible role in a later essay of mine, 'The Methodology of Positive Economics'" (Levy 1992). This story illustrates how breakthroughs can come from almost random face-to-face meetings. It also shows how Friedman was coming to view economics as defined by its scientific methods rather than by its topic.

But Friedman himself would continue to work primarily on topics at the heart of economics, such as monetary policy and consumption. It was Becker, the twenty-three-year-old graduate student, who grasped that if economics was defined by its methods, not by its topics, then a whole new world had opened up. In 1952, Becker had already penned an early version of "Competition and Democracy," which used the tools of industrial organization to think about the functioning of democracy. This paper did have a major precedent. Hotelling (1929) used his model of market competition to predict that "the competition for votes between the Republican and Democratic parties," leads each party "to make its platform as much like the other's as possible" (54).

Yet Hotelling was really just trying to show the widespread applicability of his model, not to make serious predictions about the functioning of the political system. Becker (1958, 109) presented a logically coherent argument about how free competition among parties and candidates would generally lead to policies that appealed to a wide number of voters, but "monopoly and other imperfections are at least as important, and perhaps substantially more so, in the political sector as in the marketplace." As I will discuss later, this conclusion helped shape Becker's contributions to the policy perspective of the Chicago School. At this point, I just want to emphasize that Becker was groping toward applying economic tools to the understanding of politics.

Becker's PhD dissertation on racial discrimination provided an even greater break with traditional economic topics. Economists were not publishing papers about racial discrimination in their journals, despite the fact that terrible racial divisions and inequities were among the most striking and troubling facts about America in the 1950s.

Becker grasped the importance of the topic and that the tools of economics could make predictions about discrimination and its future. He started by assuming that discrimination reflected racist tastes on the part of white employers, workers, and customers. Nonstandard preferences become a signature part of Becker's work. He would start with homo economicus and then add on racism or altruism or a taste for being in the same place as the cool kids.

By contrast, Becker showed little interest in the frailties of human cognition and typically assumed faultless maximization. With decades of hindsight, I am less sure that permissive attitudes toward modeling preferences combined with absolute strictness about human reasoning yield better predictions than a more parsimonious approach to preferences combined with a greater openness to intellectual error. While Becker's model yields predictions that are sharply different from those of a statistical discrimination model in which employers refuse to hire African Americans because they rationally and correctly believe that there is a productivity gap, the data rule in Becker's favor if the marginal African American worker hired is more productive than the marginal white worker hired.

Yet employers who just don't like African Americans, as in Becker's model, are behaviorally identical to employers who believe incorrectly that African Americans create problems in the workplace. In that case, a new African American employee may indeed be more productive than her white counterpart. Unlike Beckerian taste-based models, an erroneous belief-based model demands an explanation for why profit-seeking firms don't bother to learn the truth. Yet even that criticism can be a strength because this generates an added falsifiable prediction for error-based models of discrimination: discrimination will be far less common when erroneous beliefs are more expensive. Consequently, discrimination based on the beliefs of workers or customers may be more durable than discrimination based on the beliefs of employers.

This very logic, of course, is just a slight permutation on Becker's own analysis of discrimination by employers, workers, and customers. The basic mathematics of optimization mean that employers who maximized profits without considering race would earn (weakly) higher profits than employers who maximized profits and some other discriminatory objective. In a hypercompetitive environment, this should lead the racist employers to go bankrupt, but employer racism could easily persist if employers own physical or entrepreneurial capital and are willing to accept a lower return on that capital. Racist preferences among employees and customers are more likely to lead to segregated workplaces and stores and may persist indefinitely in equilibrium unless there is legal action to forbid such segregation.

It is not that economists had never thought about segregation. Gunnar Myrdal published his monumental *An American Dilemma: The Negro Problem and Modern Democracy* in 1944. Myrdal had a PhD in economics and wrote significant papers in economic journals, but to him "economic viewpoint" was more a synonym for "pecuniary viewpoint" rather than suggesting any particular methodological approach (e.g., Myrdal 1938). Consequently, while *An American Dilemma* was and is recognized as a magisterial work of social science that opened people's eyes to the evils of segregation, few reviewers even described the book as a work of economics.

Becker's work on segregation was followed by seminal papers on education, fertility, marriage, the allocation of time, and crime and punishment. In later years, he would turn to addiction, persuasion, fads, and the endogenous formation of preference parameters. The range of his work is illustrated also by the essays contained in this volume. He encouraged students to work on anything that seemed interesting and important, and the profession came to widely accept a Beckerian framework that accepted methodological but not topical limits on economists.

While Becker was principally a theorist, his major works all confront the real world and many of them contain data. His masterpiece on education, *Human Capital*, published in 1964, is full of facts that serve to both motivate and test his theory. His "An Economic Analysis of Fertility," published in 1960, contains five data tables and confines his model's maximization problem to a footnote. Becker never wavered in his view that the point of economic theory was to make sense of the human condition.

A second common feature of many of his most important papers is that they examine the implications of altering the budget set. Most important, Becker embraced a time budget set that accompanied the more common financial budget set. After applying Walras's Law, this yields a single budget set where the purchase of goods and the use of time outside the workplace must be less than the income that could be earned by spending all of one's time working. His work "On the Interaction between the Quantity and Quality of Children" highlights that the effective price of children increases with the amount the parents want to invest in those children. Consequently, increased demand for better-educated progeny will tend to reduce the number of those progeny.

One of my favorite examples of Becker's wizardry with budget sets comes in his analyses of commuting costs, which will rise with income because the opportunity cost of time rises with wage levels. This produces his famous conclusion that "an increase in income increases the time spent commuting if and only if [the income elasticity of demand for housing] > 1." Becker (1965) then took the fact that "in metropolitan areas of the United States higher-income families tend to live further from the central city" to "imply that outdoor space is a 'luxury'" (512). Subsequent work has typically found that the elasticities of land owned with respect to income are typically far less than one. Becker's insights are vindicated, however, within a model that includes different transportation modes (e.g., cars and buses), and when we note that the rich actually typically live closer to the city center and control for the means of getting to work.

There is a final, more elusive aspect to Becker's classic work that is particularly hard to reproduce. The basic structure of a Samuelson-inspired model starts with assumptions about maximizing agents, imposes equilibrium conditions, and then generates predictions by taking comparative statics. Becker's papers do this, of course. *Human Capital* contains a particularly charming footnote about how the implication that human capital investment should rise with expected lifespan explains why circuses have been known to spend a great deal of time training elephants. Yet these papers often grasp an insight from the model that does not come from a comparative static.

The insight that employers with discriminatory tastes will always earn less than employers who just try to maximize profits is one example of such an insight. Another example of Becker's insights based on logic rather than differentiation is his lengthy advocacy of replacing prison time, which represents pure social loss, with fines, which are a transfer, in "Crime and Punishment: An Economic Approach." The Rotten Kid

Theorem, put forward in Becker's *Treatise on the Family*, provides another example. This "theorem" demonstrates that if parents are sufficiently altruistic toward their child, then even the most selfish child will care somewhat about the well-being of his parents, because their wealth translates into that child's well-being.

In Becker's hands, the algebra took life and became a full-blooded representation of human interaction. He got so much out of that algebra because he never thought of it as algebra. These were people in his models, and he never stopped thinking about how they would attempt to improve their own situations. His methodological greatness lay in his grasping the full power of economic model-building to add to our understanding of every facet of human existing.

The Normative Gary Becker

In the decades after World War II, the Chicago economics department became known both as a place of remarkable intellectual creativity and as a bastion of support for free markets. Becker was also one of the trio of economists who built and maintained that reputation for decades along with Milton Friedman and George Stigler. Friedman was the public face of Chicago economics, whose columns, books, and television shows were read and seen by millions. Becker and especially Stigler contributed more to the economic analysis of actual government behavior.

Since at least Adam Smith, the case for economic freedom has been made by praising the virtues of markets and noting the failures of the public sector. Smith famously wrote that every selfish, ordinary person is "led by an invisible hand to promote an end which was no part of his intention," and consequently "by pursuing his own interest he frequently promotes that of the society more effectually than when he really intends to promote it" (1904, 421). Smith makes the point that when we try to become wealthy, we supply goods and services that people want and consequently serve the general welfare. This represents a core element in the positive case for free markets.

But Smith was also keenly aware of the limitations of the public sector. He was a member of the Scottish Enlightenment, which was by no means convinced of the benevolence of their Hanoverian overlord who ruled from London. Smith famously wrote that "it is the highest impertinence and presumption, therefore, in kings and ministers to pretend to watch over the economy of private people, and to restrain their expense," for "they are themselves, always and without any exception, the greatest spendthrifts in the society" (1904, 328). Smith does not base his case for limited government on the perfect decision-making of private individuals. Instead, he claims that public decision-makers are particularly bad at making decisions. Ever since Smith the case for limited government has been made on the basis of both the strengths of markets, as articulated eloquently by Milton Friedman, and the foibles of government, as described by the work of George Stigler.

The University of Chicago economics department had conservative elements before Milton Friedman came to the university to study economics. J. Laurence Laughlin led the department for its first twenty-four years. Laughlin came to Chicago from Harvard, where he had been a protégé of Frank Dunbar, Harvard's first professor of political economy. Laughlin shared Dunbar's "conservative" views on the gold standard. Dunbar, in turn, had been brought to Harvard to provide a sound-money alternative to the ideas of Francis "Fanny" Bowen, who taught Harvard's first economics classes and alienated wealthy donors with his support for loose monetary policy. The Chicago economics department, consequently, had its roots in the teaching of a Milton Friedman–like opponent of inflationary monetary policy.

Like Becker, Friedman, and Stigler, Laughlin also wanted Chicago to have the best economic researchers, regardless of their political or policy views. The iconoclastic Thorstein Veblen was an early recruit to the department, but there would also be voices for limited government. Jacob Viner came to Chicago in 1916, just as Laughlin was stepping down, and he provides the crucial link with Becker, Friedman, and Stigler. Viner had studied at Harvard under Frank Taussig, who was another hard money protégé of Frank Dunbar.

At Chicago, Viner taught the iconic introductory price theory course, later taught by Friedman and Becker, to Friedman and Stigler. He was also one of the most intellectually successful opponents of Keynesianism during the 1930s, and his skepticism would pass to his students. When Viner moved to Princeton, he taught and advised Becker as an undergraduate. Becker's first published paper, "A Note on Multi-Country Trade" (Becker 1952), is replete with references to Viner, who clearly played an outsized role in the formation of the young economist.

While Viner was the teacher of all three of these Chicago School icons (and Paul Samuelson as well), their role in the intellectual case for limited government was quite different from his. Friedman's most important contributions in this area can be grouped into two broad categories. First, he made seminal contributions to macroeconomics that pushed back against the active fiscal and monetary policy that were central to Keynesian interventionism. Second, his more popular writings, including both *Capitalism and Freedom* and *Free to Choose*, strongly advocate the virtues of free markets.

Friedman's *A Theory of the Consumption Function* (1957) forced economists to think more clearly about how spending decisions are linked to
intertemporal optimization. It also concluded theoretically and demonstrated empirically that temporary shocks to income, such as government transfers during a recession, will be saved as much as they are
spent. This finding cast doubt on the ability of the government to smooth
the business cycle by just handing out cash during a downturn.

Friedman and Anna Schwartz's *Monetary History of the United States*
provides a panoramic overview of the link between American money
supply and business fluctuations. The book demonstrates that restric-
tive money supply policies, often chosen by the Federal Board itself, were
responsible for "severe contractions in industrial production." These
facts lent support to Friedman's view that the right monetary policy is
a limited monetary policy that largely targeted the growth of the money
supply.

That view also meshed tightly with his 1968 American Economic Association presidential address which makes the case that monetary policy "cannot peg interest rates for more than limited periods" (Friedman
1968, 5). Friedman argued that temporary, unanticipated inflation can
indeed temporarily lower the unemployment rate by lowering the real
cost of labor for employers, but if inflation becomes permanent, it will
get baked into wage growth and have no real effects. This argument
struck squarely at the Phillips Curve, which was such a central part of
mainstream Keynesian macroeconomics. As it turns out, Friedman was
splendidly vindicated by the "Stagflation" of the 1970s, where high inflation rates were accompanied by high unemployment rates.

These three contributions changed macroeconomic orthodoxy, but
Friedman's broader body of work spoke for the virtues of markets more
generally. For example, in his 1946 essay "Roofs or Ceilings," which was
co-written with George Stigler, Friedman advocates using the price mechanism to allocate housing, because "in a free market, there is always
some housing immediately available for rent—at all rent levels," "the bid-
ding up of rents forces some people to economize on space," "the high
rents act as a strong stimulus to new construction," and "the rationing
is conducted quietly and impersonally through the price system" (9).
Friedman and Stigler might have added that the price system also allo-
cates housing to those people who value it most. Friedman had an even
larger impact with the show and television series *Free to Choose*. Millions
watched as Friedman extolled the virtue of free markets where people
and firms get to make their own decisions. *Free to Choose* may have been
the most important intellectual basis for the Reagan Revolution.

Stigler's home field was industrial organization, not macroeconomics, and his impatience with the public sector developed over time. Becker titled his 1991 appreciation of Stigler in *Businessweek* "A Trustbuster Who Saw the Light." Industrial organization begins with an interest in market imperfections, such as monopoly power, and so Stigler was not an unalloyed cheerleader for free markets. Instead, he was a wise and skeptical observer of government, whose work on regulations echoes the Adam Smith quotation above in its doubts about the perfection of public decision-making.

For example, in 1951, Stigler wrote, "monopoly is a devious thing," and "only by fabricating cable could the Aluminum Company of America sell cable at less than the ingot price in competition with copper, while maintaining a higher price on less competitive products" (191). Stigler was too good a student of history to question Adam Smith's line that "people of the same trade seldom meet together, even for merriment and diversion, but the conversation ends in a conspiracy against the public, or in some contrivance to raise prices" (130). Stigler began his "A Theory of Oligopoly" by accepting that "oligopolists wish to collude to maximize joint profits" (44). Yet he saw plainly that regulation could be worse.

Stigler's early writing against regulation documented the measures' harm but did not evince a full theory of public motivation. In "Roofs or Ceilings," Stigler, together with Friedman, concluded that "rent ceilings, therefore, cause haphazard and arbitrary allocation of space, inefficient use of space, retardation of new construction and indefinite continuance of rent ceilings, or subsidizing of new construction and a future depression in residential building." Stigler's growing distrust of government is indicated by the next sentence: "formal rationing by public authority would probably make matters still worse" (21). In the same year, Stigler (1946) took on minimum wages in the pages of the *American Economic Review* and argued that "the legal minimum wage will reduce aggregate output, and it will decrease the earnings of workers who had previously been receiving materially less than the minimum" (361). His later empirical work on electricity regulation failed to "find any significant effects of the regulation of electrical utilities" (Stigler and Friedland 1962, 11).

Yet Stigler moved from being a chronicler of regulation's imperfections to studying the causes of regulation. In his "The Theory of Economic Regulation," Stigler (1971) wrote that "as a rule, regulation is acquired by the industry and is designed and operated primarily for its benefit." Stigler (1972) provides an early economic analysis of political competition and concludes that a "minority," such as an industrial group, "that feels intensely the need for a particular policy can pay a sufficient price to obtain it even with normal, legal democratic procedures." Stigler's Nobel Prize citation noted in its first paragraph that his "studies of the forces which give rise to regulatory legislation have opened up a completely new area of economic research" (Sveriges Riksbank Prize in Economic Sciences in Memory of Alfred Nobel, 1982). The mid-twentieth-century Chicago School had ample space for Friedman's buoyant celebration of the virtues of private markets and Stigler's skeptical view of public motives.

Becker had been Viner's student at Princeton. He would be Friedman's greatest PhD student at Chicago. He then left Chicago to be with Stigler at Columbia, but Stigler returned to Chicago just at the moment that Becker arrived in New York City. After Becker returned to Chicago in 1970, he would be Stigler's colleague and coauthor. Their most cited joint paper, "De Gustibus Non Est Disputandum," makes the very Beckerian methodological point that "tastes neither change capriciously nor differ importantly between people," and consequently "the economist continues to search for differences in prices or incomes to explain any differences or changes in behavior." They make this point by showing how "addiction, habitual behavior, advertising and fashion" are compatible with utility maximization and stable preferences (Stigler and Becker 1977).

In 1973, they wrote another important paper, "Law Enforcement, Malfeasance, and Compensation of Enforcers" (Becker and Stigler 1974). On one level, this paper was a natural follow-up to Becker's earlier work on the economics of crime and punishment. In that work Becker had not thought seriously about "the diligence and honesty of enforcers," but Stigler's insight about how regulators get captured by their industries made it natural to ask about how police officers get "captured" by criminals. Like Becker's earlier work, its focus is more normative than positive, providing a guide about how to design the compensation of police in order to reduce bribery and corruption.

The paper is something of a landmark in the history of incentive theory and mechanism design. Before Steven Shavell and Bengt Holmström wrote their pioneering papers on principal-agent theory, Becker and Stigler were working on how wages can be structured to improve employee performance. Becker and Stigler (1974) actually began the modern literature on efficiency wages. The way to reduce police susceptibility to corruption was "to raise the salaries of enforcers above what they could get elsewhere," because then the threat of dismissal from the police force "can more than offset the gain from malfeasance." They went beyond this simple insight by writing down a dynamic programming model that they solved with backward induction. To provide incentives for the police at a minimum cost to taxpayers, they concluded that "the appropriate pay structure has three components: an 'entrance fee' equal to the temptation of malfeasance, a salary premium in each year of employment approximately equal to the income yielded by the 'entrance fee,' and a pension with a capital value approximately equal also to the temptation of malfeasance" (9). The insight that good behavior can be enforced by back-loaded wages was then used by Edward Lazear (1979) to explain why so many firms once had mandatory retirement rules.

Unlike Friedman, who personally tutored Ronald Reagan, and Stigler, who played an outsized role inspiring the deregulation of the late 1970s and 1980s, Becker influenced policy more indirectly, through teaching and the long-term impact of his research. He was less directly engaged with policy-related battles, and he worked on topics where economists rarely get final say. The states of the Jim Crow South were not going to read Becker's dissertation and conclude that they should end discrimination. Society was not going to change its mores around polygamy because Becker's model concluded that it was often actually beneficial for women. Economists have the most power in fields that only economists study, such as macroeconomics and industrial organization, and Becker's great task was to use the tools of economics to understand a far greater range of human behavior.

Yet Becker's work on crime and punishment did eventually become part of the public conversation. Indeed, his most important role in the Chicago School came from his studies of politics and government. Gradually, the view that prisons can rehabilitate lost its sway. The need for sharp incentives to deter crime became more acknowledged during the 1980s. Economists who entered into debates about crime, such as Steven Levitt, all did so in the shadow of Gary Becker.

Becker entered the public arena only in 1985, when he began to write a monthly column for *Businessweek*, as part of a rotating foursome of economics commentators. These columns allowed Becker to speak on a variety of subjects, and his public voice was somewhat different from either Stigler's or Friedman's. Unquestionably, Becker was "opposed to big government and central planning," but he also favored "selling the right to immigrate legally" and "cracking down on fathers who fail to pay child support" (Becker and Nashat Becker 1997). He agreed with Friedman that markets had considerable virtues and with Stigler that the public sector got many things wrong, but he was more interested than either of his mentors in making government more effective through the power of incentives.

Inspired by Becker's teaching, I have long thought that there are three fundamental axioms that lie at the heart of economics. One of these axioms is normative, that it is desirable to expand people's choice sets: freedom is good. In a sense, this axiom was at the heart of Milton Friedman's public message. The other two axioms are positive: that incentives have an impact on behavior, and that there is no such thing as a free lunch. While Becker was interested in the implications of no-arbitrage equilibria, for example in marriage markets, he was even more interested in how all aspects of human life can be connected to the effective prices that people face. His first-year PhD course was titled "Price Theory," and he made it clear from the first lecture that the price of something meant far more than money.

Becker's confidence in the power of incentives fueled his work on crime and punishment, and it is a leitmotif that runs throughout his *Businessweek* columns. Extreme libertarians, who have fully embraced Stigler's views about the problems of the public sector, shy away from empowering the state with the ability to impose extreme punishments. Becker favored "strong punishment for extreme crimes, especially when committed with guns" (Becker and Nashat Becker 1997). He favored strong incentives to deter crime, and he trusted that strong incentives imposed on law enforcement officials could curtail state malfeasance. He recommended renewable terms for judges, for example, so that poor performance could result in dismissal.

In a sense, he was more engaged with the project of making government better than either Friedman or Stigler, who were both far more concerned with making government smaller. Becker's direct engagement with policy advocacy began only in the mid-1980s, when Ronald Reagan was in the White House and the case for limited government had already been well-made. Becker certainly did argue, early and often, for reducing regulation and privatizing public services. But he also argued for reforming government by embracing incentives.

Immigration was among Becker's favored topics, and he had a clear policy proposal. Becker thought that the generosity of the US and EU welfare systems made open borders impracticable, because "a significant fraction of people will move to try to take advantage of welfare benefits and other economic goods provided by a government" (Becker and Coyle 2011). The incentives created by welfare benefits would, in his view, attract both an inefficiently large number of immigrants and immigrants who preferred public benefits to working. Instead, Becker argued that selling visas would attract "skilled people, young people and those who want to make a commitment to the country." Government could be made more efficient through the power of prices.

Becker was also quite comfortable with using prices to ration scarce resources, like access to fish. In one 1995 column, Becker accepted that "environmentalists made a persuasive case that restrictions on fishing could help restore the stock" of "stripers" off the coast of Cape Cod (Becker and Nashat Becker, 1997). He thought that instead of restricting fishing by imposing a commercial quota, Massachusetts should charge fishermen for their catch. The column's title answers its question "How to Scuttle Overfishing?" with the subheading "tax the catch," and Becker is essentially endorsing a Pigouvian tax on the externalities created by overfishing. He titled another column "Don't Raise the Drinking Age, Raise Taxes," and it had a similar theme. Diehard libertarians generally oppose incremental restrictions on fishing or drinking, partially because of the Stiglerian fear that the public sector will abuse any tools that it is given, but Becker accepted public intervention as long as it took the form of incentives rather than quantity regulation.

Becker's belief in reforming the public sector is perhaps most evident in his essay "Federal Pay: Only Top-to-Bottom Reform Will Do." He argues that "we need a full reform of the federal pay structure," and that "federal pay should be determined by what it takes to attract qualified personnel, not by the size of the budget deficit" (Becker and Nashat Becker 1997, 215). He broadly supported the "Quadrennial commission's recommendation to raise the pay of top government officials." He viewed government as an organization to be effectively managed, and consequently supported paying salaries that would attract effective leadership. He is once again arguing for getting the prices right, and he is accepting the need to go beyond simply shrinking the public sector.

I do not want to overstate the case for Becker's differences from Friedman or Stigler. Most of his columns argued for less government, not better government. He wanted to get prices right, and most of the time, public intervention worked against that objective.

The Plan of This Book

This book begins with two public speeches by Becker. The first is a more general speech on the occasion of Becker's receiving a Bradley Award. This piece provides a high-level view of how Becker understood the larger implications of his work on crime, discrimination, and human capital. The second speech specifically highlights his connection to the University of Chicago.

The second part contains four pieces on preferences. The first and longest essay concerns preference formation within the family. Endogenizing preferences was one of Becker's big ambitions during the early 1990s, and it is particularly associated with Casey Mulligan and their joint work. In some cases, Mulligan and Becker thought about individual preference formation, but in this paper, Becker focuses on parental investment in the preferences of children. He thinks about a positive investment that just makes children happier, but that plays little role in the paper. I suspect that this "love" investment appears in the paper so that parents' preference formation can do more than just make their children unhappy.

The primary preference formation lies in "guilt formation," which reduces the welfare of children but increases their returns to transferring resources to their parents' later in life. This preference formation can solve an incomplete contracts problem. If returns to human capital investment are high, then there is an efficient bargain where parents invest significantly in their children's education and children repay their parents when they are adults. However, parents can't enforce this repayment and so they end up saving for their own retirement instead of investing in their kids. Guilt solves this problem by ensuring that the children will repay their parents.

This paper is my favorite essay in the book, partially because it is based on a pure Beckerian price theory and partially because it has a real empirical bent. If any readers want to take this work further, I would urge them to embrace the empirical literature in psychology that looks at emotional development in childhood. Parental preference formation remains a lively research area that often focuses on political and cultural tastes.

The second essay also focuses on investment in the utility functions of others. In this case, Becker looks at rational indoctrination and persuasion and his focus is again on the incentives that lead actors to invest in indoctrination. Becker's approach to "behavioral economics" emphasized the interaction between market incentives and human psychology. The key point is not that we can be persuaded, but rather who ends up persuading us in equilibrium.

As Becker emphasized the market, he tended to work with stark assumptions about the technology of persuasion and indoctrination. He just assumed that with sufficient effort, the utility function could be changed. This is a reasonable modeling choice, but the profession has gone in a different direction. Persuasion and indoctrination have instead been taken to mean changing beliefs and not preferences. Some models of persuasion continue to assume, like Becker, that people understand and correctly use the laws of probability. Other theorists have increasingly come to believe that human cognition is far more flawed, which enables persuaders to propagate persistent errors, such as false beliefs about particular ethnicities.

Even in his dissertation on discrimination, Becker took a hard line on beliefs, which he always considered hyperrational, but a permissive line on preferences, which could take almost any form. The weakness of treating discrimination, persuasion, and advertising as shaping an amorphous utility function is that there are no implications that come from the technology of the human mind. The modern literature that microfounds these phenomena with some model of belief updating yields more predictions about what forms of error are easier to create and persist. Yet to truly address the world, that literature must do more to follow Becker and focus on the equilibrium supply of error.

The third essay contains some helpful notes about drug policy and rational addiction. The most novel thing in those notes is Becker's focus on peer pressure in drug compensation and the possibility for multiple equilibria in the drug market. The limits of Becker's libertarianism are visible in these pages, where he grapples with the problems of teenage drug use.

The fourth essay looks at the impact of a taste for power on tournaments within organizations. Again, Becker just assumes a taste for power. I think in modern work on contracts and organizations it would be more natural to assume that "power" confers a noncontractible ability to allocate workplace amenities. In this treatment, worker's appreciate power not because it has intrinsic worth but because it is instrumental in achieving benefits. Of course, most of us probably do intrinsically value power. Moreover, the impact of an instrumental power benefit on tournament design can be made to fit Becker's intrinsic benefit model.

Becker organizes the paper around the question of why organizations pay more to their more powerful employees, given that workers should be willing to accept lower wages in exchange for more power. This question is a variant of a standard compensating differential question: why do jobs with better amenities get higher wages? Again, the logic is that workers are willing to accept lower wages in exchange for higher amenities. The most classic answer to this question, which is probably largely right for the case of power as well, is that more able workers receive higher wages and higher amenities. Indeed, as long as amenities are a normal good, then wealthier workers should be willing to give up more of their earnings for on-the-job benefits, including power.

Becker makes this point in the first page of this paper, and then goes on to focus on a totally different point. If power and earnings are complements in the utility function, then firms might want to run a lottery where some workers get high wages and high levels of power and other workers do not. This is a variant of Bergstrom's (1986) point that a draft lottery can be optimal if the marginal utility of earnings is low for soldiers. Becker loved this point and was sure that it explained something big. I am not sure that it explains the high wages paid to company presidents, but I agree that the complementarity between wealth and different attributes or place or employers can explain certain forms of risk-taking.

The third part of the book focuses on human capital and the allocation of time. The first essay in this part is a 1957 piece on whether the military should pay to train skilled personnel. This essay, written for the RAND Corporation in the summer of 1957, is an intellectual landmark because it illustrates the beginnings of Becker's thinking on human capital theory and incomplete contracts. The paper is motivated by the high quit rates among soldiers who have been given serious skills by the military, such as the ability to pilot large aircraft. The paper argues that the army should make its workers pay a share of the costs of their training by giving them lower wages and do more recruitment of skilled workers from outside.

The link between this paper and Becker's later work on human capital is obvious, especially his later distinction between firm-specific human capital and general human capital. Becker is correctly credited with being a pioneer in the literature on imperfect contract enforcement because he argued that firms that provide general human capital risk losing their trained workers to other employers. This paper shows that this point came from empirical observation, and that it was Becker's grappling with the personnel problems of the army that led him to realize the problems that come along with an ability to commit to stay at a firm.

The second paper reflects on Becker's work on the allocation of time, with about fifty years of hindsight. The third paper connects the theory of time allocation with optimal insurance against shocks to physical and human capital. The key assumption is that every unit of consumption is produced with a units of income and c units of time. In this case, an individual with a wage of w, t total units of time, and v units of unearned income can consume a total of $(wt + v) / (wc + a)$ units of consumption.

Introducing time does nothing to the implied optimal insurance for shocks to physical capital or v: access to fair insurance implies full insurance. If the shock affects w rather than v and has no impact on household productivity, then households "overinsure" against the shock in the sense that their welfare is higher if a negative shock occurs. This result reflects the fact that lower wages make it effectively cheaper to purchase the good in the case of the negative shock. Conversely, if the shock to the wage has an equal impact on household productivity, then full insurance is again optimal.

This result bears similarities to the general algebra of state-dependent preferences and insurance, where full insurance is optimal only with shocks that are essentially pecuniary. Negative shocks that have no impact on the marginal utility of cash do not lead to insurance. Negative shocks that lead the marginal utility of money to decline, perhaps the death of a child, should lead to negative insurance since money is valued more in the good state than in the bad state. Becker's allocation-of-time model makes the point that changes in the value of time act in a similar way to state-dependent preferences.

The fourth and fifth papers in this part concern the rise in the returns to skill and intergenerational mobility. As the editor's introduction to that part makes clear, these essays were motivated partially by Alan Krueger's "Great Gatsby Curve," which links high levels of inequality within a generation with lower levels of upward mobility across generations. As an aside, I would like to remind readers that the title character of F. Scott Fitzgerald's masterpiece, Jay Gatsby, was born poor, and so he should serve as an example of how great upward mobility can exist during a time of extreme inequality, rather than the reverse.

Becker's two, closely linked, essays show that when a rise in the returns to skill leads to higher inequality, then we should also expect the link between parental and children's income to increase, as long as parental income is tied to children's schooling. That link might reflect a shared genetic aptitude for schooling, or the greater willingness of rich parents to invest in their children. As long as education provides a primary means of investing in children, then a rise in the returns to education should both heighten inequality and ensure that income differences persist over generations.

The fourth part contains two rather technical essays. The first paper provides a positive theory of economic redistribution, based on an assumed "political preference function." This provides an interesting alternative path to the political economy of redistribution that essentially microfounds this function with assumptions about the political process. There is a parallel here to the earlier distinction between Becker's just assuming an "indoctrination function" and the literature's embrace of a specified learning process. It is useful to think about when Becker's reduced-form approach either outperforms or underperforms an approach that models the behavior of voters or other sources of political power.

The second paper makes a really nice point about lump-sum redistribution. Becker's Theorem is that if leisure is a normal good and if people differ only because of their wage rates, then optimal lump-sum redistribution will ensure that the individuals with the highest wages, who had the highest welfare level before redistribution, have the lowest welfare levels after redistribution.

Becker's proof is a neat trick using the expenditure function. I will produce here an equivalent statement of his core result with a more canonical and plodding approach. I assume that there are I consumers, each of whom has an individual specific wage rate w_i and each of whom receives an individual specific transfer from the government t_i. Each individual maximizes $U(w_i(1-L)+t_i, L)$, where L represents leisure and the time budget has been normalized to 1. Utility functions are identical, and the government maximizes the sum of utilities across individuals subject to the constraint that $\Sigma_i t_i = 0$.

Making the usual Beckerian assumptions that ensure that first-order conditions exist and characterize an interior maximum, we have two conditions for each consumer: $U_L(w_i(1-L)+t_i, L) = w_i\lambda$, and $U_C(w_i(1-L)+t_i, L) = \lambda$. I follow the usual convention that $U_C(.,.)$ refers to the derivative of $U(.,.)$ with respect to consumption and $U_L(.,.)$ refers to the derivative of $U(.,.)$ with respect to leisure, and λ refers to the multiplier on the government's balanced budget constraint.

Welfare is declining with wages if and only if $1 - L + dt_i/dw_i$ is negative because that expression captures the direct effect of wages on welfare, including the relationship between wages and transfers but excluding the impact of wages on labor supply (which is irrelevant because of the envelope theorem). Differentiating the first-order conditions with respect to w_i, holding λ constant (which is asking how do things change within a fixed income distribution), we get $1 - L + dt_i/dw_i = \lambda(w_i U_{CC} - U_{CL}/U_{LL}U_{CC} - U_{CL}^2)$.

We would typically assume that $U_{LL}U_{CC} > U_{CL}^2$ to ensure that the first-order conditions for consumers reflect a maximum, and $w_i U_{CC} - U_{CL} < 0$ is exactly the condition that ensures that leisure is a normal good or equivalently that an exogenous increase in unearned income causes hours worked to fall. Hence leisure being a normal good implies that optimal lump-sum redistribution reverses the welfare ranking among consumers. The logic of this conclusion is that with optimal lump-sum redistribution, it is optimal for high wage earners to work more but not to consume much more. Indeed, if $U_{CL} < 0$ and work and consumption are complementary, then it is optimal to have high wage earners both work more and consume less than their low-wage equivalents.

The only exception occurs when work and consumption are strong substitutes. Consider, for example, the somewhat perverse utility function $U = (C + L - K)^\alpha C^\beta$, assuming that $w_i < K < 1$ and $\alpha + \beta < 1$. This odd function is typically used to produce Giffen goods, where K would represent calories that can be satisfied by meat and potatoes (C substitutes for meat here and L for potatoes), but people enjoy eating meat. It is hard to imagine what this function would represent with leisure and consumption, but it does satisfy the standard requirements for utility maximization. After optimization over L, the indirect utility function is a constant times $(w_i + t_i - K)^{\alpha+\beta} w_i^{-\alpha}(1-w_i)^{-\beta}$ and the first-order condition for lump-sum taxation makes $(w_i + t_i - K)^{\alpha+\beta-1} w_i^{-\alpha}(1-w_i)^{-\beta}$ constant across individuals. This implies that $w_i + t_i - K$ is rising with w_i if and only if $w_i^{-\alpha}$

$(1 - w_i)^{-\beta}$ is rising with w_i, which occurs if and only if $w_i > \alpha / \alpha + \beta$. If this condition holds, then $w_i + t_i - K$ and $w_i^{-\alpha} (1 - w_i)^{-\beta}$ are both rising with w_i, and hence $(w_i + t_i - K)^{\alpha + \beta} w_i^{-\alpha} (1 - w_i)^{-\beta}$ is also rising with w_i, and lump-sum taxation does not switch the order of utility levels.

The reason for this exception is that at this utility level, for these parameter values, consumption and leisure are close substitutes, and an increase in unearned income will reduce leisure. The effective price of utility is lower for high-wage individuals in this example, since they can satisfy the K constraint with consumption rather than having to rely on leisure, and so giving them cash delivers more marginal utility.

I have indulged in this arithmetic to make the point that equalizing marginal utilities of cash need not mean that higher-wage individuals receive less overall utility, although it seems likely that they will. The importance of this logic for actual tax systems is far from obvious, although as Becker notes, it is perhaps more relevant within the household, where redistribution is far more efficient. Indeed, it is quite possible that the most productive household members can have the lowest levels of welfare because they do much more work.

The fifth part provides some brief notes on the economics of the family. The book ends with a chronology of Becker's life, a list of his publications, and a summary of the dissertations that he chaired. The fact that my dissertation is not included in that list only proves that he had an enormous impact on many people who are not included in the list.

References

Becker, Gary S. 1952. "A Note on Multi-Country Trade." *American Economic Review* 42, no. 4: 558–68.

———. 1958. "Competition and Democracy." *Journal of Law and Economics* 1: 105–9.

———. 1965. "A Theory of the Allocation of Time." *Economic Journal* 75: 493–508.

———. 1976. *The Economic Approach to Human Behavior*. Chicago: University of Chicago Press.

———. 1983. "A Theory of Competition among Pressure Groups for Political Influence*." *Quarterly Journal of Economics* 98, no. 3 (August 1): 371–400. https://doi.org/10.2307/1886017.

———. 1997. "Federal Pay: Only Top-to-Bottom Reform Will Do." In Becker and Nashat Becker 1997.

Becker, Gary S., and Diane Coyle. April 13, 2011. "The Challenge of Immigration: A Radical Solution." SSRN Scholarly Paper. Rochester, NY: Social Science Research Network. https://doi.org/10.2139/ssrn.1846567.

Becker, Gary S., and George J. Stigler. 1974. "Law Enforcement, Malfeasance, and Compensation of Enforcers." *Journal of Legal Studies* 3, no. 1: 1–18.

Becker, Gary Stanley, and Guity Nashat Becker. 1997. *The Economics of Life: From Baseball to Affirmative Action to Immigration, How Real-World Issues Affect Our Everyday Life*. New York: McGraw Hill.

Bergstrom, T. 1986. "Soldiers of Fortune." In *Equilibrium Analysis: Essays in Honor of Kenneth J. Arrow*, ed. Walter P. Heller, Ross M. Starr, and David A. Starrett, 57–80. Cambridge: Cambridge University Press.

Friedman, Milton. 1953. "The Methodology of Positive Economics." In *Essays in Positive Economics*, 3–43. Chicago: University of Chicago Press.

———. 1957. "A Theory of the Consumption Function." Princeton University Press. https://www.nber.org/books-and-chapters/theory-consumption-function.

———. December 29, 1968. "The Role of Monetary Policy." Presidential Address presented at the Eightieth Annual Meeting of the American Economic Association, Washington, DC. https://www.andrew.cmu.edu/course/88-301/phillips/friedman.pdf.

Friedman, Milton, and George J. Stigler. 1946. "Roofs or Ceilings? The Current Housing Problem." Irvington-on-Hudson, NY: Foundation for Economic Education.

Hotelling, Harold. 1929. "Stability in Competition." *Economic Journal* 39, no. 153: 41–57. https://doi.org/10.2307/2224214.

Lazear, Edward P. 1979. "Why Is There Mandatory Retirement?" *Journal of Political Economy* 87, no. 6: 1261–84.

Levy, David. 1992. "Interview with Milton Friedman | Federal Reserve Bank of Minneapolis." Accessed June 6, 2022. https://www.minneapolisfed.org:443/article/1992/interview-with-milton-friedman.

Myrdal, Gunnar. 1938. "Population Problems and Policies." *Annals of the American Academy of Political and Social Science* 197, no. 1, May 1: 200–215. https://doi.org/10.1177/000271623819700118.

Smith, Adam. 1904. *An Inquiry into the Nature and Causes of the Wealth of Nations*. Ed. Edwin Cannan. 2 vols. London: Methuen.

Stigler, George J. 1946. "The Economics of Minimum Wage Legislation." *American Economic Review* 36, no. 3: 358–65.

———. 1951. "The Division of Labor Is Limited by the Extent of the Market." *Journal of Political Economy* 59, no. 3: 185–93.

———. 1971. "The Theory of Economic Regulation." *Bell Journal of Economics and Management Science* 2, no. 1: 3–21. https://doi.org/10.2307/3003160.

———. 1972. "Economic Competition and Political Competition." *Public Choice* 13: 91–106.

Stigler, George J., and Claire Friedland. 1962. "What Can Regulators Regulate? The Case of Electricity." *Journal of Law and Economics* 5, 1–16.

Stigler, George J., and Gary S. Becker. 1977. "De Gustibus Non Est Disputandum." *American Economic Review* 67, no. 2: 76–90.

1

JUST THE BEGINNING

*Gary Becker and Applications of
the Economic Approach*

*[Economics] is judged ultimately by how well it helps us understand the world,
and how well we can help improve it.*

—GARY S. BECKER, inauguration of the Becker Center on Chicago Price
Theory, founded by Richard O. Ryan, 2006

*Always the true scholar, Becker stayed with a problem until he understood and
solved it, even if it took years or even decades. Often he returned to some of the
same issues, such as those involving human capital, fertility, and social interactions, several times over his career. He read, cited, and extended the full literature
on each of these problems. His goal was to advance science, not to lengthen his
curriculum vitae.*

—JAMES HECKMAN, ED LAZEAR, and KEVIN M. MURPHY, "Gary Becker
Remembered," 2018

Gary Becker was one of the most original and influential economists in
the history of economics as a science. These words by James Heckman
(Nobel Laureate in Economics, 2000) on the occasion of his memorial
provide a measure of his contribution to economics: "Gary Becker transformed economics by broadening the range of problems considered by
economists and by creating new analytical frameworks. He founded
flourishing fields of economics and public policy. It is said that Helen of
Troy was 'The Face that Launched a Thousand Ships.' It can be said of

Gary Becker that his ideas launched the production of hundreds of data sets and thousands of empirical and theoretical studies."[1]

Becker viewed the economic approach as a method of analysis, as an instrument limited only by the imagination of the practitioner. In his words, "the economic approach is a comprehensive one that is applicable to all human behavior."[2] With this idea in mind, Becker applied the economic approach to a wide range of social issues, most of them outside the traditional boundaries of economics, such as marriage, fertility, crime, racial discrimination, the use of time, social interactions, politics, and drug addiction. Before Gary Becker, these topics were considered noneconomic. Today, they are in the mainstream of economics.

Becker's economic analysis of these and other topics far outside the traditional range of economics launched and guided a massive body of empirical research in economics. According to George Stigler (Nobel Laureate in Economics, 1982), "[Gary Becker] may well go down in history as the chief architect in the designing of a truly general science of society."[3] In the preface to the first edition of his *Economic Theory* (1971), Becker explained that he used "the perhaps presumptuous title of *Economic Theory* . . . instead of a title like Micro Theory or Price Theory because of my belief that there is only one kind of economic theory, not separate theories for micro problems, macro problems, nonmarket decisions, and so on."[4]

In the wake of Becker's accomplishments, it might seem that little would remain to do on the subject of understanding and predicting human behavior with the traditional tools of economic theory. He had extraordinary talent and, for example, undertook the study of human capital just before the market value of human capital was about to take off. But Becker taught that human capital has many elements that have increasing returns, that initial learning many times increases the incentive to pursue additional learning. The same goes for learning the economic approach to explaining human behavior. The genesis of this book lies in the learning that remains.

When it came to politics, the role of families in developing a person (her skills and preferences), fertility, and inequality, Becker was confident that some of the finest applications of economics had not yet arrived. He kept working to find breakthroughs. We hope that readers will find that the chapters provide good advice as to directions for important future research, or at least agree with Becker that these questions need to be revisited with the economics toolkit.

The atmosphere of ongoing inquiry is typically subtle in published work, which is traditionally distributed as "finished" and reveals little about the intellectual journey that preceded publication. We believe that reading Gary's unpublished work provides a more genuine experience of what it was like to work with Gary at Chicago or Columbia. The draft academic papers put the reader into Gary's research process in real time. Few of them have the polish of finished Becker essays. That being said, they are filled with worthwhile ideas—and even more valuably, they illustrate Becker's mind at work.

We believe that there is an important value in making these manuscripts available to the public, especially for young scholars. This book increases the legacy of Becker's work by demonstrating his process—including instances when his process didn't pan out. It aims to show the famous economist's missteps and evolutions. What we hope we have produced is an inspirational book for young people.

Many of the papers included in this collection are half-formed—early drafts that point to lines of research that emerged later and that have a value in illustrating "the craft of economic theory." They are not unfinished projects that Becker left in May 2014; most of those papers have already been published by his coauthors. The exception is an unfinished note on his seminal paper "A Theory of the Allocation of Time" that he was preparing for the 125th-anniversary issue of the *Economic Journal*. Some of the papers are exercises that start with an idea or a topic and then craft a simple but effective model.

The nontechnical reader can get a good sense of the ideas of the papers by skipping the math and following Becker's discussion and intuition of the technical analysis. As usual in Becker analysis, all new concepts are empirically motivated and introduced with examples from the world we live in. Becker firmly believed that "fields become sterile when the source of inspiration for additional work is simply the literature in the field rather than the world out there. We can see many fields where it is the literature that generates what gets done, not the problems encountered in the world."[5]

The unpublished public lectures offer his synthesis and his vision for the future. In this book, we include the drafts of two of them: on drugs, addiction, families, and public policy delivered at the meeting of the Mont Pelerin Society in Santiago de Chile in 2000, and on economics and the family delivered at the conference "Economic Dimensions of the Family" in Madrid in 1999.

We prepared a chronological academic biography, a bibliography, and a list of dissertations chaired by Becker at Columbia University and the University of Chicago. This will allow the reader to learn more about Becker's approach to economics and his work over different stages of his amazing academic career and to connect them with his unpublished manuscripts. These materials are included at the end of the book.

The manuscripts included in this collection have a great variety of styles—speeches, commentary, opinion, academic-style articles, simple early-stage models, more developed models that are interacting with data, largely empirical ruminations. We decided to organize the documents under four main topics: Accounting for Tastes, Household Production and Human Capital, Income Inequality and the Public Sector, and Family Economics.

In what follows of this introductory part, we include two acceptance speeches, for the Bradley Award and the Alumni Medal of the University of Chicago, where Becker provides his own view about his research and contributions and about the "The Spirit of the University of Chicago." In part 2 Gary looks at the effects of social security on parental efforts to affect the preferences of children. This part also includes unpublished works on rational indoctrination; the relationship between power, job hierarchy, and earnings; and a speech on drugs, addiction, the family, and public policy. Part 3 includes a 1957 RAND document on whether the military should pay for training of skilled personnel that represents perhaps his first written discussion of on-the-job training. It also includes an unfinished note for his seminal paper on the allocation of time prepared for the 125th-anniversary issue of the *Economic Journal*, two short notes on the relationship between schooling of parents and children inequality, and a very early draft of a paper that uses his household production approach to think about insurance of market and nonmarket human capital. Part 4 uses the economic toolkit to understand how redistribution by the public sector affects inequality and how economic circumstances shape public policies intended to change it. The economics of the family is the subject of part 5.

Acceptance Speech at Bradley Award Ceremony

June 4, 2008

GARY S. BECKER

[It is a] Great honor for me to be chosen this year as one of four recipients of a Bradley Prize. I join many distinguished previous and present recipients—many of the prior recipients are also present tonight. I have interacted in a very positive way with the Bradley Foundation for many years, so this is a special pleasure for me.

I would like to express my thanks not only to the Bradley Foundation, but also to my teachers, especially Milton Friedman, George Stigler, and T. W. Schultz, and to students and colleagues at Columbia and Chicago. Most of all, however, I am indebted to my wife, Guity Nashat Becker, for her support and insights into human behavior. I would not be here tonight but for her influence.

I was chosen for my contributions to economic and social life, so I will use the short time available to me to discuss briefly what I have tried to do.

Economics offers a powerful analysis of incentives based on the assumption that individuals make choices to try to promote their well-being and that of others who they are concerned about—such as family and friends. Also crucial is the assumption that competition and markets are powerful forces that induce companies usually to serve the public interest even when that is not their goal. Early in my career I became convinced that this "economic approach" could be highly valuable in analyzing a much larger set of issues and concerns than had been common in economic discussions. I will use this occasion to give three examples of help provided by this broadening of the scope of economic reasoning in analyzing public policy issues of great importance.

In my doctoral dissertation I considered discrimination against minorities based on race, sex, and other characteristics, a major topic that had strangely been neglected by economists. This study recognized that prejudice exists and has been prevalent, and it analyzed how such prejudice interacts with various types of market and political forces. A surprisingly large number of interesting implications about the incidence of discrimination flowed from a very basic approach.

To take one example, the study showed that competition does not eliminate discrimination, but competition does combat prejudice and moderates the manifestation of prejudice in the form of observed discrimination against minorities. The reason for this is that companies that do not want to discriminate much if at all have a sizable competitive advantage in the pursuit of profits over companies that are strongly prejudiced. So equal opportunity employers and those with only weak desires to discriminate are more likely to remain producing in industries with strong competitive pressures. Since this analysis distinguishes competitive from more monopolistic situations, it helps explain why monopolistic industries discriminate more than competitive industries.

To take another example to illustrate the power of economic reasoning, crime rose rapidly from the end of the 1950s through the '70s. During those decades the dominant view among intellectuals, many psychiatrists, and others was that punishments did not deter crime, that overcoming alienation of many criminals from society was the only effective way to fight crime. I challenged this view, and showed that economic reasoning supported common sense in implying that criminals responded to incentives as strongly as did professors and others did in choosing their occupations. That is, potential criminals in effect consider the costs as well as benefits from crime in deciding whether to become criminals.

One implication of the economic approach is that better education reduces crime by raising earnings from legal activities, and hence the opportunity cost of spending time at criminal activities. However, greater likelihood of apprehending and punishing criminals also reduces crime by raising the cost to potential criminals of engaging in crime. On this view, the "stick"—that is punishment—is effective along with the "carrot"—better and more available jobs—in deterring crime. Research has confirmed the powerful effects of apprehending and punishing criminals on the crime rate. Greater apprehension and punishment of criminals helps explain why US crime rates declined during recent decades while those in Western Europe increased greatly.

My final subject is perhaps my favorite: the role of human capital in economic life. The human capital revolution put people rather than machines or natural resources at the center of modern economies. Investments in the human capital of men and women take many forms, especially schooling, health, and on the job training. These investments account for about 30 per cent of GDP, which is a larger share than that of investments in physical capital. Investments in schooling raise earnings, but greater education provides greater knowledge and information, and skills at processing information, that also improve many other aspects of life. These include health and how long individuals live, their skills at investing in their children, the quality of the marriages they make, their response to shocks, such as hurricane Katrina.

The benefits of a college education have greatly increased since 1980, as reflected in a much larger earnings premium to college graduates compared to persons who did not go to college. This is basically a good development because it means higher returns on capital in the form of a college education. At the same time, however, the increased college earnings premium has been a major contributor to the rise in income inequality during the past 25 years. Greater attention needs to be paid to improving the preparation of young students, so that they can finish high school and go on to college. The challenge is especially acute for boys since girls are more likely to finish high school, and girls are now far more likely to remain in and finish college.

A number of steps can be taken that together could greatly improve the quality of K–12 education for those who are being shortchanged by the present system. One major advance would be a widespread voucher system of financing the education of poorer students that would stimulate the entry of schools geared to their educational needs.

I hope my brief discussion gives a flavor of the types of questions I have addressed, and of the power of economic reasoning. The analysis of economic and social issues will surely greatly improve over time, but I am confident that the economic approach will continue to provide deep insights that take some of the mystery out of human behavior.

The Spirit of the University of Chicago

Nobel Laureate Forum, Beijing, China,
September 14, 2010

GARY S. BECKER

I have been a student and faculty at the University of Chicago for over 45 years. It is hard for me to put into words what this university has meant to me. I entered the University of Chicago as a 20-year-old fresh out of Princeton, a very good school too. But the University of Chicago opened my eyes to true intellectual discourse and interaction across disciplines. The vitality of the discussions among faculty, among students, and between faculty and students was both eye-opening and tremendously exciting.

Of course I mainly studied economics. My teachers taught me that economics was not a game played by clever academics, but a serious subject that helped us understand what went on in the real world, and to prescribe changes through public policies that would improve the economy's functioning. Prescription built on understanding, a lesson I have never forgotten.

I had several economics teachers that I am greatly indebted to, including T. W. Schultz, Greg Lewis, Jacob Marschak, and Al Harberger.

But Milton Friedman clearly had the greatest influence on me and other economics graduate students. Milton was an outstanding researcher who made enormous contributions to economics. He was also a controversial public intellectual. But aside from these contributions, he was an absolutely marvelous teacher, the most stimulating teacher I ever had.

I was fortunate, in addition to my economic studies, to sample courses in other fields where I encountered other outstanding intellectuals and teachers. I attended lectures by Rudolf Carnap on Philosophy of Science, I took a magnificent course by Jimmie Savage on Math Statistics, I attended the famous course by Edward Levi and Aaron Director in the Law School, I attended various evening seminars organized by Friedrich Hayek from the Committee on Social Thought. The topic for discussion differed each year, and Hayek invited the great physicist Enrico Fermi, the great biologist Sewall Wright, Friedman, and other remarkable faculty members to give lectures.

I listened to lectures by sociologists, anthropologists, political scientists, and others from various fields. The vitality and commitment of the lectures and discussions were remarkably stimulating to a young student.

My research took me in controversial directions, starting with my doctoral dissertation on the economics of discrimination against minorities, continuing with my research on human capital, crime, the family, and other topics. I faced considerable opposition on all these topics from the great majority of economists. I do not believe I would have persevered without the strong support both as a student and later on as a teacher and researcher I continued to receive from Milton Friedman, Ted Schultz, George Stigler, Gregg Lewis, and other giants at Chicago.

After leaving Chicago for about 12 years to be a professor at Columbia University, I returned in 1970 as a professor at Chicago. My research continued to be influenced by what I learned from colleagues at Chicago and their general support of what I was doing.

In addition, and very crucial to my work, I have had over the past 40 years at Chicago a series of remarkable students. They were not only very able, but curious, creative, and willing to strike out in innovative directions. They also were not afraid to challenge me and other teachers. The Chicago tradition in economics, and elsewhere in the university, is not to accept the claims of authorities, but to challenge these claims, no matter how distinguished the authorities, if they are not backed up by coherent analysis and evidence.

I could cite hundreds of such students, many having gone on to distinguished careers. However, I would like to single out two former students from China who will be participating in our panel on economic development tomorrow. One is Dr. Justin Lin, Chief Economist at the World Bank, founder of the China Center for Economic Research at Peking University, and a major contributor to the theory and empirical analysis of the process of economic development.

The other is Dr. Y.C. Richard Wong, Professor at Hong Kong University, former Vice-Chancellor of that university, my former research assistant at Chicago, and an important contributor to economic development and public policies for developing countries and regions.

But the most precious gain to me from my University of Chicago experience is that I met my wife, Guity, who is present today. She received her PhD from the Department of History at Chicago. We have a deep common bond of attachment to this university. Moreover, we preserve in our home the Chicago tradition of discussion, debate, and sometimes disagreement on vital world subjects.

I truly believe that I owe whatever success I have had as a social scientist and intellectual to my long time at the University of Chicago as a student, teacher, colleague, and to my wife.

Thank you exceedingly, University of Chicago, for all you have given me.

2

ACCOUNTING FOR TASTES

The Formation of Children's Preferences, Rational Indoctrination, Addictions, and the Preference for Power in Organizations

This extension of the utility-maximizing approach to include endogenous preferences is remarkably successful in unifying a wide class of behavior, including habitual, social, and political behavior. I do not believe that any alternative approach—be it founded on "cultural," "biological," or "psychological" forces—comes close to providing comparable insights and explanatory power.

—GARY S. BECKER, "Accounting for Tastes," 1996

From very early, Becker's challenge was to evaluate the robustness and scope of the economic approach to human behavior. In "Irrational Behavior and Economic Theory" (1962), he shows that the law of demand, one of the most fundamental results in economics, does not require the assumption that the consumer is a rational maximizing being, but that it arises, mainly, from the scarcity of resources that people face. "Irrational Behavior and Economic Theory" shows the importance of resource constraints and the strength they provide to economic analysis, while also serving as a trigger for Becker to think about the role of people's preferences.

Modifying the usual assumptions about preferences, avoiding utility functions, indifference curves, transitivity, and "other paraphernalia of modern analysis," "Irrational Behavior" can be considered a behavioral economics paper, in which deviations from the standard assumptions on preferences and beliefs, extending the motives of people, are possible. Becker started questioning and modifying preferences, something that was "not allowed" in the traditional analysis, in his doctoral dissertation of 1955 on the economics of discrimination, where he incorporated a taste for discrimination in the standard preferences used by economists (see Acceptance Speech at Bradley Award Ceremony in part 1). An important distinctive feature of Becker's broad approach is that the focus is on how this "new type" or "extended" preferences (e.g., including prejudice, altruism, education, social capital) "[interact] with various types of market and political forces."

A further step in the analysis developed by Becker jointly with Kevin M. Murphy and George Stigler was to understand the structure of preferences, the formation of wants. The analysis endogenizes preferences by recognizing that they depend on an individual's past and future consumption as well as on the behavior of other individuals and economic actors: "For example, whether a person smoked heavily or took drugs last month significantly affects whether he smokes and uses drugs this month. How a person votes depends very much on the way friends and others in the same peer group vote. Successful advertising for a product increases the desire for that product. The clothing people wear depends crucially on what others wear."[1]

Efforts to persuade are an important part of economic activity. Advertising, promotions, political campaigns, and parental teachings within a household are just a few examples of economic persuasion. The first essay in this part analyzes the effect of parents' influence on the preference formation of their children on their own behavior. For example, if their smoking raises the likelihood that their children will smoke, they may decide not to smoke because they do not want their children to take up smoking. The essay was written in 1992, the year Becker was awarded the Nobel Prize in Economics. It was prepared for presentation at a session on the topic "What Happens Inside Families?" at the 1993 Allied Social Science Associations (ASSA) Annual Meeting in Anaheim.

In his Nobel Lecture, Becker includes parts of this essay in three appendices. He notes that "many economists, including myself, have excessively relied on altruism to tie together the interests of family members. Recognition of the connection between childhood experiences and future behavior reduces the need to rely on altruism in families. But it does not return the analysis to a narrow focus on self-interest, for it partially replaces altruism by feelings of obligation, anger, and other attitudes usually neglected by models of rational behavior."[2]

Rational parents maximize their utility, which is conditional not only on their resources, but also on their past experiences and their attitudes toward their children. With this idea in mind, Becker analyzes family values, investment in human capital, old age support, and how changes in economic and social conditions and public policies, such as social security, may affect parental efforts to affect the values of children.

In a more recent paper,[3] Becker extends this idea jointly with Kevin M. Murphy and Jörg L. Spenkuch. "The Manipulation of Children's Preferences, Old-Age Support, and Investment in Children's Human Capital" shows that manipulation of child preferences acts as a commitment device and may end up helping children and parents. If children are altruistic, then even selfish parents will make the optimal investment in their children's human capital, a new result that they call "Rotten Parent Theorem." This is exactly analogous to the situation in Becker's "Rotten Kid Theorem," first stated in "A Theory of Social Interactions" (1974), where selfish children perform actions that raise the income of their altruistic parents, and parents later more than compensate the children for their actions.

The second paper analyzes indoctrination of youth and adults by advertisers, dictators, religions, and governments. The literature of indoctrination has a long history, but this is the first attempt to analyze the problem under the assumption that both the indoctrinator and the public behave rationally. Individuals are indoctrinated not in the abstract but through a process. In this approach, advertising, sermons, government propaganda, and other types of indoctrination do not change preferences, but they increase or decrease the individual's well-being by stable preferences. Using this approach, Becker shows that indoctrination is greatest when individuals can be forced to submit to the indoctrination process; it is lower when indoctrinators are monopolists who cannot make subjects worse off than they would be without indoctrination, and it is lowest when indoctrinators have to compete for the opportunity to indoctrinate.

This paper is closely connected to "Norms and the Formation of Preferences" (1996), in which Becker "takes a different approach to explain how one class—usually the upper class—creates norms to influence the preferences of other classes. In this approach the upper class does not 'brainwash' other classes, for they voluntarily allow their preferences to be influenced. But a member of the lower class must be compensated for such changes in his preferences if they lower his utility by discouraging behavior that would benefit him. The approach to the formation of norms . . . assumes that one class decides whether to 'instill' particular norms in members of other classes, who in turn must decide whether to 'allow' the norms to become part of their preferences."[4]

The analysis of the link between childhood experiences and adult preferences presented in the first essay of this part is closely related to Becker and Murphy's work on rational habit formation and addictions.[5] "The formation of preferences is rational in the sense that parental spending on children partly depends on the anticipated effects of childhood experiences on adult attitudes and behavior."[6] The third manuscript in this part is about addictions and the structure of families. In these notes, prepared for a talk at the 2000 General Meeting of the Mont Pelerin Society in Santiago de Chile, Becker uses the economic, or rational choice, approach to addictions to analyze how demand for drugs and other addictive substances could have responded to the sharp changes in family structure during the second half of the previous century. Becker combines this analysis with his work with Kevin Murphy on social economics to discuss the role of social pressure in determining the effects of decriminalization of drugs.[7]

One of his last posts on the Becker-Posner Blog was called "Why Marijuana Should be Decriminalized." In the post he concludes, "The present spending of substantial resources on trying to combat marijuana use would be replaced by considerable revenue from taxing its use. A good use of the tax revenue would be on education and other efforts to point out the harm from becoming addicted to drugs. Some of the revenue could also be used to support drug clinics and other private groups that are trying to both treat addictions and to discourage individuals from becoming addicts. These are far better uses of government revenues than are the expenditures on police, courts, and prisons to apprehend and punish individuals who consume marijuana."[8]

In book 1, chapter 10, of *The Wealth of Nations*, Adam Smith identifies the job attributes that could account for differences in wages: "The five following are the principal circumstances which, so far as I have been able to observe, make up for a small pecuniary gain in some employments, and counter-balance a great one in others: first, the agreeableness or disagreeableness of the employments themselves; secondly, the easiness and cheapness, or the difficulty and expence of learning them; thirdly, the constancy or inconstancy of employment in them; fourthly, the small or great trust which must be reposed in those who exercise them; and fifthly, the probability or improbability of success in them." In the last essay of this part, building on Smith's idea, Becker incorporates power as a job attribute valued by workers to analyze the relationship between power, job hierarchy, and earnings. The analysis uses the economic approach to think about power relations and the allocation of power in the organization, an issue overlooked by economists and traditionally dominated by sociologists. To perform the analysis, Becker extends the preferences of workers by incorporating the fact that people care about the power associated with different positions in an organization. He appeals to the idea that "Men and women want respect, recognition, prestige, acceptance, and power from their family, friends, peers, and others."[9]

Preference Formation within Families

June 1992

Prepared for Presentation at the Meetings of the American Economic Association, January 6, 1993

GARY S. BECKER

1. Introduction

Children are born with their genetic makeup and their experiences in the womb, but are largely a tabula rasa compared to the effects of a lifetime of future experiences. One does not have to accept the Freudian emphasis on very early childhood and early sexual fantasies to believe that childhood and teen-age experiences have an enormous influence on adult preferences. Basic values, preferences in food and clothing, attitudes toward the opposite sex, ambitions, and other parts of preferences all get influenced by what happens to a person when young.

And no one has a greater influence on preference formation than parents and other close relatives. They usually determine practically all the experiences of children during their first few years of life, and many of their experiences through the teens. What parents do and do not do has a great influence on the preference formation of their children.

Most parents are aware of this, if only vaguely. To the extent they care about what their children's preferences will be, they incorporate the effects on children in their decisions concerning what they do. For example, if their smoking raises the likelihood that their children smoke, they may decide not to smoke because they do not want the children to take up smoking. Or they may go to church only because they believe church-going will improve the values of their children.

Of course, what parents want to do is constrained also by their preferences, as influenced by their own childhood experiences. Rational parents maximize their utility, conditional not only on their resources, but also on their past experiences, and their attitudes toward their children.

Sections 2 and 3 of this paper are organized around the issue of support of parents in their old age. Parents will accumulate assets to help provide for their old-age needs. Whether they also want their children to help support them depends on their altruism toward children. I will show that the desire for support also interacts with whether parents invest the optimal amount of human capital in children.

How can parents insure that their children will want to help them if they need help? One way is to try to influence the formation of children's preferences so that they want to help out. Parents can try to make their children love them, or feel guilty toward them, or have other preferences that lead children to help out.

If parents can rely on children to help out, they have an incentive to invest more in their children's human capital. That is, expectation of old age support by children will tend to lead to more efficient levels of investment in children's human capital. However, it also leads parents to save less for their old age support since they will rely more on help from their children.

As discussed in Section 4, governments may help the elderly through a social security system. Since that reduces the need to rely on children, social security will influence parental efforts to affect the preferences of children. As a result, families may be less closely knit because of the reaction of parents to the government program. Selfish parents are particularly likely to do less for their children when the government does more for the parents.

It is not only parents who greatly influence the preferences of children, for children also influence parental attitudes. In particular, children can affect how much their parents like them by acting "cute," by doing what their parents want them to do, by visiting parents when they are older, and in many other ways.

Section 5 considers the effect of children on the altruism of parents toward the children. Parental altruism is made endogenously dependent on the behavior of children. And children try to manipulate this altruism, so that they can benefit. For example, children may study a lot, even though they do not want to, because that leads their parents to be more generous to them.

2. The Model

I assume that everyone lives for three periods: youth (y), middle age (m), and old age (o). Everyone has one child at the beginning of his adult period, so that a child's youth overlaps his parent's middle period, and the child's middle age overlaps his parent's old age. The parent's utility is separable in the utilities he gets at each of these stages of the life cycle. Parents may also be altruistic, and the utility they get from children is also separable from the utilities they get from their own consumption.

Therefore, the utility function of parents (V_p) can be written as

$$V_p = u_{mp} + \beta u_{op} + \beta a V_c,\tag{1}$$

where β is the discount rate, and a is the degree of parental altruism toward children. Selfish parents have an $a = 0$, and the degree of altruism rises with a. I do not permit parents to be sadistic toward children, although the analysis can be easily generalized to include that as well.

Each person works and earns income only during middle age. Hence it is necessary to save to provide resources that can be consumed in old age. He can accumulate assets with a market-determined yield of R_k, which equals 1 + the interest rate on the asset. A parent also is responsible for providing for his children's earning power by investing in their human capital. The marginal yield on his investment in human capital (R_h) is defined as

$$R_h = dE_c / dh,\tag{2}$$

where E_c is the earnings of children at their middle age. This yield is assumed to decline as more is invested: $dR_h / dh \leq 0$, where h is the investment.

Parents must also decide whether or not to give a bequest to their children, which is denoted by k_c. The amounts consumed by parents at middle and old age are denoted by Z_{mp} and Z_{op}. If parents can consume at different ages, leave bequests, or invest in the child's human capital, their budget constraint would be:

$$Z_{mp} + (Z_{op} / R_k) + h + (k_c / R_k) = A_p,\tag{3}$$

where A refers to the present value of resources.

One first order condition to maximize parental utility is

$$u'_{mp} = \beta R_k u_{op} = \lambda_p,\tag{4}$$

where λ_p is parents' marginal utility of wealth. Another condition determines whether they give bequests:

$$\beta a V'_c \leq \frac{\lambda_p}{R_k} = \beta u'_{op},\tag{5}$$

and the last determines investment in the human capital of children:

$$R_h \beta a V'_c = \lambda_p.\tag{6}$$

Equation 6 assumes that the first order condition for investment in human capital is a strict equality; that some human capital is always invested in children. One way to justify this is with an Inada-type assumption that small investments in human capital yield very high rates of return. In a rich economy like the United States, investments in basic nutrition of children, etc. presumably do yield a very good return. As long as parents are not completely selfish—as long as $a > 0$—then an Inada condition does imply positive investment in human capital. However, I do permit parents to be completely selfish, so for them one may want to interpret equation 6 as an inequality.

Equation 4 determines parental consumption in middle and old age. Parents accumulate some capital assets to help finance their old age consumption. Would they also like old age support from their children? That is determined by equation 5. If this equation is a strict inequality, parents do not want to leave bequests to children. By equation 5, that happens when

$$aV'_c < u'_{op}. \tag{7}$$

We can write this equation in a more revealing way. If children allocate their resources to maximize their utility, then the envelope theorem enables us to write this equation as

$$au'_{mc} < u'_{op} \text{ since } V'_c = u'_{mc}. \tag{8}$$

Equation 8 has a simple interpretation. Parents do not want to give bequests if the utility they get from their children consuming a dollar more at middle age is less than the utility parents get from having a dollar more to consume at their old age.

Obviously, this inequality holds for completely selfish parents since the left hand side of equation 8 would be zero when a is zero. The less altruistic parents are, the less likely they are to give to children.

By combining equations 5 and 6, we get

$$\lambda_p / R_h \leq \lambda_p / R_k, \text{ or } R_h \geq R_k. \tag{9}$$

Equation 9 states that the marginal rate of return on human capital equals the return on assets when parents give bequests, while it is greater than the asset return when parents do not want to give bequests. Parents can effectively give bequests in two ways: either by investing in the human capital of children, or by leaving them assets. Since they want to maximize the advantage to children given any cost to themselves— they are not sadistic—they want to leave bequests in the most efficient form.

Consequently, if they are not leaving assets—if strict inequality holds in equation 9—then the marginal return on human capital must exceed that on assets, for otherwise they would give assets and less human capital. If they are giving bequests as well as human capital, then they must get the same marginal return on both, which is what an equality in equation 9 states (these results have already been stated in Becker [1967], Becker and Tomes [1986], and Becker and Murphy [1988]).

If a strict inequality held in equation 9, parental investment decisions are not efficient, for both parents and children could be better off with greater investment in human capital. For suppose parents were to invest a dollar more in children and save a dollar less for their old age support. Children's earnings would increase by R_h, while parents' resources available for their old age support would fall by $R_k < R_h$. Consequently, if children agreed to give their parents $R_k < g < R_h$ in old age support, both parents and children would be better off if parents had spent a dollar more on children and a dollar less on their old age savings. The same argument can be repeated to show that both could be made better off by further investment in children's human capital unless $R_h = R_k$.

But parents and children may not be able to write a contract specifying that children provide a certain amount of old age support in return for parents agreeing to increase their investments in children's human capital. For what government would enforce a contract made with children under age 14, or even older? And if children are selfish toward their parents and otherwise unconcerned about their parents' welfare, they may not keep any promise to help out when the time comes to do so.

Equations 7 and 8 imply that parents do not want to give bequests when $R_h > R_k$. Indeed, they want some old age support from their children because the marginal utility they get from middle age consumption exceeds the marginal utility *they* get from middle age consumption of their children. They would like to take resources from their children, but I assume that is not possible, nor is it possible to write a contract to get efficient investments in children. What, if anything, can parents do?

3. The Formation of Preferences, Efficiency, and Commitment

This is where the influence of parents on the preferences of their children enters the analysis. Parents may be able to influence the adult preferences of children, so that children are willing to help out when parents are old, even without a contract. Whether parents want to do this depends on whether they want old age support, and how costly it is to reduce such desires of children.

Suppose parents can take actions x and y when their children are young that affects the children's preferences. To model in a simple way the effects of these actions on children, write the utility function of children as

$$V_c = u_{mc} + L(y) - G(x, g) + \beta u_{oc} + \cdots. \tag{10}$$

I assume that $L' > 0$, and $G_x > 0$. This means that an increase in y raises the utility of children, but an increase in x lowers their utility. Why then would a non-sadistic parent spend any resources on x? Interpret G as the amount of "guilt" that children feel in regard to relations with their parents. Then an increase in x makes children feel guiltier, which lowers their utility.

The key to understanding why even altruistic parents may want to make their children feel guiltier is the role of the variable g. For g measures the contribution of children to the old age support of parents. I assume that $G_g < 0$; an increase in their contributions makes children feel less "guilty." If $G_{gx} > 0$, then a greater x may stimulate more giving by children as they try to cut down their guilt.

The budget constraint of parents now becomes:

$$Z_{mp} + h + y + x + (Z_{op} / R_k) + (k_c / R_k) = A_p + (g / R_k). \tag{11}$$

The first order condition for the optimal y is

$$\beta a L' \leq \lambda_p. \tag{12}$$

It is easy to understand why an altruistic parent may try to affect children's preferences through y since an increase in y raises children's utility ($L' > 0$).

The first order condition for optimal x is more interesting. Since an increase in x makes children guiltier, it may stimulate them to take actions when they are adults to reduce their guilt. The actions of most immediate relevance to the analysis is to increase g, contributions to parents. An increase in these contributions raises the utility of parents in their old age. It also has an opportunity cost to children that equals the marginal utility of wealth to children.

The first order condition for x to parents is then:

$$\frac{dV_p}{dx} = \frac{dg}{dx}\beta(u'_{op} - au'_{mc}) - \beta a \frac{dG}{dx} \leq \lambda_p. \tag{13}$$

where dG / dx incorporates the induced change in g. The second term in the middle expression is negative to altruistic parents because an increase in x raises children's guilt, which lowers the utility of altruistic parents. However, an increase in their guilt induces them to increase their old age support of parents, and parents try to anticipate this response as they decide whether it is worthwhile to try to make children feel guiltier.

Increased old age support from children has two effects on the welfare of altruistic parents that have opposite signs. On the one hand, it raises parental old age consumption, which raises their utility, as given by u'_{op} in equation 13. On the other hand, increased old age support lowers the resources that children have available to spend on themselves, which lowers the utility to altruistic parents, as given by the term $-au'_{mc}$ in equation 13.

In deciding whether to make children feel guiltier, parents must try to solve the children's maximization problem to determine how much children will increase their old age support when they feel guiltier; that is, parents must estimate dg / dx. Since parents "move" first as they decide expenditures on young children (although see the discussion in section 5), this game has a natural sequential decision structure.

If parents decide to make children feel guilty because the gain to parents outweighs their evaluation of the loss to children, then equation 13 becomes an equality. Note, however, that altruistic parents who make bequests to their children will never try to make them feel guiltier. For the term in parentheses in equation 13 equals 0 for these parents since they get the same marginal utility at old age from their own and from their children's consumption. Since guiltier children have less utility, such altruistic parents do not want to create any more guilt.

Parents who do not make bequests may be willing to make their children feel guiltier because they get more utility from an increase in their own consumption than they lose from an equal reduction in children's consumption. In particular, completely selfish parents may well be willing to raise the guilt of children because they do not care about children's utility. For them, equation 13 reduces to the simple condition

$$\frac{dV_p}{dx} = \frac{dg}{dx}\beta u'_{op} \leq \lambda_p, \text{ or } R_x = \frac{dg}{dx} \frac{\lambda_p}{\beta u'_{op}} = R_k. \tag{14}$$

Equation 14 gives a very simple condition for selfish parents. They are willing to spend resources to make children feel guiltier as long as the rate of return on these expenditures through the induced increase in old age support from children is larger than the rate of return on accumulating assets for old age. As it were, affecting children's preferences to make them guilty enough to want to support their elderly parents is an alternative way to save for old age that may substitute for accumulating assets for old age.

This implies that even selfish parents may spend time with children and otherwise treat them well if it pays off later. They invest in the "good will" of their children. Of course, children may see through the facade and recognize that their parents were nice to them for selfish reasons alone. Whether or not children can see through to the deeper motivation may have a crucial effect on the size of dg / dx, or how much guiltier children would feel if they do not help their elderly parents a lot. It may be much easier for parents who genuinely like their children to create guilt than for parents who only pretend to like them.

There are no real limits on how much guilt selfish parents would be willing to create, but there are sharp limits for altruistic parents. As children increase their giving, that lowers u'_{op} and raises u'_{mc}. As these get closer together, the term in parentheses in equation 13 gets smaller. Altruistic parents stop creating guilt *before* they are indifferent between increases in their own and in their children's consumption. They *would* like additional support from their children, but they are not willing to create any more guilt to get it. These parents would not mind at all if children voluntarily were willing to give more.

Richer parents invest more in the human capital of their children because such "goods" tend to be positively related to income. Consequently, richer families are more likely to be at the point where $R_h = R_k$. This means they are more likely to leave bequests for their children, an implication of the analysis that is clearly supported by the evidence. Hence, our analysis implies that rich families are less likely to want to create guilty children since they do not need to rely on children for old age support.

It is often remarked that the rich seem "cold" to their children, while the middle classes and many of the poor have a "warmer" family atmosphere. Our analysis may be able to explain this, for these latter families have greater *need* of warmth.

Since they do not plan to leave bequests to children, they have to rely on old age support. To insure that such support will be forthcoming at the appropriate time, they work at creating family warmth as mediated through children's guilt, affection, etc.

In other words, wealth does not automatically bring coldness. It does so indirectly by affecting whether a family wants to go through the effort to create a warm atmosphere. A rational choice approach to preference formation need not take "coldness" and "warmth" in a family as given, but can explain why they are related to family wealth, parental altruism, and several other variables.

Old age support from children has implications for the other decisions even of altruistic parents. Increased support from children lowers u'_{op}, which reduces parents' incentives to save assets for their old age. For why save so much if children will be helping out? Of course, as parents save less, they have more incentive to create guilt since lower saving raises u'_{op}. This lowers saving still further, etc., until a new equilibrium is reached.

Asset accumulation and guilt-creation are alternative ways for parents to save for old age. If they are good at creating guilt, they will tend to save little, and instead rely on help from their children. So one might expect parents to either save a lot and rely little on children, or save only a little and rely mainly on support from children.

Old age support from children also has implications for investments in the human capital of children. Recall that the only parents who may be willing to make their children guilty are those who do not give them bequests. And these are the parents who invest less than the optimal amount in their children's human capital. The first order conditions equations 5 and 6 imply that

$$\frac{u'_{op}}{au'_{mc}} = \frac{R_h}{R_k}.$$ (15)

An increase in the old age support from children lowers the left hand side of equation 15 by lowering the numerator and raising the denominator. In the new parental utility-maximizing position, the right hand side must also fall. Since R_k is given by market conditions, the only way the right hand side can fall is by R_h falling.

But R_h can fall only by increasing h, the amount invested in children. Hence, a rise in old age support from children encourages a more efficient level of investment in children's human capital. Even fully selfish parents might decide to invest in their children if they anticipate that old age support is sufficiently responsive to children's wealth. For if the initial investments in human capital yield a very high return, children might spend enough of their higher wealth on their parents to make this a better investment for selfish parents than the accumulation of assets.

However, greater old age support due to guilt can never lead altruistic parents to *fully* efficient levels of human capital investment. Parents always prefer at the margin their own consumption to their children's consumption *if* the only way they can increase support from children is by making them guiltier.

The increased investment in children's human capital induced by greater children support of parents raises children's earnings, which makes them better off. However, the increased support was induced by greater children guilt, which makes them worse off. It is possible that the net result is that children are made *better* off by parental efforts to make children guiltier. This is more likely, the slower R_h declines as h increases, the less sensitive G (their guilt) is to x, and the more sensitive g is to x.

It seems strange that children might become better off by being made to feel guilty. However, the explanation is straightforward: parents are not making the optimal investment in children's human capital. Parental spending on creating children's guilt is harmful, and would not be used if a first best way was available. But barring contracts, etc., guilt-creation could be a good second best way to increase not only parental utility, but children's utility as well.

A better way might seem for children to agree that they will *act* later on as if they were guilty. That would save the resources lost on guilt-creation, but it would not work. For children would refuse to help when the time came later on for them to do it since they would not want to help.

By affecting preferences, the creation of guilt *commits* children to helping out when their parents need help. If preferences are conditional on past experiences, the past partly commits future actions (see the more extended discussion in Becker [1991]).

This is one important reason why parents try to influence the preferences of their children. I have discussed this in the specific context of providing old age support, but the argument applies much more broadly. Parents try to be good examples and take other actions that, in part at least, are motivated by the desire to influence children's preferences. They may want children to become committed in the future to being honest, conscientious, thrifty, trustworthy, and so forth.

Parents can help push the process in the right direction by taking the appropriate actions. Altruistic parents who are also forward looking will do the best they can to commit children's preferences along the right path. And as we have seen, the "right" path could include commitment by children to provide old age support since that commitment could make children as well as parents better off.

4. Social Actions: Norms and Governments

In many traditional societies, children help elderly parents partly because of social norms; that is, social pressures exerted against children who do not do well by their parents. The analysis in this paper shows how these norms might have developed.

Many, perhaps most, families in traditional societies want to influence their children's preferences so that they are willing to help when parents are old. They may preach family loyalty, work to create guilty and altruistic children, and so forth. They may also form and join various organizations where the message to help parents is conveyed to groups of children. Religions, schools, and other group activities may preach this message in many ways that use peer pressure to help form the preferences of the young.

It is easier to get children to help if they come to believe it is the "right" thing to do. Religions and other group activities reinforce this view. And once people believe that they do something because it is the right behavior, they will look down on anyone who behaves differently. This is what norms are all about.

In this case, a norm developed because parents have an interest in helping it to emerge. Parents have an incentive to influence their children's preferences to support their own elderly parents. They also have an interest in getting this attitude reinforced by pressure from other families. But why do not parents free-ride on the pressure created by other families, and save the resources involved in creating guilt among their children? This is the fundamental question in the theory of norm-creation.

This is where religions, schools, and similar organizations play an important role. By "pricing" membership appropriately, they can give families the incentives to create the right attitudes toward old age support among their children. For families with the right attitudes find it easier or cheaper to gain membership. Appropriate entry requirements to gain membership can eliminate—or at least greatly reduce—any incentive to free ride on the efforts of other families.

It is sometimes claimed that the welfare state helped break up the family in the Western world. It is clear enough that governmental programs like unemployment insurance, social security, and health insurance reduce the need to rely on family members to cover these hazards (see Becker [1991, Chapter 11]). But why do such programs affect family *preferences*? Should one expect these programs to make families less closely knit?

One affirmative answer is provided by our analysis of the formation of preferences within a family. Without public programs to take care of elderly, sick, or unemployed persons, parents may spend resources to influence the attitudes of children to make them willing to help out when other family members are experiencing difficulties. If governments began to help, families will have an incentive to save resources by spending less on inducing their members to want to help.

Consider family spending on making children willing to provide old age support. Equation 13 shows that the incentive to spend depends on the term $u'_{op} - au'_{mc}$. Government payments to the elderly that are financed by pay as you go taxes on the working population lower u'_{op} by raising the resources of the elderly, and raise u'_{mc} by taking away some resources of the middle-aged. Consequently, the difference between these marginal utilities is reduced.

But a smaller difference reduces the gain to parents from spending resources to affect the preferences of children so that they want to help out. As a result, children will feel less guilty, altruistic, etc., toward their elderly parents when a social security program is put in place. The welfare state in this case would indirectly affect how close-knit families are.

Parents who leave bequests to children have no incentive to create guilt, etc., among the children to make them want to help out when the parents are old or otherwise in need. The reason is that they do not need help since they give to children rather than want to take from them. The attitudes toward each other in such families would not be affected by social security. That is, preferences within Ricardian-equivalence families would not be much affected by such government programs.

It is the families who do not want to leave bequests who are most affected by social security. These are the families who most rely on children to help out when parents are elderly or otherwise in need. Consequently, preferences in precisely those families where the government programs make the largest differences are most influenced by these programs.

We have seen that these are more likely to be middle class and some poorer families. Therefore, social security and related programs are most likely to affect the closeness and warmth in these families: it is "middle class values" that are wounded by welfare state programs. The coldness of the rich and the family disorganization of the very poor are not much affected.

One should not jump to the conclusion that these welfare state programs are necessarily bad because they adversely affect middle class family values. Government *may* be better than children at caring for the elderly. After all, many children do not help very much, and the guilt that leads others to help may harm their mental health. The point is that it is less efficient to have middle class family values when the welfare state is in full swing. But a comparison of governments and families at caring for family members raises many issues that are beyond the scope of this article.

5. The Influence of Children on the Preferences of Parents

I have been assuming that parents affect the preferences of children, and have ignored the effect of children on their parents' preferences. Yet everyone who has dealt with children knows that children also can alter parental attitudes toward them. By acting cute, considerate, affectionate, angry, hurt, needy, selfish and so forth, children affect their parents guilt, love, concern, and other attitudes. And these attitudes influence children's behavior by changing parental actions that have an impact on children's welfare.

I will illustrate how this can be done by considering parental altruism. I have taken the degree of altruism—the term a in the parental utility function V_p—as given, but altruism may be determined partly by children's behavior. To show this, it is necessary to allow children to take actions that influence parental preferences which have an impact on children's well-being.

To allow parental altruism to be affected by children's behavior, I assume that parents' utility depends not only on their own consumption and children's utility, but also on the behavior of children:

$$V_p = V(Z_p, V_c, X_c), \tag{16}$$

where X_c are the choices of children that influence parental utility. Parents are not only altruistic but are also "paternalistic," and prefer that children consume a large quantity of X; that is $\partial V_p / \partial X_c \geq 0$. Parents may prefer that children study hard, act thrifty, obey orders, visit often, marry someone they like, and so on.

What is important for our present purposes is that how well children conform to parental wishes may have a large effect on how much parents like their children. The degree of altruism now becomes endogenously related to whether children satisfy the paternalistic desires of parents. This is incorporated into the analysis through the assumption that

$$\partial^2 V_p / \partial V_c \partial X_c \geq 0. \tag{17}$$

This assumption means that paternalism and altruism are *complements* in the parental utility function. An increase in either raises the marginal utility to parents of the other. One need not assume that paternalism and love are competing attitudes of parents toward children, for they can coexist and even reinforce each other (the discussion in this section is based on Becker [1991, pages 10–13]).

Children's utility depends on X_c and Z_c, where the latter goods do not directly affect parent's utility. Children maximize their utility $V_c(Z_c, X_c)$ subject to their budget constraint:

$$Z_c + p_x X_c = I_c + g_p, \tag{18}$$

where p_x is the price of X, and g_p are gifts from parents to children that are motivated by their altruism. Presumably, gifts are larger when parents are more altruistic. Since altruism depends on children's consumption of X, g_p should also depend on such consumption.

Children begin to realize that how nicely they are treated depends on whether they behave in ways that their parents like. They have an incentive to take actions that lead to better treatment even if these actions are not very pleasant for them. For an increase in X_c could lead to an increase in g_p that makes children better off, even if the increase in X lowers their utility.

To model the feedback effects between X_c, g_p, and children's behavior, I again assume a simple sequential game. Children first choose Z_c and X_c, and then parents choose Z_p and g_p. Children try to anticipate how their choices affect gifts from parents because these gifts change their total resources. If children can accurately anticipate parents' gifts because they can solve the parents' maximization problem, then one can assume a perfect foresight equilibrium where children know how gifts depend on their choices.

The relevant first order condition for children is

$$\frac{\partial V_c}{\partial X_c} = \frac{\partial V_c}{\partial Z_c}\left(p_x - \frac{\partial g_p}{\partial X_c}\right) = \frac{\partial V_c}{\partial Z_c}\pi_x, \tag{19}$$

where π_x is the marginal price of X after subtracting out the effect of additional X on gifts from parents. If the complementarity between altruism and paternalism summarized by equation 17 implies that parental gifts rise when children consume more X, then X becomes effectively cheaper to children. This induces children to choose a greater quantity of X than they would do otherwise.

Note that equation 19 implies that children may consume a positive quantity of X even if this reduces their utility—if $\partial V_c / \partial X_c < 0$. Children may intensely dislike studying, but may study a lot because it has a negative net cost since parental gifts rise enough when they do study to compensate for children's disutility.

In a way parents can be said to "punish" children who do not consume what parents want them to. But such punishment is not directly conditioned on children's behavior, but operates indirectly, or automatically, through parental preferences. Children's behavior influences parents' preferences, which induces parents to respond *automatically* in particular ways. No bargaining or threats need by involved, for everything depends on the formation of parental preferences through children's choices. And rational children take these effects into account in deciding what they do.

In this example, parental altruism is endogenously related to children's behavior. And the endogeneity of their altruism *commits* parents to particular responses that may serve a useful purpose in the perennial game between parents and children.

Consider a wasteful child who anticipates that his parents will help him out when his resources run low because they love him. He would then have little incentive to be frugal. If, however, they love him *less* when he is wasteful, they may then not be willing to help him out very much. And their reluctance to help feeds back on his behavior and discourages him from being as wasteful as he would otherwise be.

The endogeneity of altruism in this case leads to more efficient behavior by cutting down waste. It does this through generating a commitment that may otherwise be difficult to obtain. And the commitment is automatic because it comes through preferences. The argument is similar to that in the earlier sections, where children became committed to helping parents in their old age because parents affected their preferences regarding guilt and the like.

This analysis of endogenous altruism can help explain why parents are more altruistic to their *own* children than to other people's children. In addition to the biological preference for own children, there is also the fact that own children have more opportunity to influence their parents' preferences. Since they are raised by their parents, they can take actions that positively affect the degree of altruism of their parents. They act lovable and do other things that raise parental altruism. They do these things not necessarily out of any love for their parents, because we have shown how children can benefit if they increase their parents' love for them.

We are not denying that own children start out with an advantage over other children regarding their parents' love. But these differences get magnified over time as children reinforce their initial advantage with behavior that increases parental altruism toward them. It is easy to exaggerate the *intrinsic* differences in altruism by observing simply the differences in altruism toward own and other people's children after the children have lived for at least several years.

Siblings have much less of an intrinsic advantage over each other than they have over other people's children. And they may be forced to compete for the limited good will of their parents. For an increase in the degree of altruism toward one child may lead to lower giving to the other children.

If there are n children, one could replace the parental utility function in equation 16 with

$$V_p = V(Z_p, V_c^1, V_c^2, \ldots, V_c^n, X_c^1, X_c^2, \ldots, X_c^n). \tag{20}$$

V_c^i refers to the utility of the ith child, and X_c^i refers to the paternalism-influencing choices of the ith child. It is natural to assume that an increase in X_c^i raises parental gifts to the ith child because X_c^i and V_c^i are complements in the parental utility function.

It is also reasonable to assume that the altruism that parents feel toward different children are substitutes, so that a child gets his parents to love him more partly at the expense of reducing the love toward siblings. Therefore, if an increase in X_c^i raises gifts to the ith child, that tends to lower gifts to siblings. So children have to compete for the limited affection of their parents by their choices of paternalism-satisfying consumption.

One could model the competition among siblings by assuming that the children move simultaneously, and afterwards parents select the gifts to all their children. One looks for Nash equilibrium among the children's choices that are contingent on the gifts from parents, which are in turn contingent on the paternalistic-satisfying choices of all the children. There is no reason to expect a unique equilibrium, but there would be a tendency for children to do "too much" to satisfy their parents, as they try to get an edge on their siblings (see Bernheim et al. [1988] for a related model of competition among siblings).

Not only do children, in effect, choose the degree of parental altruism toward them, but this example also brings out that in a fundamental sense, parents also choose their own altruism. Suppose that *other things the same*, parents would get the same pleasure from changes in the utilities of many different children, including several that are not their own. And suppose too that the altruism toward the different children are close substitutes.

Parents have to decide in which directions to cultivate their altruism through gifts, frequent contacts and in other ways. Given their limited time and other resources, cultivation of altruism toward some children will tend to mean less altruism toward other children. Which children should they cultivate?

It is clear that other things the same, they want to cultivate those children who can benefit them the most, which gives these children an edge over the others who are competing for the affections of adults. Own children clearly can in general benefit them more since they interact much more with own children. They live in the same household, and in other ways generally have much more contact with their own children.

So in effect, we can say that parents partly *choose* to be more altruistic to own than to other children. And among the own children, they *choose* to be more altruistic toward the children whose behavior can be most favorably influenced by parental altruism. By "most favorably influenced" is meant the children who can respond more with paternalistic-satisfying choices, or the children who are most likely to support the parents when they get old, etc. (see also Rotemberg [1994] for a discussion in other contexts of the choice of altruism).

References (added by the editors)

Becker, Gary S. 1967. "Human Capital and the Personal Distribution of Income: An Analytical Approach." Woytinsky Lecture, no. 1. Ann Arbor: Institute of Public Administration.

———. 1991. *A Treatise on the Family*. Cambridge, MA: Harvard University Press.

Becker, Gary S., and Kevin M. Murphy. 1988. "The Family and the State." *Journal of Law and Economics* 31 (April): 1–18.

Becker, Gary S., and Nigel Tomes. 1986. "Human Capital and the Rise and Fall of Families." *Journal of Labor Economics* 4, no. 3, pt. 2 (July): S1–S39.

Bernheim, B. Douglas, and Oded Stark. 1988. "Altruism within the Family Reconsidered: Do Nice Guys Finish Last?" *American Economic Review* 78 (December): 1034–45.

Rotemberg, Julio J. 1994. "Human Relations in the Workplace." *Journal of Political Economy* 102, no. 4 (August): 684–717.

Rational Indoctrination and Persuasion*

Preliminary, March 2001†

GARY S. BECKER

1. The Nature of Indoctrination and Persuasion

There is a long history of concern with indoctrination and persuasion, but few discussions take the approach of this article, which assumes that persons being persuaded or indoctrinated are rational. For purposes of this article I simply mean by "rational" that individuals maximize their utility, including their decisions about indoctrination and persuasion.

Individuals are indoctrinated or persuaded not in the abstract, but through a process. For example advertisers use television commercials for particular products that surround these products with athletic, sexual, or other symbols that are designed to stimulate greater demand. Parents may use their behavior or lectures to indoctrinate their children into concern for others, especially for other member of their family.

The processes used may attempt to indoctrinate and persuade by changing either the information and beliefs, or the attitudes and tastes, of the persons they are trying to influence. Advertisers may provide information about the health-enhancing properties of their products, or they may simply show attractive individuals consuming these products. Parents may try to explain why honesty is a good policy, or simply repeatedly emphasize that their children should be honest.

Whether information or attitudes are to be affected, indoctrination and persuasion would be welcomed rather than resisted if the process used raised the net expected utility of those being persuaded and indoctrinated. By "net" utility is meant after deducting the time and other costs of being exposed to the process. Similarly, rational individuals would resist any indoctrination and persuasion that made them worse off.

*I had valuable comments from Edward Lazear, Richard Posner, Ivan Werning, and Sherwin Rosen shortly before he passed away. My research was supported by the Olin Foundation and the Stigler Center at the University of Chicago.
†Not to be cited without permission.

Note that if the process itself makes a person better off, then a rational person must be even better off after the adjustment in his behavior caused by the effects of the process. For he could stand pat and not adjust his behavior, so that any adjustment must make him even better off than he would be simply from exposure to the process alone. For example, if a rational person likes an ad, he is even better off from any induced increase in consumption of the goods being advertised. If he likes the rituals and doctrines of a particular religion, he is made even better off from any induced increase in religiosity due to the rituals and doctrines.

If a process itself lowers utility of recipients, then adjustments in their behavior induced by the process would reduce the negative effect on their utility. It is possible that the positive effects on utility from these adjustments could be larger than the negative effects of the process. However, such induced net increases in utility are unlikely, so I lump these cases with those where the process itself raises utility.

Processes that lower utility may seem strange and unlikely, but there are many examples. Television ads for life insurance that show a destitute wife and children after a father dies without life insurance may be unpleasant, but they are presumed to stimulate demand for life insurance. Children may not like to hear lectures from their parents on the need to support them when they get old, but these lectures could stimulate guilt and love by the children that significantly raises their support (see Becker, 1992). Preachers who sermonize about temptation and the devil may make the congregation feel uncomfortable, but such sermons could stimulate better behavior and greater religiosity. Sometimes citizens are forcibly exposed to government propaganda that disturbs them, as when it asserts that loyalties lie with the government rather than with families or religions, but this may reduce their other loyalties. Tardy employees may become unhappy when they hear lectures by their employers on the necessity of arriving to work on time, but they also may begin to feel guilty about being late.

The analysis of indoctrination and persuasion is far more challenging when it lowers rather than raises utility. For it is easy to understand why even rational individuals permit themselves to be indoctrinated and persuaded if that makes them better off. But why would rational persons endure a process that makes them worse off? To try to answer that question, this essay ignores utility-raising indoctrination and persuasion.

I also concentrate on indoctrination and persuasion that operates through attitudes and preferences rather than through beliefs and information. I believe that most of the implications that are derived would also apply to the beliefs case, but I do not attempt to show that.

2. A Model of Indoctrination

From now on I use the term "indoctrination" to stand for either persuasion or indoctrination. The approach used to discuss indoctrination is to expand the utility function to include the indoctrination processes themselves. For example, parental efforts to change the attitudes of their children toward them would be included in the children's utility functions (as in Becker, 1992). Advertising itself would be included in the utility functions of those exposed to advertising, along with the goods advertised (as in Becker and Murphy, 1993). The pictures of dictators and the sermons of preachers would also be included in utility functions of those exposed, along with their attitudes toward the dictators, and their attendance at church and their beliefs in god.

With this approach, indoctrination does not change utility functions, but rather the indoctrination process becomes one of the arguments of these functions. In other words, in this approach, advertising, sermons, government propaganda, and other types of indoctrination do not change preferences, but they increase or decrease the utility given by stable preferences. Since there is a unique set of preferences for each individual, there can be no conflict between pre and post indoctrination preferences since they are the same.

Indoctrination directly changes the level of utility through the indoctrination process, and it also changes the marginal utilities from different consumption choices and behavior. By changing some marginal utilities more than others, indoctrination would alter the utility-maximizing consumption choices.

My approach is shown by the following utility function:

$$U = U(x, y; I\,) = u_t(x, y). \tag{2.1}$$

The *LHS*, *U*, is utility, x and y are consumption goods, and I represents the indoctrination process. The stability of preferences over time is expressed by the assumption in eq. 2.1 that the U function in the middle does not have a time subscript.

The stability of the utility function that depends on I as well as x and y implies that the utility from given amounts of x and y will change over time if I does. Therefore, u, the utility function of x and y alone, has a time subscript, which recognizes that this function would change over time if the amount of indoctrination, I, changes over time, even though the fuller function, U, were stable. We use the word "tastes" to describe the u function that depends only on consumption. Our analysis imbeds instability of tastes that depend only on consumption of different goods into a framework where preferences are a stable function of a much broader set of arguments that include indoctrination efforts.

The assumption that the preference function U is stable in one sense is a tautology since an unlimited set of variables can be included in this function. But preference stability is a very useful tautology for understanding choices and behavior since this assumption is the beginning, not the end, of the analysis of choice. In particular, this framework can explain why it is sometimes very difficult to indoctrinate others, even by powerful governments. Rational individuals can anticipate and try to counter or avoid indoctrination that they do not like. And sometimes competition among indoctrinators raises the utility of those being indoctrinated because they have to attract individuals to their indoctrination efforts.

An analysis of indoctrination depends on both the motivation of indoctrinators, and the responses of those being indoctrinated. I assume that indoctrinators want to shift tastes in favor of particular goods, concepts, beliefs, or individuals. Parents may try to make their children feel guilty if they were not to support them when they became old. Advertisers want to increase the demand for goods they produce, corporations want to raise the loyalty of their employees, preachers want to increase attendance at their services and belief in the doctrines they advocate, and dictators want to raise their esteem in the eyes of their citizens.

Indoctrinators recognize that indoctrination is usually not free, but takes their time and money. Advertisers spend well over \$100 billion in the United States on advertising, parents spend time inculcating proper attitudes in their children, and dictators spend on celebrations, outings, schools, rallies, and propaganda to indoctrinate the young and adults.

Presumably, rational indoctrinators are willing to pay these costs because they benefit from successful indoctrination. I assume that the utility of indoctrinators depends on the consumption of goods x, and that indoctrinators maximize their utility by comparing the benefits to them from indoctrination to the costs of producing the indoctrination:

$$V = B(x) - C(I), \text{ with } B' \text{ and } C' > 0, B'' < 0, \text{ and } C'' > 0. \qquad (2.2)$$

The utility of indoctrinators depends on B, the benefits to them from the consumption of x by the population being indoctrinated, and $C(I)$, the cost of indoctrinating. Indoctrinators choose I to maximize V, subject to the effectiveness of I in producing increased consumption of x. That is, the behavior of indoctrinators is subject to the relation between x and I determined by the preferences of those being indoctrinated, and the market for indoctrination.

Consider a representative person among those subject to indoctrination efforts. Advertising, rallies, propaganda, schooling, and other methods are used to shift his behavior toward the goods desired by indoctrinators. Indoctrination expenditures on I try to raise the marginal utility from x relative to y in either the U or u functions in eq. 2.1. This implies that someone successfully indoctrinated would voluntarily increase his demand for the x's desired by indoctrinators.

The concept of "indoctrination" and "persuasion" rather than compulsion implies that subjects successfully indoctrinated voluntarily choose to act in ways that benefit indoctrinators. This implies that

$$\partial U/\partial x \geq 0. \tag{2.3}$$

Otherwise, they would not voluntarily choose to increase their consumption of x either before or after indoctrination.

Since I am concentrating on negative effects of the indoctrination process on the utility of subjects, then

$$\partial U/\partial I < 0. \tag{2.4}$$

For small amounts of indoctrination, the total effect on the utility of those subject to indoctrination is entirely determined by this derivative. However, for large amounts of indoctrination, the effect on utility also depends on how the indoctrination process shifts their choices of x and y.

Moreover, even when the indoctrination process lowers utility, as in eq. 2.4, the induced shift in behavior of utility-maximizing persons toward the x's desired by indoctrinators raises the utility of those being indoctrinated (as well as that of indoctrinators). For subjects voluntarily shift their behavior toward the x's after the indoctrination process only because that raises their utility. That is, optimal consumption would shift toward x and away from y because higher I raises the marginal utility of x relative to y without changing prices or wealth. Hence

$$dx^*/dI > 0. \tag{2.5}$$

That is, the indoctrination stage must raise the utility of rational persons being indoctrinated, even when the indoctrination itself lowers their utility. This distinction between the effects on utility of the induced change in behavior, and the effects on utility of the indoctrination process itself, has been missed because indoctrination has not been discussed in a framework where those indoctrinated are assumed to behave rationally.

Most discussions of indoctrination presume that persons indoctrinated are brain-washed or in a trance, and are unable to look out for their interests. That may sometimes be true, but one can discuss indoctrination in a meaningful, and I believe insightful manner, while still preserving the assumption of rationality and utility maximization by those subjected to indoctrination.

This approach recognizes that individuals may be hurt by indoctrination efforts through a negative effect of the indoctrination process on their utility, as in eq. 2.4. But rational persons who are indoctrinated make the most of a bad deal, and they shift toward greater x because that is induced by the indoctrination process. They consume greater x not because they are brain-washed, but rather because that raises their own utility, given their exposure to the indoctrination process.

Still, it is important to also recognize that while their shift to greater x makes rational individuals better off, given that they were subject to the indoctrination process, this does not mean they are better off than they would have been without the indoctrination. Indeed, if the process itself makes them worse off, as in eq. 2.4, then they are surely worse off for small changes in the indoctrination process, and they are likely to be worse off even for large changes.

3. Indoctrination under Different "Market" Conditions

This conclusion, however, raises the fundamental question of why rational individuals would expose themselves to an indoctrination process that makes them worse off? Of course, they might not fully anticipate the harmful effects, but they would not willingly do anything that makes them worse off. Consequently, if they anticipate negative consequences, they either would have to be forced to accept exposure, or they would have to be compensated for the exposure. This section compares the equilibrium amounts of indoctrination under different conditions that determine how easy it is for indoctrinators to access the individuals they want to indoctrinate.

A. FORCE

The most attractive situation for indoctrinators is when the individuals they want to indoctrinate cannot refuse exposure to the indoctrination process. Parents have this power over their children when the children are young. Even democratic governments force children to attend schools where they can be indoctrinated (see the discussions by Bowles and Gintis, 1976, and Lott, 1999). These governments as well often require young persons to serve in the armed forces and at other activities where they are also subject to indoctrination. Totalitarian governments do all these things too, but in addition, they may require attendance at rallies and parades, indoctrinate workers at government enterprises, and use the public streets and airwaves for further indoctrination.

When subjects can be forced to be exposed to the indoctrination process, indoctrinators do not have to be concerned about the effects on the utilities of subjects. They would then choose the amount of indoctrination that maximizes their own utility in eq. 2.2 without paying any attention to the effects on the utilities of those indoctrinated. The FOC for their maximization is simply

$$B'(x)dx/dI - C'(I) = 0. \qquad (3.1)$$

The derivative dx/dI and the optimal x as a function of I to the typical person indoctrinated are then determined from his budget equation and first order maximization conditions. Given these, eq. 3.1 leads to the optimal levels I^* and x^* when force is available.

This equation shows that the amount of resources that indoctrinators want to spend on indoctrination is limited by the cost of that process, even when indoctrinators can force exposure to the indoctrination process. These costs include the time and goods that parents use to persuade their children, and the resources spent by governments on instruction in patriotism. However, the resources that indoctrinators want to spend is also limited in a more interesting way by dx/dI, the effectiveness of indoctrination expenditures in producing additional consumption of the goods desired by indoctrinators.

For example, the Soviet Union had seven decades of almost full control over schools, jobs, radio, and television to indoctrinate the young and old. That dictatorial government tried to make Russians and other members of the Union more concerned about the state's welfare than their own selfish wellbeing, and to persuade them that the state came before religion and even their families. However, the degree of success in these efforts was quite limited. Their monopoly of the communication media and other institutions were not enough to allow them to persuade most of the Soviet population that they should put State interests before their own and those of their families.

The power of the State was limited by the indoctrination of parents that offset state propaganda—even the powerful Soviet State never attempted to separate the rearing of children from their parents.

This, and perhaps basic biology, apparently were powerful forces that continued to promote self-interest against all efforts to further the interests of the State.

But while the parental monopoly of child-rearing activities gives them enormous power over the formation of their children's ethics, loyalty, and motivation, even the influence of parents is limited. For example, practically all parents in traditional societies try to instill in their children attitudes that would induce them to support their parents in old age. And most parents do succeed to some extent since the main old age support in these societies comes from children. But still, appreciable numbers of children treat their elderly parents shabbily, despite parental and social efforts at indoctrination.

B. MONOPOLY OF INDOCTRINATION

Often, individuals can avoid the indoctrination process if they want to. One situation is where an indoctrinator has a monopoly of indoctrination, so the only choice to individuals is whether to accept that indoctrination or none at all. For example, one religion may have monopoly privileges granted by the state, such as Islam in Islamic fundamentalist republics, Judaism in Israel, and Catholicism in Ireland and Poland. Individuals can choose to avoid the indoctrination of the monopoly religion only by not attending any religious service.

In such cases, rational individuals would not accept the indoctrination process if they expect to be made worse off since they can avoid the process. A monopolist indoctrinator would have to take that into account, but only to the extent of insuring that the individuals they want to indoctrinate would not be made worse off than they would be without the indoctrination.

Monopoly indoctrinators maximize their utility function in eq. 2.2, but they are subject to the incentive-compatibility condition that their indoctrination cannot make subjects worse off. If the indirect utility function of individuals exposed to indoctrination is expressed as $E(I, W, p)$, where W is their wealth, then the constraint on a monopolist indoctrinator is that

$$E^*(I^*, W^*, p) = E^*(0, W, p). \tag{3.2}$$

The RHS gives the optimal utility of subjects when they are not exposed to indoctrination, and the LHS gives their optimal utility when they are exposed to I^*.

If the indoctrination process lowers the utility of those being indoctrinated—as in eq. 2.4—they have to be sufficiently compensated by indoctrinators so that in equilibrium they are no worse off than they would be without the indoctrination. We assume that they are exactly compensated with monetary transfers, defined by $g = W^* - W$, although often they are compensated by particular goods and services. For example, advertisers on television compensate viewers who do not like their ads by providing programs that they do like along with the ads (see Becker and Murphy, 1993).

If transfers are subtracted from the indoctrinator's utility function in eq. 2.2, the FOC's for I and g to maximize that utility, subject to eq. 3.2, imply that

$$B'(x)dx/dI - c'(I) = -E_I^*/E_g^*. \qquad (3.3)$$

The RHS of this equation must be positive if the indoctrination process lowers utility since $E_I^* < 0$. Hence a monopolist indoctrinates to a point where the marginal benefits to him from indoctrination exceed the marginal costs of the indoctrination process.

Comparing eqs. 3.1 and 3.3 shows that a monopolistic indoctrinator does less indoctrinating than an indoctrinator who can force subjects to submit to the process. A monopolist has an additional cost of indoctrinating since he has to compensate subjects for any harm to them from the indoctrination process. Even when compensation is lump-sum and in a strictly monetary form, the need to compensate reduces optimal indoctrination efforts.

The technical reason for this is that equilibrium marginal benefits to indoctrinators equal their marginal costs of indoctrination when subjects can be forced to submit to the indoctrination process. These subjects are made worse off by the indoctrination process, but a powerful indoctrinator does not have to worry about their welfare. Since a monopolist, however, cannot force subjects to submit to indoctrination, he cannot lower their utility below where they would be if they were not indoctrinated.

A monopolist can raise their utility without lowering his utility by small reductions in indoctrination expenditures from the equilibrium with force available where the indoctrinator's marginal cost equals his marginal revenue. This immediately implies that a monopolist spends less on indoctrination than indoctrinators who can use force. If the utility of subjects were still below what they would have without indoctrination, a monopolist would have to further reduce indoctrination expenditures and further increase monetary compensation until the monopoly equilibrium is reached, where subjects are no worse off than without the indoctrination.

C. COMPETITIVE INDOCTRINATION

Especially in market-organized democratic societies, most indoctrination takes place under competitive conditions. Religions still try to indoctrinate, but they must compete against other religions that try to induce conversions to their own religious doctrines. Companies advertise to persuade consumers to buy more of their products, but they have to recognize that they are competing for consumers' attention and money against many other advertisers. Politicians try to develop a following, but they have to compete against other politicians trying to do the same.

The main effect of competition among indoctrinators is to allocate some of the surplus from indoctrination to the subjects who are being indoctrinated. Instead of their equilibrium utility being unchanged by indoctrination, the reallocation of some surplus to individuals being indoctrinated induced by competition among indoctrinators makes the subjects as well as indoctrinators better off from indoctrination.

The effect of this reallocation of rent can be shown by first taking the differential of eq. 3.2 with respect to E^* to get:

$$E_I^* dI + E_g^* dg = dE^* > 0. \tag{3.4}$$

One might believe that the optimal way for indoctrinators to increase the utilities of subjects would be to simply raise monetary transfers. But that would not be efficient if the marginal utility of wealth is diminishing to those being indoctrinated.

This is easily seen from the equilibrium condition for indoctrinators in eq. 3.3. If only g increased, the denominator of the RHS would be reduced with diminishing marginal utility to subjects from greater wealth. Assuming that the reduction in marginal utility of wealth does not greatly reduce the marginal disutility of the indoctrination process—greater wealth would tend to increase this disutility—an increase in g would raise the RHS of eq. 3.3. For equilibrium to be restored, the LHS must then also increase, which is only possible through reduced expenditures on indoctrination. This shows that the utility of subjects would not be increased only through an increase in monetary transfers, and that indoctrination is also reduced by competition among indoctrinators.

We can summarize the results of this section by the

PROPOSITION: The ranking of indoctrination expenditures and the amount of indoctrination is: $I_f^* > I_m^* > I_c^*$, and $x_f^* > x_m^* > x_c^*$. Indoctrination is greatest when individuals can be forced to submit to the indoctrination process, it is lower when indoctrinators are monopolists who cannot make subjects worse off than they would be without indoctrination, and it is lowest when indoctrinators have to compete for the opportunity to indoctrinate.

References (added by the editors)

Becker, Gary S. 1992. "Preferences Formation within Families." Included in part 2.

Becker, Gary S., and Kevin M. Murphy. 1993. "A Simple Theory of Advertising as a Good or Bad." *Quarterly Journal of Economics* 108, no. 4 (Nov. 1993): 941–64.

Bowles, Samuel, and Herbert Gintis. 1976. *Schooling in Capitalist America: Educational Reform and the Contradictions of Economic Life*. New York: Basic Books.

Lott, John R., Jr. 1999. "Public Schooling, Indoctrination, and Totalitarianism." *Journal of Political Economy* 107, no. S6: S127–S157.

Some Notes on Drugs, Addiction, Families, and Public Policy

May 2000

Prepared for Meeting of Mont Pelerin Society, Santiago, Chile, November 13, 2000

GARY S. BECKER

Several findings from the modern economic analysis of addiction are highly relevant in understanding the determinants of the demand for drugs, and how demand responds to changes in prices of drugs and in family structure. These notes sketch out the relevant analysis.

1. The Economic Theory of Addiction

Many substances, including tobacco, alcohol, heroin, and cocaine, have been shown to be "addictive" in the sense that increased consumption of these substances in the present encourages greater consumption in the future. However, the economic theory of addiction does not imply that heavy users of tobacco, cocaine, or other substances remain addicted forever. It can explain why most young addicts eventually throw off their addictions.

To be sure, this theory implies that addictions usually can end only by "cold turkey"; that is, only by abrupt cessation of use. Various investigations by psychologists and others support these implications of the theory.

Addictions to substances appear to begin either early in life or not at all. By early, I mean primarily from age 13 to 20. Few heavy smokers or regular users of crack cocaine appear to begin their addictions after their early twenties. Similarly, most also end their addictions, if they do, by age twenty-five or so.

The onset of substance addictions during the impressionable teen years suggests that peer and other social pressures are particularly important determinants of drug use. Consumption of many goods is heavily influenced by what others consume, but social influences tend to be particularly strong for addictive substances and for younger persons, although empirical support for social influences is hard to tease out from consumption data. Still, the circumstantial evidence is quite strong that peer pressure is important for heavy drinking, smoking, drug use, and other addictions.

The early beginning of addictions to drugs and other substances implies that parents and family structure are major determinants of whether children become addicted. Parents have an enormous influence over the formation of the preferences of their children (see Becker, 1996 for a discussion of preference formation). In particular, children are far more likely to become heavy drinkers and smokers when their parents are (see Cook and Moore, 2000).

In addition, children often become addicted to substances after the marriage of their parents breaks up, and children who grow up in homes without both parents more frequently become heavy drinkers and smokers (see, e.g., Cook and Moore, 2000). A marriage breakup increases the propensity of children to perform worse while in school, and to drop out of secondary school.

Parents also greatly influence the kind of peer pressure experienced by their children through their decisions about where to live, the schools their children attend, and whether to attend church on a regular basis. Presumably, parents take peer and other effects on their children into account in their decisions, including where to live and whether to divorce, although some parents put more weight than others do on positive or negative "spillover" effects of their behavior on children.

2. Implications of the Theory

The theory of substance use onset and subsequent addiction sketched out in section 1 has various implications about responses to price changes and other forces that are briefly considered in this section. Contrary to many beliefs about addicts, this theory implies that addictive consumption highly responds to changes in price and other forces that affect the demand for addictive goods.

The initial impact of say an unexpected permanent rise in the price of cigarettes or cocaine might be slight since addicts are "locked in" by past consumption. But over time declines in their consumption accumulate since every fall in consumption encourages further declines in the future. This implies that the long run price response would tend to be larger for addictive goods than for "similar" non-addictive goods, even though short run responses to unexpected price changes would be *relatively* small for addictive goods.

The price response of the demand for cigarettes, a highly addictive good, has been extensively studied. The evidence indicates that the long run price elasticity of demand exceeds 0.7, which is rather large compared to estimated elasticities for other goods. Moreover, even short run price responses of smoking are not small (see Becker, Grossman, and Murphy, 1994).

Grossman (2000) has recently summarized the evidence on the effects of price changes on the consumption of alcohol, cocaine, opium, and marijuana. Studies of opium price response in Taiwan and the Dutch East Indies find long run elasticities of 1.0 or more (Grossman, 2000, p. 16). Equally large price elasticities have been found for cocaine and alcohol (see Grossman, 2000, pp. 15–17). The response to changes in the price of marijuana appears to be smaller, although the estimates are not statistically reliable (see Grossman, 2000, p. 18).

The theory of social interactions implies that goods which are subject to peer group pressure also tend to be unusually responsive to common shocks that affect the consumption by each member of the group. Consider the effect of a permanent change in price that initially reduces the demand of each member. Then each further reduces their consumption because other members have done so. The total decline would be large if the "social multiplier" were sizeable (see Becker and Murphy, 2000). Indeed, the aggregate demand could change explosively since this multiplier could be large enough to create unstable demand.

Such explosive responses to price and other common shocks would be particularly likely for goods like drugs that are both addictive and sensitive to peer pressure. In that case, even moderate degrees of addiction and moderate degrees of social pressure could interact to create enormous sensitivity of aggregate consumption to changes in prices and other variables that affect all members (see Becker, 1996).

The revolutionary changes in the family during the past four decades presumably also left their mark on the demand for drugs and other addictive substances. The most relevant changes for our purposes are the sharp decline in birth rates, the rapid growth in divorce rates in most developed countries (and in many developing countries as well), the rise in the fraction of unmarried mothers, and the greatly expanded labor force participation of married women.

The decline in births presumably helped reduce the propensity of children to become addicted. For parents invest more in the preferences and human capital of each child when they have fewer children.

However, most other major changes in family structure probably raised the likelihood that children become addicted to drugs and other substances. The evidence suggests that this is an especially likely effect of the much higher divorce rates, and possibly too of the steep rise in the fraction of unmarried younger women with children.

3. A Few Policy Implications

I have generally supported decriminalization of drugs. This is partly out of libertarian beliefs, but probably even more out of the practical difficulties of generating effective policies of prohibition. A full evaluation, however, requires an appreciation of the economic theory of addiction. Unfortunately, few contributions to the discussion of decriminalization, either pro or con, incorporate these implications.

Presumably, the price of drugs would fall greatly if they became legal because the expected cost of punishment is incorporated into price. According to the theory summarized in the previous section, this lower price would initially have relatively little effect on drug use, especially if it were unanticipated. However, the long run increase in drug use would be expected to be substantial because of the sizeable long run elasticity of demand for drugs. Recall that the high elasticity is due both to the cumulative effects on demand of lower past consumption, and to the cumulative effects of the social multiplier due to peer pressure and other social interactions.

The theory, however, also offers two possibly major qualifications to this conclusion about large responses to decriminalization. When peer pressure is important, there may be "multiple equilibrium," or more than one aggregate consumption outcome at any given price. The reason is simple. A young man may use cocaine if he believes that everyone else in his peer group uses cocaine. If everyone in the group believes as he does, the result would be a large demand for cocaine mainly because of the expectation by each person that peers are cocaine users. However, if everyone expects his or her peers to be abstaining, each person might also abstain, and the result then will be little use by this group. It is possible that due to the presence of such multiple equilibrium, ending the prohibition on drugs could shift the equilibrium from one with large drug use to one with much less use through the effects of decriminalization on expectations.

This change in expectations might occur because legalization of drugs per se may affect the demand for drugs. On the one hand, some young persons might reduce their interest in drugs because buying or selling them would no longer flout governmental authority. On the other hand, some young persons who refrained from use when drugs were illegal would now become more willing to try them. If the expectations shift toward lower consumption by others because of the first effect, decriminalization could actually lower consumption despite a much lower price.

The initiation into drug use at early ages creates philosophical problems for libertarian fellow-travelers like myself. The reason is that the preferences and behavior of children and teenagers are so heavily determined by their parents, especially the values and attitudes parents convey to children. That raises no problem in most families where parents are very concerned about the effects of their behavior on the attitudes and preferences of their children.

But drug use among children tends to be greater precisely in those divorced families, and in other badly-functioning families, where less attention is paid to the influence of parental behavior on their children. I am not sure how this cuts on the decriminalization issue, but it does suggest at the very least a minimum age for the purchase of drugs so that consumers are old enough to have greater influence over their behavior. Moreover, it makes evident that the many government programs which help destabilize families have additional negative effects through the indirect stimulus given to the use of drugs.

The public policies I consider particularly harmful to families include welfare programs that encourage marital breakups of poorer families, and divorce laws, like no-fault divorce, that tend to worsen the position of divorced women, even if they do not encourage divorce. I also am concerned about weak public schools that do little to produce the marketable skills that would provide boys and girls better legal job alternatives to selling drugs, and to drug use and other destructive behavior.

Bibliography

Becker, Gary S. 1996. *Accounting for Tastes*, Harvard University Press.

Becker, Gary S., Michael Grossman and Kevin M. Murphy. 1994. "An Empirical Analysis of Cigarette Addiction," *American Economic Review*, 84 (no. 3): 396–418.

Becker, Gary S., and Kevin M. Murphy. 2000. *Social Markets*. Cambridge: Harvard University Press.

Cook, Philip J., and Michael J. Moore. 2000. "Environment and Persistence in Youthful Drinking Patterns." April.

Grossman, Michael. 2000. "The Economics of Substance Use and Abuse: The Role of Price." April.

Promotion Tournaments, Power, Earnings, and Gambling

Preliminary, July 1991

GARY S. BECKER

Sociologists always speak about the power relations among people in different jobs, social classes and ethnic groups, while economists seldom give that much attention. Yet to the extent that people value power—and presumably most people do like it—the allocation of power should be part of the allocation of jobs, etc. I will show that incorporating power helps explain a major puzzle that is less well explained by the usual analysis.

The puzzle can be seen from the model of a hierarchy in an organization—say a company. The president is at the top and has the most power in the sense that his decisions influence everyone below that. Vice-presidents have the next largest amount of power, and so on, with power declining as one descends the hierarchy. Workers at the bottom have the least power.

If power is valued as a good, the president gets the most utility from this good and the workers get the least utility, or the most disutility. Shouldn't the president receive the lowest wage, while workers get the highest wage to compensate them for their lack of power? That would surely be so if all employees ex ante were equally capable. But since the president has the most power and influence, there is a gain from putting the most capable person at the top (see Rosen [1986]). Wages as well as power might then rise through the hierarchy because ability rises.

Surely, ability and human capital do tend to rise with position in the hierarchy, but since power also rises, there is no *guarantee* from this line of argument that earnings rise rather than fall with power. The sorting of people by ability only implies that *utility* rises with position in the hierarchy. Since by definition, power rises with position, and if power raises utility, the latter could rise even if earnings fell.

Another approach to sorting in a hierarchy builds on the fact that most higher level appointments result from promotions within the organization. If private information about effort is important, a company might encourage employee effort by making them participate in a tournament with promotions going to those who win. Rosen has shown that if identical employees participate in a tournament that has stochastically determined output, then earnings have to rise with position in order to encourage effort. Ultimately, earnings must rise at a convex rate as position in the hierarchy rises.

This analysis also ignores the direct utility from power. What is really shown is that utility has to rise with position but not necessarily that earnings do.

In these tournaments there is uncertainty about pay and utility because promotions, and hence earnings, depend on stochastic variables that affect output. If the utility function were concave in earnings, the uncertainty in outcomes means that average earnings have to be high enough to compensate participants for bearing the risk from the tournament.

Consider a tournament which recognizes that utility depends on power (P) as well as earnings:

$$U = U(E,P), \quad \left. \begin{array}{l} U_e > 0, U_{ee} < 0 \\ U_p > 0, U_{pp} < 0 \end{array} \right\} \tag{1}$$

I assume that utility is concave in P alone as well as in E alone. It is reasonable to assume also that

$$\frac{\partial^2 U}{\partial E \, \partial P} = U_{pe} > 0, \tag{2}$$

that an increase in power raises the marginal utility of income. There are several ways to justify this; for example, the prestige from having a powerful job provides entree to a higher social class, exclusive clubs, etc. This assumption is important to my analysis.

Equations 1 and 2 are consistent with U being either concave or convex in E and P together. Utility is jointly convex or concave as

$$U_{ep}^2 \gtrless U_{ee} U_{pp}. \tag{3}$$

I assume first that U is convex in E and P together. Then the goal of the design in the relation between E and P would be to take advantage of such convexity to make U convex as E changes, given the relation between E and P. Such convexity is attained by having earnings rise as power rises in the hierarchy.

This is easily seen by letting earnings be linearly related to power:

$$E = a + bP, \tag{4}$$

where E and P move together only if $b > 0$. If $b < 0$, higher earnings compensate for less power. The total differential of U with respect to E, taking account of the implied change in P given by equation 4 is

$$\frac{dU}{dE} = U_e + U_p \frac{dP}{dE},$$ (5)

and

$$\frac{d^2U}{dE^2} = U_{ee} + U_{pp}\left(\frac{dP}{dE}\right)^2 + 2U_{ep}\frac{dP}{dE}.$$ (6)

By equation 4, the second order differential becomes

$$\frac{d^2U}{dE^2} = U_{ee} + \frac{U_{pp}}{b^2} + \frac{2U_{ep}}{b}.$$ (7)

Clearly, given that $U_{ee} < 0$, $U_{pp} < 0$, and $U_{ep} > 0$, equation 7 can be positive only if $b > 0$: only if earnings in a job are positively related to the power. Moreover, if U is jointly convex in E and P, it is easy to show that values of $b > 0$ do exist to make $d^2U / dE^2 > 0$. However, if U is jointly concave, then no value of b could make the right hand side of equation 7 positive.

Owners are better off when the employees in a promotion tournament have increasing marginal utility in earnings because such employees want to gamble. That is, they are willing to pay with lower expected earnings for the privilege of engaging in a tournament with uncertain outcomes about both earnings and power. In this way promotion tournaments serve two purposes: they goad workers into greater effort, but they also reduce costs by lowering the average level of compensation.

At the beginning I pointed out that a positive relation between earnings and power seems to waste a company's money, for it compensates higher level employees twice: with greater power and also with greater money. But this turns out to be the opposite of the truth in promotion tournaments where winners and losers are not known in *advance*. *Only a positive relation between earnings and power saves a company money by offering employees the opportunity to gamble over both power and earnings.*

This has been shown only when utility is jointly convex in power and earnings. I do not want to argue, nor do I have to, that convexity is plausible. Perhaps utility is concave in E and P both separately and jointly. It might seem that employees then do not want to gamble because the second order differential of their utility function is negative. That is true if the relation between earnings and power is linear. But with an appropriate nonlinear relation, a firm can make its employees want to gamble over earnings and power even when the utility function is fully concave.

If the relation between E and P is not linear, the second order total differential in equation 6 is extended to

$$\frac{d^2U}{dE^2} = U_{ee} + U_{pp}\left(\frac{dP}{dE}\right)^2 + 2U_{ep}\frac{dP}{dE} + U_p\frac{d^2P}{dE^2}. \tag{8}$$

If U is concave, the sum of the first three terms must be negative by the negative definiteness of quadratic forms for concave functions. But no restriction is placed on the term that depends on the $E - P$ relation, $U_p(d^2P / dE^2)$. This term is positive if d^2P / dE^2 is positive; that is, if E is a concave function of P.

Consequently, utility can be made convex in E—after netting out the accompanying change in P—if U_p is large enough and if E is made a sufficiently concave function of P. Then employees would be willing to *pay* for the privilege of engaging in a promotion tournament on both earnings and power even when their utility function is fully concave. Firms reduce costs by converting employees into gamblers over earnings and power together through the way they structure the earnings payoff to greater power.

Notice that such a gamble cannot be held on income alone in a lottery market since utility is concave in income alone. The gamble intrinsically requires a tie-in between income and power, and hence can only be provided by an organization—such as a firm—that brings together both these arguments of the utility function.

Note too that the concave function of power required for earnings could be consistent with Rosen's convex relation between earnings and hierarchical level. They will be consistent if power is a more convex function of hierarchical level than is earnings.

I have interpreted P as "power," but I have not introduced any properties of such power other than that it rises with position in the hierarchy. One might define $P = s(H)$, where H is position in the hierarchy, and s is the fraction of jobs below H. Then $0 \leq s \leq 1$, and $s' \geq 0$. If $E = E(H)$, so that earnings go with the job, then $P(E)$ gives the implicit relation between P and E to H.

One might as well for some purposes deal directly with the function

$$P = s(E),\ 0 \leq s \leq 1,\ \text{and}\ s' \geq 0, \tag{9}$$

where s gives the fraction of persons in the hierarchy who can earn less than or equal to E. The utility function

$$U = U(E, s(E)),\ U_s > 0 \tag{10}$$

can be interpreted as assuming that utility is produced by being a big fish in a little pond (Frank [1984]).

If everyone is identical in tastes and productivity, there is no way to compensate ex post those persons who take jobs lower down in the hierarchy since they necessarily earn less and thus also have less power. This is why Frank [1984] assumes heterogeneity in tastes.

But everyone, even if identical, might participate in a gamble that ex post *either* gives high E and s, *or* low E and s. The second derivative of U with respect to E, and hence also s, is

$$\frac{d^2U}{dE^2} = U_{ee} + U_{es}s' + U_{ss}\left(s'\right)^2 + U_s s''. \tag{11}$$

The firm would try to find a compensation structure that for a given total expenditure, makes the right hand side of equation 11 as large as possible.

By the argument given earlier, if U is jointly convex in E and s, there exists a uniform distribution of pay over jobs ($s'' = 0$) that makes the sum of the first three terms on the right hand side of equation 11 positive. If U is fully concave, this is not possible. But even then, a nonuniform distribution of E that has a rising density as the level of the job increases ($s'' > 0$) could make $d^2U / dE^2 > 0$. In other words, a sufficiently convex cumulative distribution on earnings could induce employees to pay for the privilege of participating in a promotion tournament.

Actual cumulative distributions of earnings in companies are convex over certain job regions, but probably not at the upper end. Therefore, it is not obvious that actual distributions are consistent with this analysis of what is needed to induce participants to want to pay for the privilege of participating in a tournament.

In all cases, the aim of the firm is to design a compensation schedule to maximize the expected utility of the typical employee-participant, given total spending on compensation. The market equilibrium condition then enables compensation expenditures to be reduced to the point where the maximized expected utility equals the utility a participant can get at other firms.

It might appear that each participant's gamble imposes an externality on other participants since anyone can get more power only by reducing the power of the others. But this externality is internalized by the firm. By maximizing the value of the gamble to participants—given total compensation—the firm chooses the most efficient gamble, and takes account of all externalities.

This internalization of externalities distinguishes these gambles over power and earnings within a firm from gambles in the marketplace. In market gambles where say income rank counts, each gambler does not fully internalize the negative effects on others (see Robson [1990]). Consequently, there is social value to a preference for being a big fish in a small pond compared to a preference for being a medium-sized fish in an ocean. The owner of the pond—in my example, firm—will internalize the externality from the competition to be big, whereas there is no owner of "oceans" who can internalize such competition.

Equations 1–8 use a variable called "power," but they do not utilize any properties of power—that is done in equations 9 and 10. The question arises: how much of the analysis would apply to any type of non-pecuniary payoffs from different jobs? If P refers to general non-pecuniary or hedonic attributes, it would not necessarily be reasonable that $U_{ep} > 0$. But how needed is this assumption? I showed that $U_{ep} > 0$ is required if P and E are linearly related, and if U is convex in P and E jointly.

But if U is concave in P and E, then even $U_{ep} > 0$ cannot produce a desire to gamble when P and E are linearly related. I showed that it is necessary then to have a convex relation between P and E. However, with a sufficiently convex relation, it may not be necessary to have $U_{ep} > 0$. Indeed, if $U_{ep} < 0$, then a convex partly *negative* relation between P and E might be what is called for.

Since U_p and d^2P / dE^2 in equation 8 are completely independent of the degree of concavity in U, it seems possible always to make $d^2U / dE^2 > 0$ by choice of the $P - E$ relation, no matter what the sign of U_{ep}. However, I am not sure whether this argument is fully valid. But what is clear is that the argument is not applicable with any two types of jobs (or occupations) since it relies on the second derivative of the relation between earnings and type of job.

References (added by the editors)

Frank, Robert. 1984. "Interdependent Preferences and the Competitive Wage Structure." *RAND Journal of Economics* 15 (Winter): 510–20.

Robson, Arthur J. 1990. "Status, the Distribution of Wealth, Social and Private Attitudes to Risk." Paper presented at the 6th World Congress of the Econometric Society, Barcelona, then published as "Status, the Distribution of Wealth, Private and Social Attitudes to Risk," *Econometrica* 60 (1992): 837–57.

Rosen, Sherwin. 1986. "Prizes and Incentives in Elimination Tournaments." *American Economic Review* 76, no. 4: 701–15.

3

HOUSEHOLD PRODUCTION AND HUMAN CAPITAL

On-the-Job Training, Insurance of Market and Nonmarket Human Capital, and Investment in Children

Different constraints are decisive for different situations, but the most fundamental constraint is limited time.

—GARY S. BECKER, Nobel Lecture, 1992

Modern research on the economics of education began in the 1950s with work by T. W. Schultz, Jacob Mincer, Sherwin Rosen, Gary Becker, Finis Welch, and some others. This new literature treats education as an investment that has both costs and returns. The returns analyzed are principally the increase in earnings due to greater amounts of schooling. The costs include tuition, fees, and other direct expenses from schooling, and the earnings foregone by being in school rather than at work.

In his classic study of human capital, Becker applies capital theory to explain investment in an individual's education, training, health, and knowledge, considering their effects on productivity both in market and nonmarket activities. Most of the empirical studies that have been done since then find significant effects of education on people's income and other variables such as health, childrearing, and crime.

The opening paper[1] of this part is perhaps Becker's first approximation of his theory of human capital. It was written as an internal working paper while he was at the RAND Corporation during the summer of 1957. The paper uses the economic approach to analyze the recommendations of the 1957 Report by the Cordiner Committee, which was formed to study military pay as there was concerns about low reenlistment rates among the more skilled personnel.

In his statement to Congress, Ralph Cordiner, president of General Electric Company, said, "Along with a committee of distinguished citizens, I had an opportunity to learn why it is that the most promising skilled young officers and men are leaving the Armed Forces in large numbers, and what it will take to retain them for a productive career in the service of their country." The main recommendation of the Cordiner Report was to raise military pay according to skill, talent, and responsibility as a way to solve the problem.

The twenty-six-year-old Gary Becker tackles the same problem but by addressing a different question: "Should the Military Pay for Training of Skilled Personnel?" In addressing this question, Becker took a first step toward his theory of human capital and the study of worker-firm relationships by developing the concepts of transferable and nontransferable on-the-job training. He later points out in his Nobel Lecture that "One of the most influential theoretical concepts in human capital analysis is the distinction between general and specific training or knowledge."

In this early version, Becker claims that "If the training were not transferable, the equilibrium wage rate would simply equal the marginal product; therefore non-transferable on-the-job training costs should be paid for by the employer, just like any other non-transferable training costs."[2] Later in his *Human Capital* (1964), he shows that "the final step (in the analysis) would be to shift some training costs as well as returns to employees, thereby bringing supply more in line with demand. When the final step is completed, firms no longer pay all (specific) training costs nor do they collect all the return but they share both with employees."[3]

It is interesting that Becker used the case of military service on many occasions over his career to illustrate different points. In considering the arguments against his controversial proposal to pay for organ donors in order to eliminate the organ shortage in an effective way, he compares them with the arguments about paying market wages to attract a voluntary army. Becker also learned from the experience of the drastic policy change of replacing the draft with the once controversial voluntary army proposal that efficient policy could take time to be implemented, as we will discuss in the introduction to part 4.

An important part of the study of human capital is concerned with the use of time. In "A Theory of the Allocation of Time" (1965) Becker develops a general treatment of the allocation of time for education, training, and all other non-working activities.

Becker opens the study by noting that "Throughout history the amount of time spent at work has never consistently been much greater than that spent at other activities. Even a work week of fourteen hours a day for six days still leaves half the total time for sleeping, eating and other activities. Economic development has led to a large secular decline in the work week . . . Consequently the allocation and efficiency of non-working time may now be more important to economic welfare than that of working time; yet the attention paid by economists to the latter dwarfs any paid to the former."[4]

He also notes that "the time spent at work declined secularly, partly because young persons increasingly delayed entering the labour market by lengthening their period of schooling . . . Most economists have now fully grasped the importance of forgone earnings in the educational process . . . it is surprising that economists have not been equally sophisticated about other non-working uses of time. For example, the cost of a service like the theatre or a good like meat is generally simply said to equal their market price, yet everyone would agree that the theatre and even dining take time, just as schooling does, time that often could have been used productively."[5]

Becker's theory of the allocation of time laid the foundations of the analysis of household production and of the allocation of time between and within the market and nonmarket sectors. At the heart of his theory is the idea that households are producers as well as consumers. Analysis of the allocation of time is now used in economics in discussing not only hours' work for pay, but also the time a student invests in education and other human capital and changes in the allocation of time in the course of economic development. Household production theory has become crucial to analyzing human capital and fertility decisions, and also increasingly in both micro and macro aspects of technological progress not only in markets but also in households.

The second selection in this part is Becker's reflections on the 1965 paper. It discusses the allocation of time and goods over a lifetime among three main sectors: consumption, investment in human capital, and labor force participation. The 1965 paper considered the allocation only at a moment of time among various kinds of consumption and time utilizations; this later discussion generalizes the analysis to decisions over time and to investment in human capital.

In a recent work Aguiar et al. (2021)[6] look at how video gaming and other recreating computer activities have affected hours of work by improving leisure technology. They show that these changes account for the decline of work hours of younger men, ages 21 to 30, over the past fifteen years.

Becker's reflections were to be included in 125th-anniversary issue of the *Economic Journal*,[7] where the 1965 paper was published. Becker wasn't able to finish and send the essay to the editors, and an introduction by James Heckman and an essay by Pierre-André Chiappori and Arthur Lewbel was included instead.

On the influence of Becker's theory of the allocation of time, Heckman said: "Although others had developed analytical frameworks with similar features, Becker's great contribution was to apply the model to interpret a broad array of empirical phenomena and to inspire the generations that followed in his wake to investigate the economics of home production. The concept of nonmarket production of human capital (Ben-Porath, 1967), children (Becker and Lewis, 1973; Willis, 1973), health (Grossman, 1972a, b; Becker, 2007b), the value of life (Viscusi and Aldy, 2003), the production of child quality (Leibowitz, 1974; Cunha and Heckman, 2007), transportation (Gronau, 1970), the consumption of leisure on-the-job (Juster and Stafford, 1985; Aguiar and Hurst, 2007; Aguiar et al., 2012) are just a few of the numerous applications of these ideas. Becker's article also stimulated the collection of data on time use in household production."[8]

Chiappori and Lewbel note in their conclusion that "Becker's approach to family economics is so mainstream today that it is difficult to recognize how revolutionary his models and methods were at the time. Pollak (2003) documents how many researchers were openly hostile to Becker's application of mathematical microeconomic tools to intra-household decision-making. Many believed Becker's analyses were sterile and vacuous, and it was considered cold and immoral to think about loving families in such terms. In contrast, the enormous literature on family economics that exists today vindicates Becker's methodology."[9]

In the third paper of this part, Becker uses the household production approach to analyze and distinguish between insurance of market and nonmarket human capital. The analysis extends his earlier work with Isaac Ehrlich (Ehrlich and Becker, 1972)[10] on insurance and self-protection and allows the incorporation of the time devoted to household production and its cost into the insurance problem. This is particularly important in thinking about insurance of the member of the household specialized in household production, and in accounting for nonmarket human capital and differences in health between the members of the household.

One of the main motivations of Becker to develop the theory of human capital was to understand income inequality. In the fourth and fifth essays in this part, Gary Becker assembles a simple structure to think critically about the evidence on the negative relationship between

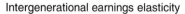
Intergenerational earnings elasticity

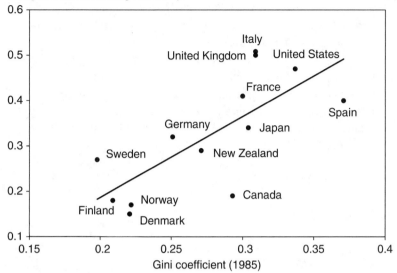

Figure 3.1 The Great Gatsby Curve: Inequality and Intergenerational Mobility.
Source: Miles Corak, "Inequality from Generation to Generation: The United
States in Comparison," https://docs.iza.org/dp9929.pdf, and OECD.

intergenerational mobility and income inequality that had appeared in
the 2012 Economic Report of the President:

> The high degree of persistence in incomes between generations in the
> United States is especially noteworthy in the context of cross-country
> comparisons. Corak (2011) makes such a comparison and finds that the
> average estimated IGE [intergenerational earnings elasticity] of 0.47 for
> men in the United States, while lower than the IGE for countries such
> as the United Kingdom (0.50) and South Africa (0.69), is much higher
> than the IGE for men in countries such as Sweden (0.27), Norway (0.17),
> Finland (0.18), and Denmark (0.15). Jäntti et al. (2006) also compare
> IGEs for men's incomes in some of the same countries and report simi-
> lar estimates.
>
> While many factors contribute to cross-country differences in inter-
> generational mobility, one clear pattern is that countries with more
> intergenerational mobility also tend to have lower point-in-time income
> inequality.
>
> As other research has shown, the finding of a positive relationship
> between IGE and inequality—a relationship that Krueger (2012) has

referred to as "the Great Gatsby Curve"—is robust to alternative choices of countries, intergenerational mobility measures, and year in which income inequality is measured (see, for example, Corak 2011; Andrews and Leigh 2009; OECD 2010). This robust relationship suggests that at least some of the same mechanisms that drive income inequality also drive intergenerational mobility.

For example, a rise in the rate of return to schooling can be expected to lead to both a rise in point-in-time income inequality and a decline in intergenerational mobility because educational attainment is positively correlated across generations.[11]

Should the Military Pay for Training of Skilled Personnel?[1]

RAND Document, D-4508, August 15, 1957

GARY S. BECKER

Rising government expenditures and low reenlistment rates have recently combined to stimulate a reexamination of military personnel
policies. On the governmental level this has culminated in the Cordiner
report; while the private sector of the economy has produced several
studies, here at RAND and elsewhere. The Cordiner report points out
that reenlistment rates are especially low among the more ("hard core")
skilled personnel; that this results primarily from low compensation relative to civilian alternatives; that this is extremely wasteful because of the
large military expenses in training men who fail to reenlist; and that a
way to solve this problem is to raise pay so that a career in the military
becomes economically competitive to a civilian career. A similar analysis and recommendation has been made at RAND by Alain Enthoven.[2]
The writer heartily endorses this recommendation as it certainly would
improve matters. However, it apparently has not been noted that this
recommendation would not lead to an optimal policy, even if it were
carried out in an ideal manner. The optimal policy would not only result
in a more efficient allocation of resources for the country as a whole, but
would also be cheaper for the military. However, some sharp changes in
military personnel procurement policies might be required.

    The model to be employed is the following. An enlistment period of
n years is assumed, and during part of this period the enlistee is trained
for a particular job, such as a pilot, radar repairman, etc. At the end of the
period he has the choice of reenlisting or resigning. The military, in order
to insure that a large fraction of its personnel reenlists, offers any man
reenlisting a time stream of payments with a present value equal to the
present value of the stream he could receive as a civilian. For simplicity
only, it is assumed that there are no net non-pecuniary advantages or
disadvantages of military life relative to civilian life, so that a military
pay equal to civilian pay guarantees that a large fraction of first-termers

reenlist. The military is assumed to behave rationally in the sense that the number of men it "hires" is such as to equalize the present value of the stream of marginal products to the present values of costs. The civilian sector is assumed to behave the same way. Finally, it is assumed that the civilian sector obtains its skilled personnel either from the military or from civilian training schools.

Let us examine the equilibrium conditions in the civilian and military sectors. Each first-termer that resigns and enters a civilian occupation receives an income with a present value of P_c and has a marginal product with a present value of MP_c; for civilian firms to be in equilibrium requires:

$$P_c = MP_c \tag{1}$$

Each first-termer that decides to remain in the military receives an income of P_m and has a marginal product of MP_m. It cannot be said that the equilibrium condition for the military is $P_m = MP_m$, for the military also has to consider the costs and productivity during the first term. Since training costs may be large, military costs are apt to be substantially larger than productivity during the first term. Let t_m represent the value at the end of the first term of the difference between the costs and productivity of first-termers. In equilibrium, total costs per person should equal marginal productivity, or

$$P_m + t_m = MP_m \tag{2}$$

Since $P_m = P_c$ and $P_c = MP_c$,

$$MP_m - MP_c = t_m \tag{3}$$

Thus it turns out that even though the civilian and military sectors act competitively and even though there are no non-pecuniary factors influencing occupational choice, the equilibrium marginal product is not the same in these two sectors, but it is higher in the military by the amount of training costs. This, after all, is not surprising. The military takes unskilled personnel and converts them at a cost into skilled personnel. Skill level determines the civilian wage and hence the amount the military must pay to hold their men; consequently, there is no way for the military to capture the gain from increasing productivity through training.

There are two important implications of equation 3. The first is that resources are inefficiently allocated, since in the model assumed here (perfect allocation in the civilian sector), efficient allocation of resources requires the equalization of the marginal product of each factor in all directions. The second is that the military pays more for skilled manpower than it needs to; the reason for this will become clear shortly. Suffice it now to point out that the military provides "free" training to men who would be willing to pay something—either directly or indirectly—for this training, since it increases their income prospects. The military could, therefore, reduce costs by charging for the training.

If the military shifted some of the costs to the trainees, the value of t_m would be reduced; if all costs were borne by the trainee, $t_m = 0$ and, consequently, $MP_m = MP_c$. The quantity t_m can be reduced in several ways; one way is to lengthen the initial enlistment period and pay a salary that is less than the marginal product during these years. To illustrate, assume that the training and enlistment period are two years and that $t_m =$ \$50,000. Suppose that the enlistment period were extended an additional three years, that the marginal product in each of these years was \$10,000, and that the military paid only \$5,000 for each of these three years. Then t_m would be reduced from \$50,000 to about \$35,000 and roughly \$15,000 training costs would have been shifted to the trainee. Probably something can be done with this technique but it also has an important limitation. Training is primarily given to young men just entering the permanent labor force. At this age they are quite experimental, trying one job and then another in the hope of determining their interests and aptitudes. It is unlikely that they would sign up for very long-term contracts, although they might sign up for five or six years instead of the present four years.

As second method is suggested by the first: to reduce the pay within a given enlistment period. However, as long as payments by the trainee to the military are ruled out, this method, too, has an important limitation: pay can be reduced to a "subsistence" level and no further. Nevertheless, something could be done in this direction and it brings to the surface an error or at least an oversight in the Cordiner report. This report recommends pay increases, particularly for more highly skilled personnel. The analysis here points out that while pay increases are desirable for periods subsequent to the initial enlistment period, a pay *decrease* may be desirable for the initial enlistment period.

Extending the initial enlistment period and reducing pay during this period involve no sharp break with current practices but only marginal adjustments. At the same time, they are apt to have too weak an effect to shift entirely the burden to the trainees, at least for those occupations—like piloting—with substantial training costs. This points to a method which enables the military to shift the entire burden to the trainees; although it involves a more drastic change in military procedure, its use by the military is not unknown. Under this scheme, the individual receiving training directly pays all training costs, so that t_m would equal zero and MP_m would equal MP_c, giving an efficient allocation of resources.

The military might continue to provide the training but would charge an amount equal to its cost, just as they now charge for goods in the PX. If the trainee could not pay these costs, the military would lend him the money at the market rate of interest. I see no difficulties in doing this, so it will not be discussed any further. Since no person could be forced to take training involving a sizable outlay, the military would have to rearrange its personnel procurement policy so as to obtain a sufficient number of persons willing to pay for training. This is an advantage rather than a disadvantage since it guarantees that the military trains people who want (as shown by their willingness to pay for it) training in order to use it later on (see my discussion on pp. 67–68). The difficulty with this procedure is that it maintains the military in the education or training industry as well as in the industry of using skilled personnel for military objectives. The military would have all the "headaches" of being in an extraneous industry and the nation and the military would be prevented from achieving the economies that result from the specialization of function. That such "headaches" and economies would be substantial can be seen from the wide variety of specialized schools which have developed in the civilian sector: these range from universities and trade schools to schools for supermarket "checkers" and bartenders.

This suggests that a wide range of training activities be contracted out by the military to the civilian economy. If the trainee is himself paying all training costs, contracting out is equivalent to buying the end product of the training process. Thus, in hiring persons to fly military aircraft, the Air Force might require, in addition to the usual things, 200 hours flying time—a requirement not unlike that used by commercial airlines today. This kind of requirement is, of course, not unknown to the military: they often require a college or high school education, they secure physicians and dentists without training their own, etc. I merely propose that this technique of buying the trained person instead of training the person be extended systematically to a much wider range of activities.

If the military did adopt this program on a large scale, many more men would have to obtain training in the civilian sector. There is little reason to expect civilian firms making use of skilled manpower to take up where the military left off, for they would run into the same problems that the military faces. There would be a development and expansion of firms or "schools" that specialize in the training of persons for various occupations. These schools would be similar to those already developed on a large scale in the civilian sector. The civilian training of such groups as pilots has only developed on a very small scale because such schools would be "competed out" by the subsidized military schools.

A perusal of the *USAF Training Prospectus* strengthens the suspicion that training expenses may be an important item in the military budget. This is a 150-page manual listing the courses offered by the Air Force alone! It includes a course in the operation of a lithographic press (5-E-23), in the grinding and polishing of lenses (8-E-5), in advanced commercial accounting (AA67270), in the operation of computing machines (AB68230), in the operation and maintenance of welding equipment (AB53230), in machine and bench work (AB53130), in modern weather techniques (XX2524), in teaching (1T75100), in directing a photographic section (OB2331), in transportation techniques (OB6031), and in hundreds and hundreds of other subjects. All these courses and many others give training in skills that are already taught in civilian schools; thus the Air Force could easily hire trained persons. Or to take a different and very controversial example, all three services have their own "colleges"; the Army has West Point, the Navy has Annapolis, and now the Air Force has an Academy. In all these institutions much non-military training is offered in the humanities, the natural sciences, engineering, and the social sciences. But this kind of training should not be given by the military; instead, they should hire men with some higher education (such as a college degree, or 2 years of college) and then give them a year or more training in military strategy, logistics and other purely military subjects. In this way, as it were, the military would go out of the college "industry" and into the post-graduate "industry," specializing in military education.

It is clear that by buying the end product of civilian schools the military eliminates the quantity t_m and thus the divergence between MP_m and MP_c, since the military and civilian sectors now *both* buy only school "graduates." Hence the change proposed here leads to an efficient allocation of resources; it could be a substantial saving to the economy as a whole. However, the military is concerned not only with the effect of any proposal on costs to the economy, but also with the effect on its own costs. Fortunately, it turns out that the military can never lose money by buying trained personnel (instead of training them) and that the savings achieved can be quite substantial, even if the military can operate these schools as efficiently as civilian firms. The savings are greater the more inelastic is the supply of persons to the occupation being considered, the more elastic is the civilian demand for persons in this occupation, and the larger the fraction of all persons in this occupation employed in the civilian sector. In particular, if the supply is completely inelastic, or if the civilian demand is completely elastic, the savings by the military exactly equal their training costs. On the other hand, if the civilian demand is completely inelastic, or if the military employs all persons in this occupation, there are no savings to the military. These results can be shown rigorously only by using some mathematics,[3] but it is not difficult to gain an intuitive understanding. The shifting of costs from the military to members of this occupation reduces the net costs to the military, reduces the net income received by these members, and increases the net costs to civilian firms using them. Hence the less responsive the amount supplied and the more responsive the civilian demand is to their "wage," the greater the number of men available to the military at this lower military "wage"; the more important the civilian sector is, relative to the military, the greater the absolute decrease in civilian demand for any given elasticity of civilian demand.

This analysis refers to training which increases the productivity of trainees in civilian jobs as well as in military ones. Other kinds of training, such as in handling a jet fighter, may only slightly affect his civilian productivity, although it significantly affects his military productivity. For this training it makes no difference whether the military or the trainee directly pays the training costs—except for the important consideration that private schools may be more efficient—since the equilibrium military pay would equal the civilian pay if the military paid for the training and would equal the civilian pay plus the training costs if the trainees paid. "On-the-job training" indicates a relatively slow increase in skill due to the experience gained while working on the job. If this training were transferable, the equilibrium wage rate during any period would equal the marginal product minus training costs; therefore, "transferable" on-the-job training costs should be paid for by the trainee, just like any other transferable training costs. If the training were not transferable, the equilibrium wage rate would simply equal the marginal product; therefore non-transferable on-the-job training costs should be paid for by the employer, just like any other non-transferable training costs.

It has been shown that if the military shifts to a policy of buying trained personnel instead of training the personnel themselves, there will be a more efficient allocation of resources for the economy, and a reduction in costs, perhaps a substantial one, to the military. Before empirically estimating these savings, it is advisable to point out some additional implications of these policy changes.

1. The military is a unique organization in that for a wide range of positions the higher positions are filled almost entirely by men who worked up in the organization. Thus the probability is almost unity that a sergeant initially started as a private, or that a colonel started as a second lieutenant. It is true that there would be a significant amount of internal promoting in the most efficiently run organization, the reason being that in a world of uncertainty, the ability of a prospective employee is not known immediately, and can be deter-

mined only after a period of employment. Nevertheless, it appears that the internal promotion is more important in the military than is necessary, and certainly greater than in the average firm. A virtue of the change proposed here is that it forces the military to hire men at intermediate levels in the enlisted and officers ranks. For example, it would be impossible to hire a skilled radar repairman as a private; he would probably have to be hired as a sergeant. It would be impossible to hire a skilled pilot as a second lieutenant, just as today it is impossible to hire a skilled physician as a second lieutenant; he usually becomes a captain or a major. This development on a large scale would bring military hiring policies closer to those practiced by efficient firms.

2. The Cordiner report and A. Enthoven have expressed concern over low reenlistment rates in the military, arguing correctly that with present personnel policies this is very wasteful of military resources. The reader should not require any detailed argument at this stage to be convinced that the main reason for this is that the military bears the costs of training, and is unable to reap any gains from those who fail to reenlist. A policy of buying trained personnel would, therefore, eliminate this cost. Of course, low reenlistment rates would still involve a cost to the military, since continuity of personnel is preferred, but the cost would be *greatly* below that incurred today.

3. Given the (relatively) costless nature of the training provided by the military and given the existence of the draft, many young men take training from the military (such as in piloting) without any serious intention of using this training later on, either in the military or as a civilian. Paying an amount competitive with that paid in comparable civilian occupations (as proposed in the Cordiner report) would not prevent these young men from resigning, since they resign not to enter comparable civilian occupations but to enter quite different civilian occupations. However, if they were forced to pay for their training, they would do so only if they had a serious intention to use the training later on. Thus this change in policy would eliminate one cause of the attrition of skilled military personnel. Of course the major cause of this attrition is the low military pay; the great virtue of the Cordiner report is that it realized this and recommended the correct solution, namely, an increase in pay for skilled military personnel.

4. This change also puts the draft in proper perspective.[4] It makes little sense to draft a man, give him expensive training, and then have him leave for a civilian job. If the military wants to use the draft to obtain skilled personnel, it makes much better sense to draft the skilled personnel; this has been done for physicians, dentists and chaplains.

There is no reason why it cannot be extended (if so desired) to a much wider range of skills. It is quite likely that such personnel would fail to enlist after the draft term expires, but as pointed out in section (2), such attrition would cost much less than the attrition of drafted personnel does today.

Further Reflections on the Allocation of Time

February 2014

GARY S. BECKER

I am delighted that the editors of the *Economic Journal* decided to include my article on the allocation of time in its special issue celebrating its 125th anniversary. The long and distinguished history of the *Economic Journal* makes this a distinct honor.

I had originally submitted an essay on the allocation of time to a distinguished American journal. They were willing to publish the paper as long as I greatly cut back its length. Since I believed that would greatly weaken the argument, I decided to submit a somewhat revised version to the *Economic Journal*. The editors were happy to accept, and also gave me various useful comments.

Unlike some of the other research I was publishing at that time, most economists rather quickly accepted the analysis in "The Allocation of Time." Some economists developed various applications, extensions, and modifications, but while maintaining the framework of time budgets interacting with goods budgets. Here I briefly describe the underlying framework in my article, and also give a few of the many interesting applications.

Time has certain properties that make it rather special, and likely the most fundamental of all resources. Days and years flow along without stopping, so that time cannot be saved for future use. This implies that individuals age as time flows by, although they can slow down their aging process by medications and personal behavior.

Time is a fundamental resource because it enters into every human activity. This includes working, reading, watching the Super Bowl, exercising, eating, sleeping, and visiting doctors. This implies that how productive is the use of time at all these different kinds of activities would be a fundamental determinant of an individual's wellbeing.

Even within a given society individuals differ greatly in the efficiency of their time use. Some "waste" a lot of their time, others are disorganized in their use of time, and still others are the height of efficiency as one activity flows seamlessly into another. My article introduced two main concepts to help analyze efficiency in the allocation of time. One is the concept of full income, which incorporates not only the spending of earnings and other income on different goods and services. It defines "full" or potential income as the maximum income that could be earned, and shows how that income is "spent" not only on goods and services, but also on consumption activities that require giving up the opportunity to earn more income.

Full income values each non-working hour at the wage rate, or the same as the value of each working hour. For persons not working it values each hour at the money value of the marginal utility of time in household production. Individuals leave the labor force when the marginal value of their time in household production exceeds its value in the labor force.

Even individuals who work 40 hours a week for every week of the year still have 128 hours per week that they spend at household production. Excluding a full 70 hours for sleep and basic personal care still leaves 58 hours to be spent in producing different commodities. Since considerably more time is spent in household production than at work even for full time workers, the implication is that for the typical adult the value of time spent in household production is much greater than the value of goods.

Just as the productivity of time spent at work varies across individuals, so does the time spent at different household activities, such as parental investments in children's human capital. To model household productivity I assumed each household has a set of production functions for different "commodities." These commodities are the determinants of utility. Commodities are produced by the two main inputs, goods and time, and by other aspects of the household's technology. The amount of time used relative to the amount of goods in the production of commodities depends on the wage rates of household members and the substitutability between time and goods in production.

"The Allocation of Time" gives several applications of the commodity and full income approach to the use of time. Subsequently, other studies have shown that time allocation is extremely important in understanding many other kinds of behavior as well. I will discuss three of the more important of these applications.

The analysis in the allocation of time article is static, and does not consider how households allocate time and goods over the life cycle. Income can be saved, so that consumption of goods in any year does not necessarily equal the money income in that year. Since time cannot be stored or saved, the amount of time used in any year must equals

8760 hours, the total hours in any year. Even though time cannot be saved, the amount of time available for non-working activities is clearly affected by choices about weeks and hours of work. Moreover, the ability to save goods means that the amount of non-working time available in any year RELATIVE to the amount of goods is not rigidly given by hours worked and the level of money income, but also depends on the amount saved in that year.

These considerations in turn help explain consumption and savings over the life cycle. Consumption seems to decline rather sharply after a person retires from the labor force. One interpretation of that decline is that individuals are not sufficiently forward-looking at younger ages, and fail to save enough to provide adequately for consumption in their old age. Another interpretation based on a time and goods analysis is that retired individuals consume less goods because they substitute some of their greater time available for fewer goods in producing the commodities they consume. Mark Aguiar and Erik Hurst examine these two competing explanations of the decline in consumption after retirement, and they show (2007) that the substitution of time for goods hypothesis can much better explain the decline in consumption of goods after retirement, and also patterns in the type of goods they consume after retirement.

The statistical value of life literature studies how much individuals are willing to pay for changes in their probability of surviving through different ages. This willingness to pay is determined by the gain in expected utility from decrease in the probability of dying. The early theory on the value of life related this willingness to pay to money income, and to future consumption. However, this approach is too narrow because it fails to account for the important contribution to utility of the time spent outside the work place in producing different household commodities. This failure is especially important for many older persons who do not work and get most of their utility from their use of time rather than their consumption of goods.

This implies that the appropriate concept for the statistical value of life is not money income but full income. Full income explains, for example, why married women who are not in the labor force because they are caring for children often behave as if their time is valuable even when their earnings potential is low. As a result, they may have a high statistical value of their life.

Since my article on time allocation, data on how individuals allocate their time among many possible categories of time use have become more comprehensive. The American time use survey, issued annually since 2003, shows in considerable detail how individuals allocate their time to various activities, such as childcare, preparing meals, socializing, and so forth. One can use these data to determine how time allocation differs between households with small children and households with grown children, between men and women, between working individuals and those who are retired, and for many other comparisons. Perhaps some day time budget accounts will stand alongside national income accounts as showing the levels of income of both time and goods, and how households and firms spend this income.

Among other valuable information time budget accounts provide information on the time parents spend with children. Some of the time parents spend with children helps the children develop knowledge, skills, and values. Especially educated mothers, and to a lesser extent fathers, tend to spend considerable time with younger children. This is an important cause of the substantial advantage that children with educated parents have over other children, even when the children have equal abilities.

References

Aguiar, M., and Hurst, E. 2007. "Measuring Trends in Leisure: The Allocation of Time over Five Decades." *Quarterly Journal of Economics* 122, no. 3, pp. 969–1006.

Becker, G. S. 1965. "A Theory of the Allocation of Time." *Economic Journal* 75, no. 299, pp. 493–517.

The Insurance of Market and Nonmarket Human Capital

First Draft, November 1980

GARY S. BECKER

Consider first a utility function that depends only on a single (aggregate) good purchased:

$$U = U(x), U' > 0, U'' < 0, \text{ and } p_x = 1. \tag{1}$$

If there are two states of the world, a and b, where a is the hazardous state involving some income loss, the expected utility from the endowed income in the different states is

$$V = p_a U_a(x_a^0) + p_b U_b(x_b^0), p_a + p_b = 1, \tag{2}$$

where p_a and p_b are the probabilities of each state.

Assume that consumption in b can be traded for consumption in a at the price $1/f$:

$$\frac{dx_a}{dx_b} = -\frac{-1}{f}. \tag{3}$$

If the many identical persons have independent risks, if there is a competitive insurance industry with negligible costs of operation, and if insurers only look at the average experience of all these identical persons (not at individual experiences), the terms of trade between states would be a constant equal to the (average) odds:

$$f = \frac{\bar{p}_a}{\bar{p}_b} = \frac{p_a}{p_b}. \tag{4}$$

The optimal insurance (s) purchased by each person is determined by maximizing

$$V = p_a U_a(x_a^0 + s) + p_b U_b(x_b^0 - fs) \tag{5}$$

subject to equation 4. The equilibrium condition is

$$p_a U'_a = p_b U'_b f, \qquad\qquad\qquad (6)$$

or

$$U'_a = U'_b . \qquad\qquad\qquad (7)$$

If the utility function is the same in both states, equation 7 implies that

$$x^0_a + s = x_a = x^0_b - fs = x_b, \text{ or } s = (1 - p_a)(x^0_b - x^0_a): \qquad\qquad (8)$$

each person fully insures his losses. Since the price of insurance is a constant to each person that does not depend on his behavior, and since he fully insures his losses, he would not spend any resources on reducing the probability of the hazardous state [see Ehrlich and Becker (1972) for a discussion of self-protection].

This analysis can be criticized in several respects. Insurance companies can partially experience-rate each individual, so that he can be offered cheaper insurance if he alone takes steps to reduce the probability of his hazard. Individual experience-ratings reduce the "external economies" of self-protection that result when only average experience determines the cost to each person, and encourages a more efficient level of self-protection [see the analysis in Ehrlich and Becker (1972)].

I will concentrate in this paper on the assumption that the utility function is the same in all states: the assumption required to go from equation 7 to 8. If an accident cripples a person, perhaps confining him to a wheelchair, equal marginal utilities in the different states [see 7] presumably implies less consumption when crippled rather than equal consumption in both states [see 8] because goods provide less utility when one is crippled [see   ].[1]

I believe, however, that the basic difficulty is not the assumption that utility functions are the same in different states, but rather the assumption that utility functions depend only on the goods purchased [see Ehrlich and Becker (1972, fn. 5)]. The household production approach implies that utility functions depend on the commodities produced by purchased goods, own time, education levels, ability, health, and other "environmental" variables. The utility function of a cripple would depend on his commodities in the same way as the utility function of a well person depends on his commodities, but presumably a cripple is less efficient at producing commodities. I will try to show that an emphasis on commodity production provides major insights into the insurability of different hazards, and in particular, implies that human and nonhuman capital must be distinguished: a crippling accident has very different consequences from theft or fire.

To develop our analysis, write the utility function as

$$U = U(Z) = U(wt + v / \pi), \qquad (9)$$

where Z is a single (aggregate) commodity produced by each household, w is his wage rate, t his total time, v his nonwage income, and π is the average shadow price or cost of Z. This price can be written as

$$\pi = a + cw, \qquad (10)$$

where a is the market goods $(p_x = 1)$ and c is the time used per unit of Z. These coefficients measure the efficiency of household production, and depend on the household environment, including the price of time relative to goods.

If a hazard (perhaps a fire or theft) reduces the value of nonhuman assets, expected utility with insurance equals

$$V = p_a U_a \left(\frac{wt + v_a + s}{\pi_a} \right) + p_b U_b \left(\frac{wt + v_b - fs}{\pi_b} \right). \qquad (11)$$

If V is maximized subject to equation 4, the equilibrium condition is

$$\frac{U'_a}{\pi_a} = \frac{U'_b}{\pi_b}. \qquad (12)$$

The cost of producing Z would be the same in both states if hours of work are positive and if w is constant. Then $\pi_a = \pi_b = \pi$ and 12 becomes

$$U'_a = U'_b, \qquad (13)$$

the same as 7. Since the utility function of commodities is assumed to be independent of the states, then

$$U'_a = U'_b => Z_a = Z_b, \qquad (14)$$

or

$$\frac{wt + v_a + s}{\pi} = \frac{wt + v_b - fs}{\pi};$$

hence

$$s = (1 - p_a)(v_b - v_a), \qquad (15)$$

the same as equation 8. This analysis implies that a working person faced with fair insurance fully insures all his losses of nonhuman capital.

The analysis begins to have novel implications when the value of human capital is affected by a hazard, and these losses are compensated by nonhuman assets. Consider first a loss in earning power (w) that has no appreciable effect on the efficiency of commodity production. One example is a shift in demand that lowers the value of a particular market skill; another example is an injury that lowers market productivity without much affecting household productivity (e.g., a knee injury to a football player). Equilibrium condition 12 is still applicable but now $\pi_a <$ π_b because $w_a < w_b$. Hence

$$U'_a < U'_b, \text{ or } Z_a > Z_b. \tag{16}$$

Actuarially fair insurance in terms of the nonhuman assets exchanged between states induces risk-averse persons to increase their consumption in the hazardous state until they would be made better off by the hazard. The explanation of this apparent paradox is that actuarially fair insurance in terms of nonhuman assets is biased insurance in terms of commodities because these can be produced more cheaply in the hazardous state where time is cheaper. This explains why a *market* "cripple" is better off than a well person.

Since each person is made better off by the hazard, he has an incentive to *increase* the probability of the hazard. That is, if

$$p_a = p_a(h), p'_a > 0, \tag{17}$$

where h are expenditures on self-protection, he would choose the level of h that maximizes expected utility subject to equation 4. The equilibrium condition is

$$p'_a(U_a - U_b) = \frac{U'_b}{\pi_b}. \tag{18}$$

Expenditures on "negative" self-protection are socially optimal because everyone is made better off by the hazard. The amount spent as determined by 18, however, is socially excessive because each person imposes costs on others when he raises the probability of his hazard because the cost of market insurance is raised to them.

If a crippling accident reduces both wage rates and household productivity to the same extent so that the cost of producing commodities is unchanged, then $\pi_a = \pi_b$, and equation 12 implies that $U'_a = U'_b$ and $Z_a = Z_b$. Hence, a crippling accident with such "neutral" effects on household productivity induces a level of insurance that raises the utility and commodity consumption of cripples to the level of healthy persons.

Their insurance does not simply replace the actual earnings lost but the *potential* earnings lost:

$$s = (1 - p_a)(\Delta w)t > (1 - p_a)(\Delta w)t_w, \tag{19}$$

where t is the total time available and t_w are hours worked. The common argument that becoming a cripple lowers utility even with fair market insurance goes wrong by not considering the effect of becoming a cripple on the cost of household time, and by not recognizing that the optimal level of insurance exceeds the money income foregone.

A crippling accident would make a person worse off when market insurance is actuarially fair only if the cost of producing commodities is raised because the accident reduces household efficiency by more than the cost of time. Equation 12 implies that

$$Z_a < Z_b \text{ if } \pi_a > \pi_b \text{ and } f = \frac{P_a}{P_b}. \tag{20}$$

The explanation is that actuarially fair insurance in terms of nonhuman assets would be biased against the hazardous state in terms of commodities. The amount of insurance chosen would then be less than the amount that equalizes consumption in both states, and persons experiencing the accident would be made worse off. Resources would then be spent to reduce the probability of the accident that makes one worse off. In equation 18, $p_a' < 0$ and $U_a < U_b$.

Note that it is reasonable to say that $\pi_a = \infty > \pi_b$ when someone dies, so that persons dying would have zero consumption and would be made worse off. If $U(0) = 0$, the value placed on a small change in the probability of dying would then be

$$\frac{dv}{dp_b} = \frac{-U_b \pi_b}{U_b' p_b}. \tag{21}$$

Equation 21 reproduces the result that wealthier persons and those more likely to die would pay more for a small increase in the probability of living [see Rosen (1980)].[2] Equation 21 also has the new result that the "value of life" is greater for persons with larger costs of producing commodities. In particular, (household) crippled persons would place a *larger* value on their life than equally wealthy persons with the same probability of dying.

The traditional sexual division of labor has meant that married women have specialized in human capital that raises household productivity and married men have specialized in human capital that raises market productivity. Consequently, a crippling accident that destroys much human capital would tend mainly to reduce the market productivity of married men and the household productivity of married women. The analysis in this paper that distinguishes the effects on market and household productivity implies that married men buy more actuarially fair market insurance than married women against personal risks, an implication strongly supported by the evidence. Married women spend more than married men on reducing the probability of personal risks because women are less protected against these risks by market insurance. This could explain why women have fewer accidents, are healthier, and live longer than men. The same analysis implies that single men insure more and experience more accidents and are less healthy than single women, and perhaps also than married men, because the productivity of married households is mainly determined by the productivity of wives. As the sexual division of labor between market and household productivity continues to become less important, sexual differences in insurance, accidents, and health should become smaller.

These differences between men and women follow from the general implication of the analysis that nonmarket risks are less "insurable" than market risks even when actuarially fair market insurance in terms of nonhuman assets is available. A further application is that the "pain and suffering" is less insurable than earnings even with fair insurance if "pain and suffering" implies some reduction in nonmarket productivity. Still another application is that pets would not be readily insurable, whereas racehorses and other animals that produce income would be.

Some risks mainly reduce the effective amount of available time; Grossman (1972) assumes that ill-health reduces the time available for the production of commodities and utility. A reduction in the available time of employed persons would be fully insured with actuarially fair insurance. That is, $U'_a = U'_b$ and $Z_a = Z_b$ because $\pi_a = \pi_b$, which implies that

$$s = (1 - p_a)w(t_b - t_a), \tag{22}$$

where $w(t_b - t_a)$ is the loss in *potential* earnings due to the reduction in time available $(t_b - t_a)$.

Persons not in the labor force would not fully insure reductions in available time because their costs of producing commodities are not constant but equal to

$$\pi = a + \mu c, \tag{23}$$

where μ is the shadow price of time. Since μ increases when the amount of goods increases relative to the available time, a reduction in the available time would not be fully insured because π would increase as the amount of insurance increased. This is another reason for distinguishing market and nonmarket effects, and implies that the ill-health of retired and other persons out of the labor force—including those induced to leave by their ill-health—would not be fully insured even with fair market insurance in terms of nonhuman assets.

References (added by the editors)

Ehrlich, Isaac, and Gary S. Becker. "Market Insurance, Self-Insurance, and Self-Protection." *Journal of Political Economy* 80, no. 4 (Jul.–Aug. 1972): 623–48.
Grossman, Michael. "On the Concept of Health Capital and the Demand for Health." *Journal of Political Economy* 80, no. 2 (1972): 223–55.
Rosen, Sherwin. "Valuing Health Risk." *American Economic Review* 71 (1981): 241–45.

On Whether Intergenerational Mobility Has Declined in US While Inequality Has Increased

March 2012

GARY S. BECKER

To model the process of income generation, assume that each parent has one child, so that one can examine the relation between parental and children's earnings. Further assume, as in the labor economics literature, that the log of earnings is related to years of schooling, as in

$$\ln I_p = a + bS_p + e_p \tag{1}$$

$$\ln I_c = a + bS_c + e_c, \tag{2}$$

where I is income of parents or children, S is schooling of parents and children, b measures the return to schooling, and e refers to other determinants of the earnings of parents and children.

I also assume that the schooling of children depends on the schooling of their parents, perhaps as mediated through the abilities of parents and children. I assume this relation is linear, as in

$$S_c = c + h(x)S_p + v_c, \tag{3}$$

where v_c are other determinants of the schooling of children, and h is the degree of "inheritability" of schooling from parents to children. Income does not enter eq. 3, so I am assuming basically perfect capital markets. I make h a function of variables x, that may be partly controlled by parents through the childhood investments parents make in children. This endogeneity of the degree of inheritability of schooling is crucial for understanding why the degree of intergenerational mobility may have decreased over time.

In the US, the return to schooling increased greatly since 1980, especially return to college and post-college education. I take this as implying that the coefficient b in the earnings generating equations 1 and 2 increased greatly over time. We can find the effect of an increase in b on the relation between the earnings of parents and children by substituting eq. 3 into eq. 2 to get the earnings of children as a function of parental schooling. By then substituting the earnings of parents for their schooling as given by eq. 1, we end up with a relation between the log of the earnings of parents and children:

$$\ln I_c = (a(1-h) + bc) + h\ln I_p + bv_c + e_c - he_p \qquad (4)$$

Note that the coefficient of parental earnings in the eq. determining the earnings of children does not depend on b—the returns to schooling—but depends directly only on the "inheritability" of schooling from parents to children. The residual term that is correlated with parental earnings, $-he_p$, also does not depend on b. So while an ordinary least squares estimate of h is biased downwards, the bias does not directly depend on b.

Suppose we measure inequality in earnings by the variance of the log of earnings. If earnings inequality is in a steady state, then the equilibrium degree of earnings inequality is given by the simple expression

$$\text{var}(\ln I) = \frac{b^2 \text{var}(v)}{(1-h^2)} + \text{var}(e) \qquad (5)$$

Clearly, the inequality in earnings does directly depend on the returns to schooling. It is also positively related to the degree of inheritability (h).

Although eq. 4 shows that the degree of intergenerational mobility depends only on the "inheritability" of schooling, h, that coefficient is not exogenous. It depends, among other things, on the inheritance of abilities from parents, and investments made by parents in their children. Let the direct inheritance coefficient be ß, the investment coefficient be ∂b, and assume these effects are additive, so that the relation between the schooling of parents and children can be written as

$$S_c = c + (ß + \partial b)S_p + v_c, \text{ where} \qquad (6)$$

$$h = ß + \partial b. \qquad (7)$$

Eq. 7 implies that when returns to schooling are low, parents make few investments in their children—for example, investments are 0 when returns are 0—and that more educated parents are more productive investors in their children than less educated parents. Then eq. 4 can be written as

$$\ln I_c = (a(1-h) + bc) + (ß + \partial b)\ln I_p + bv_c + e_c - he_p \qquad (8)$$

Now the relation between the earnings of parents and that of children does depend on the returns to education, as measured by the coefficient b. Other things the same, an increase in these returns, as occurred after 1980 in the United States, would not only increase inequality at any moment in time, but would also reduce the degree of intergenerational mobility. Inequality at any moment greatly increased, but there is controversy over whether intergenerational mobility also increased.

In addition, eq. 7 implies that the effect of a rise in the returns to education on steady state inequality in earnings would be even greater. For not only would inequality in eq. 5 rise directly when the coefficient b rises, but steady state inequality would rise by more because of the induced increase in the degree of intergenerational inheritance, h. We can see this by totally differentiating eq. 5 with respect to b to get

$$\frac{d(\operatorname{var}(\ln I))}{db} = \frac{2b\operatorname{var}(v)}{(1-h^2)} + b^2\operatorname{var}(v)(1-h^2)^{-2}(2h)\frac{dh}{db},\text{where}\frac{dh}{db} = \partial \quad (9)$$

The total effect on inequality of earnings of an increase in the returns to schooling is greater when the degree of inheritability is greater, and when an increase in returns to schooling stimulates a larger increase in parental investments in their children, as measured by ∂.

Eq. 6 implies, for example, that elite schools are now more likely than in the past to be filled with students with high cognitive and noncognitive abilities, and that parents and children are now both likely to go to schools of the same caliber, such as elite or second tier schools. More generally, the stratification of families by education and other characteristics will tend to have grown over time.

We have so far considered the implications of an increase in the returns to schooling for steady state inequality in earnings, and for the steady state degree of intergenerational mobility in earnings. This analysis also has some interesting implications about the effect of an increase in the returns to schooling during the transition to new steady states. Let us now distinguish between b_p and b_c, the returns to schooling in the parents' and children's generations. Then eqs. 1 and 2 become

$$\ln I_p = a + b_p S_p + e_p \quad (1')$$

$$\ln I_c = a + b_c S_c + e_c, \quad (2')$$

If eq. 3 remains the same, we can still derive a relation between the earnings of parents and children, but now we have to use separate returns to schooling for parents and children. By entering the schooling relation into earnings equations, we get

$$\ln I_c = \left(a\left(1 - h\frac{b_c}{b_p}\right) + b_c c\right) + \frac{b_c}{b_p}h\ln I_p + b_c v_c + e_c - \frac{b_c}{b_p}h e_p \quad (4')$$

If the returns to schooling are higher in the children's than in the parent's generation, as happened after 1980 in the US, eq. 4' shows that the degree of intergenerational mobility would decline during this transition period, even if parents do not adjust their investments in their children because of the higher return to schooling that children receive. The magnitude of the transitional decline in intergenerational mobility depends on how much higher returns to schooling are in the children's than in the parent's generation.

Links Between Intergenerational Mobility and Inequality Within a Generation

An important question is what, if any, is the connection between inequality at any moment, or inequality over lifetimes, and inequality between generations, as measured by the degree of intergenerational mobility? The analysis we have given indicates that for two basic reasons, these different types of inequality tend to be positively related. Equation 5 shows that there is causation from greater inequality across generations, or greater intergenerational mobility—as measured by a larger value of h— to greater steady state inequality within a generation. The explanation is that inequality within a generation is stretched out over time when children of high-income parents tend to have relatively high incomes, and children of low-income parents tend to have relatively low incomes.

There is also a more subtle relation that involves choices between inequality within a generation and inequality across generations. We have shown that an increase in the returns to education does not affect the degree of intergenerational mobility in earnings if the degree of inheritability of education from parents to children, as measured by h, is unchanged. However, we have also shown that if more educated parents are more effective investors in children, then they have an incentive to invest more in their children's human capital when the returns to education as measured by b are higher—see eq. 6.

Parents with higher schooling may invest more in goods and time, or their investments may have higher productivity. Eq. 6 attempts to capture in a simple way both features by introducing a term that affects the schooling of children through the schooling of their parents, and a term that is complementary with schooling that depends on the returns to schooling, b. As a result, the degree of inheritability of schooling, h in eq. 7, depends positively on the returns to schooling. In this way, an important component of inequality within a generation, the returns to human capital investments, affects the degree of inequality between generations.

This relation very much depends on more educated parents being more effective investors in their children's human capital. Considerable research shows that education of parents is an important determinant of investments in children's human capital at different stages of their childhood. It is not surprising that this affects the degree of intergenerational relation between the education and earnings of parents and children. It is perhaps more surprising that it also affects the degree of inequality within a generation.

This analysis can help us understand why the degree of intergenerational mobility in the US may have declined, and within generation inequality definitely increased, after returns to schooling and the education of women increased after 1980. It also helps explain why countries, like the Scandinavian countries, that have low within-generation inequality also have a high degree of intergenerational mobility.

Consider also the rapid growth in the higher education of women during the past 30 years. Women are now much more likely to have a college education, college-educated women are much more likely to marry than they did decades ago, and they tend to marry college-educated men.

This greater stratification of families by education affects investments in children. Presumably, college-educated families are now more effective investors because both parents tend to be college educated. In our equations, this increased degree of sorting by education would raise the productive coefficient, ∂, in eq. 6 that generates children's schooling from parental schooling. And an increase in ∂ increases h and the degree of intergenerational mobility.

Derivation of Relation Between Schooling of Parents and Children and Inequality

April 2012

GARY S. BECKER

Assume a production function for the production of the human capital of children that depends on the amount, y, spent on children's human capital formation, and the human capital of parents, H_p. If y and H_p interact, and if the function is quadratic in y, we can write the production function of H_c as

$$H_c = g + ky + eyH_p + dH_p - my^2 + v_c, \tag{1}$$

where v is a random component in the production of human capital. We assume v is revealed only after parents invest y in their children, and that parents are risk-neutral. If m is positive, this has diminishing returns to investments in children. Later on we introduce an H_p^2 into household production.

Parents who care about the earnings of their single child optimally choose the level of y. Suppose parents maximize their utility:

$$U_p = u(C_p) + aV_c(E(w_c)), \tag{2}$$

where C is parental consumption, a is parental altruism, and $E(w_c)$ is the expected earnings of children; that is, the earnings before v_c is revealed. If y is measured in the same units as C, the budget constraint of parents is

$$C_p + y = W_p \tag{3}$$

The earnings generating function is simply

$w = rH$, where r is the earnings per unit of H. (4)

The optimal y, y^*, would be determined from the maximization of eq. 2, subject to the budget constraint in 3, the expected production function in eq. 1, and the earnings generating equation in 4. The FOC can be expressed as

$$u'(w_p - y^*) = arV'(E(w_c))f_y(y^*, H_p),^1 \tag{5}$$

where y^* refers to the optimal value of y. By substituting eq. 1 into this eq. and using eq. 4, we get

$$u'(rH_p - y^*) = aV'(r(g + ky^* + ey^*H_p + dH_p - my^{*2}))\, r\, (k + eH_p - 2my^*) \tag{6}$$

We take a first order approximation of y^* of the form

$$y^* = n + \beta H_p \tag{7}$$

β can be derived by totally differentiating equation 6 with respect to y and H_p and evaluating it at y^*:

$$\beta = \frac{dy}{dH_p} = \frac{(-ru'' + aV're) + \left(aV''r^2\left(k + eH_p - 2my^*\right)\left(ey^* + d\right)\right)}{D[>0]} \tag{8}$$

The first bracketed term is > 0, and is the substitution effect of a rise in H_p. The second bracketed term is < 0, and it is the income effect. Hence β can be either greater or less than zero depending on whether the substitution effect or the income effect dominates.

By substituting eq. 7 into the production function in eq. 1 we get

$$H_c = K + hH_p + jH_p^2 + v_c, \text{ where } j = e\text{ß} - m\text{ß}^2, h = en + d + k\text{ß} - 2nm\text{ß}, \text{ and } K = g + kn - mn^2 \tag{9}$$

This equation is a quadratic in H_p. To simplify the initial discussion, we assume that ß $= 0$ because income and substitution effects of greater H_p exactly offset each other. We then have a stochastic linear relation between human capital of parents and children:

$$H_c = K\,(= g + kn - mn^2) + h\,(= en + d)\,H_p + v_c \tag{10}$$

Since $w = rH$, by substitution of w_c for H_c and w_p for H_p in eq. 10, we get

$$w_c = rK + hw_p + rv_c \tag{11}$$

This is a stochastic linear intergeneration mobility equation that relates the earnings of parents and their children. The expected degree of mobility, measured by h, depends solely in this case on the interaction parameter and another parameter from the household production function, and the optimal investment in children, given by n.

The coefficient h does not *directly* depend on the returns to human capital, given by r, although both the intercept and the random term do directly depend on r. The term en may depend on r through its effects on n, but there are offsetting income and substitution effects of r on n. Unlike some claims in literature (see Council Report, 2012)[2] an increase in returns to human capital does not affect the degree of intergenerational mobility in earnings, *given* the transmission coefficient in the relation between parental and children's schooling.

The analysis also has implications for inequality within a generation. If sig_v denotes variance of v, then steady state inequality of earnings is

$$sig_w = \frac{r^2 sig_v}{1 - h^2}. \tag{12}$$

Obviously, steady state inequality in earnings depends on the inequality in the error term in the production function. It also depends positively on the value of a unit of human capital (r) since that magnifies the effect on H_c of the variability in v. Steady state inequality in earnings also depends positively on the degree of persistence in earnings across generations of a family (h). The greater the persistence, the more inequality in one generation is directly transmitted to the next generation along with the inequality created by the variance in v.

Eq. 12 gives an interesting relation between inequality within a generation and the degree of intergenerational mobility (measured by $1 - h$). The greater this mobility, then the smaller is the equilibrium inequality within a generation, given the return on human capital (r), and the variance in the random coefficient in household production. On the other hand, the greater the return on human capital, and hence greater earnings inequality does not directly affect the degree of intergenerational mobility since h would not be directly affected by a change in r. To be sure, h might be indirectly affected by r through its effect on n and y^* but even the sign of that effect is ambiguous.

The importance of the degree of intergenerational mobility for inequality of earnings gives an added reason to better understand the determinants of the degree of mobility across families in different generations. Not surprisingly, h depends on the direct effect of parental human capital on the human capital of their children (given by d), and the effect of parental human capital on the productivity of investment in children—given by the interaction term, e. It also depends on the optimal investment in children, as measured by n.

These effects on intergenerational mobility remain if we allow β in eq. 7 to be $\neq 0$, but additional determinants of intergenerational mobility in human capital and earnings become relevant. With $\beta \neq 0$, the intergenerational transmission of earnings equation becomes

$$w_c = rK + hw_p + jw_p^2/r + rv_c, \tag{13}$$

where $j = e\beta - m\beta^2$, $h = en + d + k\beta - 2nm\beta$, and $K = g + kn - mn^2$.

The relation between earnings of parents and children is no longer linear, but is quadratic. The quadratic coefficient, j, depends on β, the interaction between H_p and y in the household production function (e), and the degree of diminishing returns to investments in the human capital of children (m). If $\beta < 0$, so that an increase in parental human capital lowers their investment in children, the quadratic term j is also < 0, and there would be a concave relation between w_p and w_c (see figure 1).[3] On the other hand, if β is positive but not too large—that is, if $\beta < e/m$—then there is a convex relation between w_c and w_p (see figure 2). A sufficiently large β again gives a concave relation between these earnings because diminishing returns to investments in children, as determined by m, then creates the concavity.

Perfect Capital Markets for Human Capital Investments

The analysis above assumes that parents self-finance investments in their children's human capital. That is true for many families, but there is considerable debate over whether limits on capital are important constraints on investments in human capital in richer countries. So in this section we go to the other extreme and assume perfect capital markets for human capital investments in the sense that the equilibrium marginal return on these investments in all families equals the given return on other capital:

$$rf_y^i = R_y^{*i} = R_k, \tag{14}$$

all i, where R_k is the return on other capital, and R_y^{*i} is the equilibrium marginal return on y for the ith family.

Equation 14 enormously simplifies the derivation of the relation between the human capital of parents and children. We still assume the quadratic production function for human capital in eq. 1. Then eq. 14 becomes

$$r(k + eH_p - 2my^*) = R_k, \text{ or} \tag{15}$$

$$y^* = (k/2m - R_k/2rm) + (e/2m)H_p = n^* + \beta^* H_p, \tag{16}$$

with $\beta^* > 0$, and the parameters must be such that n^* also > 0.

Eq. 16 gives an exact linear relation between y^* and H_p. By substituting this eq. for y into the production function we derive a quadratic relation between H_c and H_p:

$$H_c = K^* + h^* H_p + j^* H_p^2 + v_c \tag{17}$$

where $h^* = d + ke/2m$, and $j^* = e^2/4m > 0$.

Eq. 17 shows that in a perfect capital market, the relation between H_c and H_p is necessarily convex, with the degree of convexity increasing in the degree of interaction in production between y and H_p (e), and decreasing in the degree of diminishing returns to y (m). The linear term (h^*) also depends positively on e and negatively on m, but in addition, h^* depends positively on both the direct effect of y on H_c (k) and the direct effect of H_p on H_c (d).

Combination of Imperfect and Perfect Capital Markets for Human Capital

The data indicate that bequests of assets tend to be concentrated in middle and upper income families. The theory of investment in human capital by altruistic parents indicates that families that leave bequests act as if the capital market for human capital is perfect, as defined by eq. 14. When bequests are effectively zero, as in the lower income families, they act as if they are in imperfect capital markets for human capital. Their behavior is determined by the FOCs in eqs. 5 and 6, and the first order approximation for the relation between y and H_p in eq. 7.

The then merger of two sections would determine the overall relation between the human capital of parents and children. The upper section—with greater parental human capital and bequests > 0—would be given by eq. 17, and the lower section, with lesser parental human capital and bequests = 0, by the linear approximation in eq. 9. Eq. 17 suggests that the persistence in human capital from parents to children would be rather high among middle and richer families, and gets higher the greater parental human capital.

The picture is less clear at the lower end of the human capital distribution since the relation between the human capital of parents and children in this group depends on the strength of offsetting income and substitution effects. If these effects completely offset each other, the intergenerational relation in human capital is linear and the degree of persistence is not so high. If income effects dominate, the relation is concave in parental incomes.

Figure 1 gives a likely relation. We assume that for all $H_p > H_p^*$, bequests are positive and the relation is convex, while bequests are zero for $H_p <= H_p^*$, and the relation is concave. There is a kink and convexity in the overall relation at $H_p = H_p^*$.

4

INCOME INEQUALITY AND
THE PUBLIC SECTOR

Many people, especially academics and other intellectuals, find the phrase "good inequality" jarring because they can hardly think of any aspect of inequality as being "good." Yet a little thought makes clear that some types of economic inequality have great social value. For example, it would be hard to motivate the vast majority of individuals to exert much effort, including creative effort, if everyone had the same earnings, status, prestige, and other types of rewards.

—GARY S. BECKER, Becker-Posner Blog, 2011

Since his beginnings as an economist, Becker was concerned and thought about major public policy issues with the objective of having a positive impact on the debate, of improving public policy. In the analysis, Becker always tried to understand the political and economic process involved in the adoption of new policies, and why efficient policies may meet resistance in the beginning.

Very early, in 1957, he wrote "The Case Against Conscription," during a summer stay at RAND Corporation, at a time where there was a fierce opposition to a fully voluntary military. He did not publish the paper, because he "felt that the opposition to a fully voluntary military was so powerful that the United States would never abandon the draft." Only twelve years later, the Gates Commission was formed, and soon after that conscription was eliminated from US military recruitment. "This experience taught me that ideas and policies that are politically impossible at one time can come to fruition later if events and circumstances change.

Analyzing defects in public policies can create intellectual ammunition, if you will, for dramatic policy changes not yet on the horizon."[1]

In 2014, he published with one of the editors of this volume a controversial piece, "Cash for Kidneys: The Case for a Market for Organs," in the *Wall Street Journal*. "Initially, a market in the purchase and sale of organs would seem strange, and many might continue to consider that market 'repugnant.' Over time, however, the sale of organs would grow to be accepted, just as the voluntary military now has widespread support. Eventually, the advantages of allowing payment for organs would become obvious. At that point, people will wonder why it took so long to adopt such an obvious and sensible solution to the shortage of organs for transplant."[2]

The distribution of income has received an enormous amount of attention during the past decades and is a theme that has long preoccupied economists. The great recession of 2007–9 focused attention on longer-term trends in wealth and income inequality around the world and heated the debate on inequality that has produced deep economic and political divisions. This debate was invigorated following the publication of the book *Capital in the Twenty-First Century* by Thomas Piketty of the Paris School of Economics.

Even though inequality is not a bad thing per se and in many contexts could be good, as Becker explains in the initial quotation of this part, many inefficient policy proposals have been discussed, and some of them implemented, to reduce inequality, including increases in the minimum wage, taxing heavily the top 1 percent.

In the first paper included in this part, Becker develops a positive theory of the redistribution of income by the state. The theory assumes that governments are not irrational or inefficient, but rather that governments maximize as fully and as successfully as private firms and households. For example, a government that imposes a tax reducing aggregate consumer welfare is not said to be irrational or ignorant of these effects, but is presumed to receive a political advantage that outweighs the reduction in consumer surplus. This theory does imply an "optimal" redistribution of income, but this optimum should not necessarily be considered "just" or ethically satisfactory. Rather it is the result of a balance between the political advantages from additional redistribution and the cost in consumer surplus or efficiency.

Public policy has to come to some decision. The analysis has to take account of the fact that any project will benefit some people and make others worse off. In Becker's view, to make sensible public policy, you have to take into account the effects on different groups.

Here Becker proposes a division into rich, poor, and middle classes that is endogenously determined in the model.

He proposes the use of a political preference function as an alternative to the traditional social welfare function, a function that ranks alternative states of society as less desirable, more desirable, or indifferent.

When redistribution is costless, equity and efficiency can be dealt with separately. However, when redistribution is costly, this is no longer true. The analysis allows us to understand questions like (or shows that is difficult to distinguish between): is the redistribution from higher-income whites to lower-income blacks in the United States limited by the cost of redistribution or by the greater marginal political power of a white person vis-à-vis a black person?

This also explains why in some cases inefficient methods of redistribution are rationally adopted. Becker returned to these subjects in his pressure-group papers, part of a lifelong interest in applying the economic approach to politics. As recently as 2014, Becker believed that some of the finest political applications of economics had not yet arrived. It is not an accident that public-sector topics are among his unpublished work.

This part's second paper is a note on optimal taxation that Becker wrote in 1982. He later realized that the results were already included in *Lectures on Public Economics* by Anthony B. Atkinson and Joseph E. Stiglitz (1981). The emphasis of Atkinson and Stiglitz is on noticing that utilitarianism is not synonymous with egalitarian principle. That is, an optimal utilitarian policy is not egalitarian.

In the note on optimal first best taxation, the second paper of this part, Becker shows a paradoxical implication of optimal lump-sum or first best taxation that was unnoticed by the optimal tax literature. The paradoxical implication is that lump-sum taxation will reverse the ranking of different individuals by utility level, or well-being.

There is a sense among a lot of economists and other social scientists that for a long time income distribution was not a topic of interest among Chicago faculty. These pieces show that Gary was very interested in the subject and was willing to do important work on it.

A Positive Theory of the Redistribution of Income

Working Paper No. 0006, Center for the Study of the Economy and the State, University of Chicago, April 1978

GARY S. BECKER

I. Introduction

The "just" distribution of income has received an enormous amount of attention during the last decade, the most influential contribution being Rawls's contractual approach to "justice" when individual incomes are subject to considerable uncertainty (see Rawls 1971). A first approach to a reasonable theory of the actual distribution of income has also developed, a theory that combines intergenerational preferences, investments in the human capital of children, bequests and gifts of assets to children, and inherited endowments of abilities and other characteristics (see Becker 1967, Becker and Tomes 1976, Loury 1981, and Blinder 1976). However, a positive theory of the redistribution of income by the State is still lacking. By a "positive" theory is meant not a theory of what a "just" State will do, but a theory of what actual States do.

The theory in this paper is an outgrowth both of an earlier comment on government redistribution (Becker 1976a)[1] and of an analysis of income redistribution within a family (Becker 1974). The theory assumes that governments are not irrational,[2] subject to whim, or inefficient, but rather that governments maximize as fully and as successfully as private firms and households.[3] For example, a government that imposes an excise tax reducing aggregate consumer surplus (producing "waste") is not said to be irrational or ignorant of these effects, the social scientists' usual evaluation, but is presumed to receive a political advantage that outweighs the reduction in consumer surplus. This is no different from saying that workers choosing jobs with lower wages than those available elsewhere are not ignorant or irrational, but are presumed to receive offsetting favorable climate, good working conditions, or other psychic benefits.

This theory does imply an "optimal" redistribution of income, but this optimum should not necessarily be considered "just" or ethically satisfactory. Rather it is the result simply of a balance between the political advantages from additional redistribution and the cost in consumer surplus or efficiency. "Justice" can indirectly affect the optimum by affecting the political advantages from redistribution.

II. The Model

A. THE POLITICAL PREFERENCE FUNCTION

The basic and highly controversial assumption of this approach is that the political sector maximizes a function that measures the political advantages of different outcomes (see Peltzman 1976). Since outcomes are measured by the utilities of different persons, the "political preference function" can be written as

$$P = P(u_1, \ldots, u_n),\tag{1}$$

where u_i is an index of the utility of the ith person.

One of the properties assumed for this political preference function is thai

$$\frac{\partial P}{\partial u_i} \geq 0 \text{ for all } i.\tag{2}$$

A political decision that makes some members of a particular society better off without making others worse off will receive more votes, allegiance, political contributions, or whatever determines the ordering of outcomes. Presumably, a change in the welfare of someone who is not a member of this society, or is *effectively* disfranchised even though he is a member, would not affect the ordering of outcomes; that is, for this kth person, $\partial P / \partial u_k = 0$. For example, an action of the US government that harmed or benefitted persons in say Thailand without directly or indirectly affecting the welfare of persons in the United States would have no political value here. On the other hand, political decisions can be affected by the welfare of disfranchised persons, such as poor persons in England before the reform act of 1832, blacks in the South before the 1950s, or women in most countries before the twentieth century, if their welfare directly or indirectly affects the welfare of franchised persons because of altruism, or fear of rebellion and disobedience.

Condition (2) does not assume away envy and spite in the political process. If i is envious of j in the sense that an increase in j's income lowers i's utility, then an increase in j's income with i's and everyone else's held constant would both raise j's utility and lower i's utility. j's utility alone would increase only if an increase in j's income were accompanied by a sufficient increase in i's income to compensate i for his increased envy. Such a "compensated" increase in j's income would be politically advantageous whereas an increase in j's income alone might not be.

A more controversial property imposed on the political preference function is that of transitivity:

$$P^1 \geq P^0 \text{ and } P^2 \geq P^1 => P^2 \geq P^0, \tag{3}$$

where $\geq$ means "not less preferred than." The assumption of transitivity will disturb those who believe that political choices depend on the ordering of agendas, (   )[4] or on which decisions are made by referendum, legislative act or executive order. I believe, however, that this loss in "realism" is more than offset by the implication of transitivity that outcomes can be completely ordered from worst to best. This immensely simplifies the analysis of the effects of changes in various political parameters on political decisions. Note that I do not assume that the political preference function is necessarily everywhere concave, and it could well be convex in many sections.

The last important property of the political preference function is its stability with respect to shifts in political opportunities. Of course, political upheavals, such as the Russian revolution, may change the political preference function along with political opportunities. The assumption of stability implies only that more ordinary changes in political opportunities do not significantly affect political preferences.

It is also important to be clear about what is *not* assumed about the political preference function because positive and normative aspects of political choices continue to be hopelessly confused. The political preference function does not necessarily embody any attractive ethical rule, whether based on individualistic or organic considerations. Therefore, the Rousseau, Bentham, Rawls and countless other discussions of what the State *should* do to redistribute income and otherwise affect outcomes are not directly relevant to political behavior and political preferences. Some of these discussions may, however, be indirectly relevant because they have helped determine the underlying political structure that does determine the shape of political preferences.

In other words, the political preference function is not to be confused with the social welfare function of modern welfare economics that shows how different outcomes are ranked by a particular ethical belief.[5] Consequently, the normative issues raised by the social welfare function— should individual preferences "count" or should the function be "completely (or very nearly) symmetrical with respect to the consumption of all individuals" (Samuelson 1947, 224)—are not relevant in considering the properties of the political preference function. Since this function explains *actual* political choices and since the votes and other expressions of political support by members of a political constituency are assumed to be guided by their own utility functions, these individual utility functions necessarily affect political preferences.

A political preference function is helpful in understanding political choices in fascist and communist dictatorships as well as in democracies and oligarchies. To be sure, the preferences of a Hitler or a Stalin counted much more in Nazi Germany or Soviet Russia than do the preferences of any person in the United States, but the difference when analyzing political choices is one of degree only. Even in the United States, the preferences of more educated persons count more than those of the less educated because education increases the propensity to vote and become politically active (Filer 1977), the preferences of union workers count more than those of non-union workers because of the political contributions and other political activities of unions, and the preferences of owners of trucks count more than those of owners of say delicatessens because truck owners influence the regulatory activities of the ICC (see Moore 1972).

The assumption in consumer economics that each household has a well-ordered preference function has been useful in explaining household behavior even though these preferences have not usually been derived from the interaction between the preferences and resources of different household members (but see Becker 1974); similarly, a clock is used to allocate time during a day even when the operation of the springs, gears, quartz crystals, and other parts of a clock's machinery is not understood. In the same way, a political preference function can be useful in analyzing political choices even when one does not understand how this function is produced by campaigns, votes, elections, lobbying, logrolling, filibustering, regulatory agencies, executive orders, and the other political machinery. Admittedly, political machinery appears to be more complicated than a household or clock machinery. Moreover, an understanding of the underlying political machinery might lead to additional restrictions on the shape of political preferences, in the same way that the derivation of household preferences from interactions among household members has provided additional restrictions on household behavior (Becker 1974, 1976b, 1979). Nevertheless, excessive attention has been paid to political machinery compared to the effort spent on analyzing the implications of "given" political preferences.

The subsequent discussion is simplified without any significant loss in generality by the assumption that political preferences depend only on the real full incomes of different persons:

$$P = P(I_1, \ldots, I_n). \tag{4}$$

Since I have little to say about "income" effects, I also assume during much of the discussion that the political preference function is homothetic: the relative marginal political influence of each person is unaffected by equal percentage changes in all incomes, or

$$\frac{\partial P/\partial I_i}{\partial P/\partial I_j} = \varphi_{ij}\left(\frac{I_1}{I},\dots,\frac{I_n}{I}\right), \text{ for all } i,j, \qquad (5)$$

where $I = \Sigma I_i$ is aggregate real full income.

The transition from equation 1 to equations 4 and 5 does not require the additional assumption that utility functions depend only on own incomes, for they could also depend positively ("altruism") or negatively ("envy") on the incomes of other persons. However, the transition from the assumption in equation 2 of a non-negative political effect of a rise in the utility of any person to the assumption of a non-negative effect of a rise in his own income does require the additional assumption that envy has less political influence than selfishness.[6] To simplify, I usually do assume that P rises when any I_i does.

Different sets of political indifference curves are shown in Figures 4.1 and 4.2 for any two persons. Those in Figure 4.1 are everywhere negative and convex to the origin, indicating that an increase in the income of each person always has a positive political value, and that its relative value declines as his relative income increases. The indifference curves in Figure 4.2 are positive in certain regions and negative and concave to the origin in certain other regions, thereby indicating that an increase in someone's income may have negative political value—perhaps because of envy—and that the relative value may increase as someone's relative income continues to increase.

A society will be said to be fully democratic if political power does not depend on race, sex, religion, family background, and other such personal characteristics, that is, if the political preference function is symmetrical in the incomes of all persons. Among other things, this definition implies that persons with equal incomes have the same political power in the sense that equal (small) changes in their incomes would change the value of the political preference function by equal amounts. That is, political indifference curves in a fully democratic society have a slope of −1 at all points along a 45° line from the origin. Therefore, if political indifference curves were everywhere convex, as in Figure 4.1, rich persons would have *less* political power than poor persons in a democratic society in the sense that small changes in high incomes would change the value of the political preference function by less than would equal changes in low incomes.

B. POLITICAL EQUILIBRIUM

Political choices depend not only on the political preference function but also on political opportunities. I assume that the political system is led through elections, campaigns, lobbying, and so forth to choose that point from all points in the set of opportunities that is on the highest political indifference curve. If indifference curves were everywhere negatively inclined, as in Figure 4.1, the equilibrium position would necessarily be on a negatively inclined section of the boundary of the opportunity set, as at point e; any point in other regions would be on a lower indifference curve. On the other hand, if the indifference curves were sometimes positively sloped because of envy, the equilibrium position could be on a positively inclined section of the boundary, as at point e^* in Figure 4.2, because points with higher incomes for everyone would be on lower indifference curves.

III. Optimal Redistribution

A. LUMP-SUM REDISTRIBUTION

The political opportunity set depends on the productive governmental activities that are feasible, including investments, regulations, and taxes, and also on the "dead weight" loss resulting from various redistributions of income. If incomes could be redistributed without any dead weight

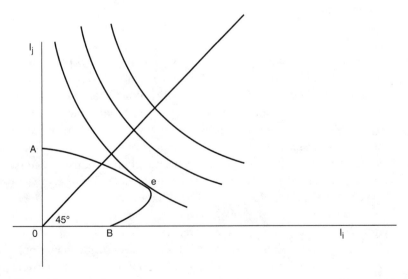

Figure 4.1

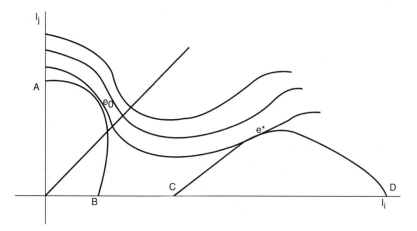

Figure 4.2

loss—by "lump-sum" taxes and subsidies that do not affect incentives—redistribution would be dollar for dollar: one dollar would be transferred for each dollar taxed away. If point E in Figure 4.3 gives the "endowed" incomes provided by the private sector, the boundary of the opportunity set when redistribution is socially costless would be a straight line through E with a slope of -1.

The political process would tax away ΔI_i from i so that equilibrium would be at point e, where the slope of a political indifference curve also equals -1. Note that the political equilibrium is independent of the endowed position when transfers are socially costless—it is the same, for example, when the distribution provided by the private sector is represented by point E' rather than E. The amount redistributed, however, closely depends on the initial conditions: the amount taxed away directly depends on the difference between the initial inequality and the inequality in political equilibrium. Indeed, a 100 percent tax is levied on the income of i or j in excess of I_i^e or I_j^e, respectively, and a 100 percent subsidy is provided on the income below I_i^e or I_j^e, respectively.

If political indifference curves were always either concave to the origin or positively sloped, socially costless redistribution would tax away the whole income of all persons but one, and transfer these taxes to him. After-tax incomes of many persons would be positive only if these indifference curves were sufficiently convex in some region. In particular, if redistribution were socially costless in a fully democratic society, all after-tax incomes would be equal if the indifference curves were convex in a region around this point. Incomes would be equalized in a full democracy because convexity of the indifference curves implies that rich

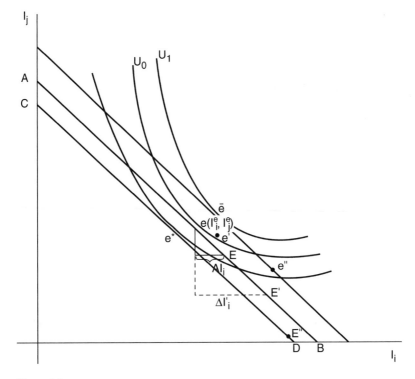

Figure 4.3

persons have less political power than poor persons in the sense that the political support from the division of a given total income is maximized when all incomes are equalized. Moreover, in *all* societies with socially costless redistribution, the *marginal* political power of rich and poor persons would be the same because a small change in the incomes of rich persons would have the same political value as an equal change in the income of poor persons.

Are productive political activities chosen solely because of their effects on efficiency—on aggregate incomes—with political "equity" determined by the purely redistributive activities just discussed, or does equity influence decisions about efficiency? In particular, would an activity that raised aggregate incomes always be chosen even if "adverse" effects on political equity were not corrected; that is, does the political process only require the *potential* to compensate losers?

Consider, for example, a public project that raised aggregate income but reduced the incomes of poor persons. If the initial position were a political equilibrium with costless redistribution, this project would be undertaken because aggregate incomes would be raised, and the effects on the distribution of income would be irrelevant. Indeed, if the project only had "small" effects on incomes, increased efficiency would be the sole criterion even with no further redistribution of incomes. In other words, the potential to compensate losers is politically sufficient, and actual compensation need not occur when projects have "small" effects.

If the project were efficient and raised aggregate incomes, the point representing incomes prior to any additional redistribution would be raised above the initial costless redistributive path, line *AB* in Figure 4.3, because aggregate incomes are constant along that path. Since small changes in the incomes of different persons would be perfect substitutes politically at the initial equilibrium position, the new point would also be on a higher political indifference curve than the initial equilibrium position if the changes in incomes were "small." For example, point e' in Figure 4.3 is above line *AB* and is also on a higher indifference curve than point e, even though the poorer person's income (j) has fallen. Consequently, the new position would be politically preferred to the initial position even with no further redistribution to poor persons. On the other hand, if the project had "large" effects on incomes, the new point could both be above the initial redistribution path and below the initial equilibrium indifference curve, as is point e'' in Figure 4.3. The *potential* to compensate losers would no longer be sufficient politically, and the project would not then be undertaken without additional redistribution to the losers.

However, if incomes were redistributed away from the new point along a costless redistribution path, the new political equilibrium must be on a higher indifference curve than the initial equilibrium as long as the project raised aggregate incomes. For example, the new equilibrium position in Figure 4.3 is at $\bar{e}$, clearly on a higher indifference curve than e. Indeed, if everyone's welfare were a superior "good" in the system of political indifference curves, the additional redistribution of income would overcompensate losers so that all would be better off at the new political equilibrium. Consequently, public investment in new technology or in any other efficient project would be *unanimously* preferred since everyone would be better off after the politically optimal amount of redistribution.

Therefore, if redistribution were costless, public projects would be undertaken if, and only if, they were efficient; any adverse effects on equity would be ignored because they could be better handled by lump-sum taxes. Moreover, efficient public projects would receive *unanimous* political support because the politically optimal redistribution overcompensates losers and makes everyone better off. Furthermore, if incomes were only slightly affected, efficiency would be a necessary and sufficient political criterion even when losers were not compensated at all!

Costless redistribution also has a rather remarkable and neglected effect on private incentives. Each person might appear to have a private incentive to take all actions that benefit him, regardless of the adverse "external" effects on others, if those harmed were unable to get together to "bribe" him against these actions. However, since these actions "worsen" the distribution of income, the political system would redistribute income away from him to compensate those harmed. Indeed, if these actions were socially inefficient and reduced aggregate incomes and if redistribution were costless, sufficient income would be redistributed away from him so that he as well as everyone else would be made worse off. For example, if i in Figure 4.3 could raise his income and lower j's even more and thereby change endowed incomes from point E to a point E'' on the redistribution line CD below AB, i as well as j would be worse off in the new political equilibrium at e^*. Anticipating this reaction, i would not want to take the action.

In effect, all persons are discouraged from actions that reduce aggregate income by an effective marginal tax rate in excess of 100 percent. If someone lowered other incomes by more than he raised his own, the government would tax away not only the entire increase in his income, but also some of his prior income in order to better compensate the others for their losses. Consequently, if redistribution were costless, each person would have a selfish incentive to internalize fully all the "external" effects on his actions, and to refrain from those that are *socially* inefficient. In particular, he would be willing to lower his own income to raise other incomes by more because the government would automatically overcompensate him for his loss. Note that this conclusion[7] requires only that governments know the incomes of different persons and does not require that they know how incomes are determined.

B. SOCIALLY COSTLY REDISTRIBUTION

The taxes, subsidies, and regulations that redistribute income include taxes on personal or corporate incomes, excises on different goods or property, subsidies to higher education or to mail service in rural areas, aid to mothers with dependent children, food stamps, restrictions on entry into the airline industry, and the like. These are not socially costless or lump-sum interventions and do affect the allocation of resources: personal income taxes and transfers tied to income reallocate time from the market to the household sector, a tariff on foreign steel encourages the domestic production of steel, and entry restrictions in the airline industry reduce the efficiency of air transportation.

Since these methods used to redistribute income have a social cost, equity and efficiency cannot be dealt with separately. The other implications of costless redistribution are also significantly affected; in particular, if redistribution is socially costly, efficient public projects may not make everyone better off, private behavior would not fully incorporate all "external" effects, and the income inequality in political equilibrium would depend on the privately endowed level of inequality.

To simplify the discussion, I temporarily make the unrealistic assumption that the loss in consumer surplus, or the "dead weight" loss, is a constant fraction of each dollar redistributed that is determined by the misallocation of resources induced by different taxes, subsidies, and regulations. Therefore, if point E in Figure 4.4 represents endowed incomes, redistribution away from i would be along the straight line AE with a slope equal to $(1 - w) < 1$, where w is the loss in consumer surplus per dollar redistributed; similarly, redistribution away from j would be along the straight line EB with a slope equal to $1 / 1 - w > 1$. The set of redistribution opportunities would be concave, with a boundary formed by the line segments AEB.

If political indifference curves were either positively inclined or concave, there either would be no redistribution and equilibrium would be at the endowed point E, or income would be redistributed until the entire income of either i or j were confiscated, and equilibrium would be on one of the axes A or B. If income were redistributed away from E without confiscating the entire income of i or j, equilibrium must be in a convex section of the indifference curves, as at point e, where EF is redistributed away from i, $eF = (1 - w)EF$ is transferred to j, and $EF - eF = wEF$ is the total dead weight loss from the redistribution.

The indifference curve through e has a slope equal to the slope of AE, or

$$\left. \begin{aligned} -\frac{dI_j}{dI_i} &= 1 - w, \\ \text{and} \quad \frac{d^2 I_j}{dI_i^2} &> 0 \text{ by convexity.} \end{aligned} \right\} \tag{6}$$

Small changes in the "disposable" incomes of different persons would not be perfect substitutes politically, as they are with costless redistribution, for changes in the disposable incomes of persons subsidized would have greater political value than equal changes in the disposable incomes

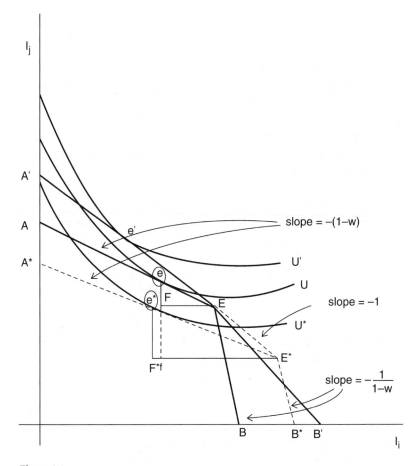

Figure 4.4

of taxpayers. Moreover, all disposable incomes would not be equalized even in a full democracy; taxpayers would have larger incomes than beneficiaries because of the dead weight cost of redistributing income.

Equation 6 and the assumption that the political preference function is approximately homothetic implies that a reduction in the dead weight loss per dollar redistributed—perhaps the introduction of the income tax in the United States in the early part of the twentieth century reduced the loss from redistribution—would increase the amount redistributed and thereby reduce the inequality in disposable incomes. For example, a reduction in w changes the boundary from *AEB* to *A'EB'* in Figure 4.4, and the equilibrium position from e to e'. The ratio of I_i to I_j is reduced in order to increase the slope of the indifference curve at the equilibrium position. As w became smaller and smaller, the boundary of the redistribution set would converge toward a straight line with a slope of −1; the equilibrium amount of inequality in a full democracy would become smaller and smaller and converge toward zero.

If the endowed inequality increased while aggregate income remained the same, the income redistributed would also increase. A shift of the endowed point from E to E^* in Figure 4.4 would increase redistribution from EF to E^*F^*. Since part of each dollar redistributed is "wasted," disposable aggregate income and political utility are reduced when additional income is redistributed: both are lower at e^* than at e. If all incomes are superior "goods" in the political preference function, disposable incomes of richer persons would also be reduced because the increase in their taxes would exceed the increase in their endowed incomes; the income of i in Figure 4.4 is lower at e^* than at e by the quantity FF^*. Indeed, if the preference function were homothetic, the relative inequality in disposable incomes would depend only on the rate of dead weight loss and would be independent of the endowed inequality, so that all disposable incomes would rise or fall by the same percent as the endowed inequality fell or rose.

If a third person g had a larger endowed income than i and if both were taxed to subsidize j, political utility would be maximized if the disposable incomes of g, i, and j satisfied

$$-\frac{dI_j}{dI_i}=1-w_i \text{ and } -\frac{dI_j}{dI_g}=1-w_g, \tag{7}$$

where w_i and w_g are the dead weight costs of taxing a dollar from i and g. Therefore,

$$\frac{dI_i}{dI_g}=\frac{1-w_g}{1-w_i}. \tag{8}$$

If the dead weight loss were the same for g and i, $w_g = w_i = w$ and equal small changes in their disposable incomes must have equal political value, which is only possible in a full democracy when their disposable incomes are equal. Therefore, if the dead weight loss were the same for everyone, a political democracy would equalize the disposable incomes of everyone paying taxes. That is to say, a 100 percent tax would be imposed on all endowed incomes above a certain level.

Similarly, if another person k had an endowed income that was below j's and if both were subsidized by taxing persons with the same disposable income, political equilibrium requires that

$$\frac{dI_j/dI_i}{dI_k/dI_i}=\frac{dI_j}{dI_k}=\frac{1-w}{1-w}=1. \tag{9}$$

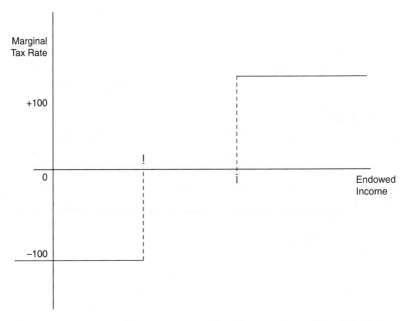

Figure 4.5 Tax Structure in a Democracy with a Constant Rate of Dead Weight Loss

This is only possible in a full democracy when their disposable incomes are equal. Therefore, j, k, and everyone else being subsidized would have the same disposable income in a full democracy, or a 100 percent negative tax would be imposed on all endowed incomes below a certain level.

If $\underline{I}$ is the maximum endowed income subsidized and $\bar{I}$ is the minimum endowed income taxed, all incomes I_p between $\bar{I}$ and $\underline{I}$ would be neither taxed nor subsidized because the slope of the indifference curve at the equilibrium point would be less than $1 - w$ between I_p and $\bar{I}$ and greater than $1 - w$ between $\underline{I}$ and I_p. Since taxes are imposed on all incomes above $\bar{I}$, continuity implies that the slope of the indifference curve between $\underline{I}$ and $\bar{I}$ would be exactly equal to $1 - w$.

Figure 4.5 shows the implied tax schedule in a fully democratic society with a constant rate of dead weight loss. All persons with endowed incomes below $\underline{I}$ are fully subsidized on the difference between $\underline{I}$ and their incomes, all persons with endowed incomes above $\bar{I}$ are fully taxed on these differences, and incomes between $\underline{I}$ and $\bar{I}$ are neither taxed nor subsidized. The distance between these intervals is determined by the dead weight loss from redistribution and the shape of the political preference function. For example, if $w = 1/2$, and if the political preference function were Cobb-Douglas, a full democracy would have $\bar{I}/\underline{I} = 2$.[8] If say

$\underline{I}$ equaled \$4000 in the United States, $\bar{I}$ would equal \$8000, and 24 percent of all persons with income would not be taxed because their incomes are between \$4000 and \$8000, 35 percent would be fully taxed on the difference between their incomes and \$8000, and 41 percent would be fully subsidized on the difference between their incomes and \$4000 (these amounts calculated from US Bureau of the Census 1976).

$\underline{I}$ would decrease and $\bar{I}$ would increase as w increased so that the number of persons taxed or subsidized would decrease as w increased. At one extreme, if $w = 0$, if redistribution has no dead weight loss because all taxes and subsidies are effectively lump-sum, then $\underline{I}$ would equal $\bar{I}$, or a fully democratic society would then equalize all disposable incomes. At the other extreme, if $w = 1$, $\underline{I}$ and $\bar{I}$ would be $-\infty$ and $+\infty$ respectively: no incomes would be taxed or subsidized because income could not be redistributed.

I have frequently used the assumption that a society is fully democratic, that the political preference function does not depend on the identity of persons. Yet the same personal characteristics that contribute to private incomes—energy, education, ability, race, sex, religion, etc.—often also contribute to political influence. If they did, a society would be undemocratic because persons with larger endowed incomes would tend to have greater political influence than other persons when their disposable incomes were equal.[9] Even redistribution with lump-sum taxes would not fully equalize disposable incomes in such a society: persons with larger endowed incomes would also tend to have larger disposable incomes.[10]

More generally, disposable incomes would be more unequally distributed—less would be taxed away from persons with larger endowed incomes—the greater the political influence of the persons. Point e in Figure 4.6 gives the political equilibrium in a democratic society with a positive dead weight loss, and point e^* gives the equilibrium in a society with the same dead weight loss that politically favors persons with larger endowed incomes. Less is taxed away from the richer person i at point e^* than at e because the undemocratic society has political indifference curves that are more favorable to richer persons.

An undemocratic society does not equalize the disposable incomes of all persons paying taxes if their endowed incomes are different. Indeed, the apparent tax system could even be sharply regressive: *total* taxes could only be slightly higher or even lower at higher endowed incomes. Similarly, an undemocratic society does not equalize the disposable incomes of all persons subsidized, and the total subsidy could even be higher at higher endowed incomes. A decline in the degree of democracy—a shift of the political preference function toward persons with larger endowed

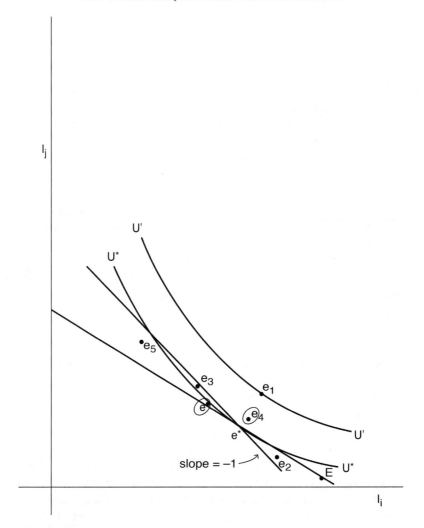

Figure 4.6

incomes—would lower the maximum endowed income subsidized, raise the minimum income taxed, increase the fraction of persons neither taxed nor subsidized, and generally reduce the amount of redistribution away from higher and toward lower endowed incomes.

However, the true marginal tax and subsidy rates applicable to any given person are much steeper than and grossly underestimated by the apparent rate in undemocratic societies. Indeed, even if the apparent tax and subsidy rates were low and perhaps even negative, the true rates would be as high in undemocratic as in democratic societies: 100 percent marginal tax rates for all persons taxed, −100 percent marginal tax rates for all persons subsidized, and a zero rate for those neither taxed nor subsidized. Consider, for example, an increase in the endowed income of a person because of changes in variables that are unrelated to the characteristics that determine his political influence, so that the political preference function would be unchanged. Since aggregate income would increase only by a small amount, the level of political utility would be approximately unchanged. If he were taxed or subsidized initially, none of the equilibrium conditions would be changed, hence all disposable incomes of persons taxed or subsidized would be approximately unchanged in the new equilibrium. Consequently, the entire increase in his income would be taxed away even if the apparent marginal tax or subsidy rate were low and even negative.

The dead weight loss can be easily estimated in a full democracy from evidence on the maximum endowed income subsidized, $\underline{I}$, and the minimum taxed, $\bar{I}$, using the formula

$$\hat{w} = 1 - (\underline{I} \,/\, \bar{I})^{1/\sigma}, \tag{10}$$

where σ is the elasticity of substitution in the political preference function. Since a decline in the degree of democracy lowers the maximum income subsidized and raises the minimum income taxed, equation 10 would overstate the dead weight loss when there is less than full democracy. A more general formula also applicable to undemocratic societies is

$$
\left.
\begin{aligned}
&\hat{w} = 1 - (b \,\underline{I} \,/\, \bar{I})^{1/\sigma} \\
\text{with} \quad &b = \frac{\partial P}{\partial I_i} \bigg/ \frac{\partial P}{\partial I_j} > 1, \text{ when } I_i = I_j,
\end{aligned}
\right\}
\tag{11}
$$

where persons (j) have the endowed income $\underline{I}$ and persons (i) have the larger endowed income $\bar{I}$.

For example, if $\sigma = 1$ and $\underline{I} \,/\, \bar{I} = .5$, equation 10 estimates the dead weight loss at .5, whereas the true loss would only be .25 if $b = 1.5$, if the marginal political influence of persons with the endowed income $\bar{I}$ were 50 percent greater than that of persons with the endowed income $\underline{I}$ when their disposable incomes are equal. This is why the observed inequality in income in different countries is explained sometimes by adverse effects of redistribution on the allocation of resources—the dead weight cost of redistribution—, and sometimes by the absence of full democracy. To take one example, is the redistribution from higher income whites to lower income blacks in the United States limited by the cost of (or "waste" from) redistribution or by the greater marginal political power of a white than a black person?

The approach in this paper has produced the progressive income tax structure shown in Figure 4.5 without requiring any assumptions about the shape of the distribution of endowed income, the number of persons at different income levels who can form a winning "coalition," or attitudes toward risky income prospects (see Rawls 1971). The main assumptions are very different; namely, that political choices are not determined by a mechanical counting of "votes," that the "intensity" of "voter" preferences determines the shape of a political preference function that is maximized by the political process, and that political equilibrium is not a "corner" because political indifference curves are effectively convex.

It is easy to show that the direction of redistribution is not determined in this model by the *number* of persons with different endowed incomes. If one person had I_0 and 99 others had $I_1 > I_0$, if all were selfish, and if political choices were determined by majority rule without regard for the intensity of individual preferences, any redistribution would be from the single poor person to the many rich persons. On the other hand, if political choices were determined by a preference function that depended on the intensity of individual preferences, and if the political indifference curve at the endowed point $(I_0, I_1^1, \ldots, I_1^{99})$ were convex with a slope $-(dI_0/dI_1^j) < 1$, for all j, any redistribution would be from the many rich persons to the single poor person. The gain to the poor person politically outweighs the sum of the losses to the rich persons, presumably because the intensity of this political response can offset their much greater number. Large changes do not always dominate politically many small ones, however, for if $I_1 < I_0$, and if the convex indifference curve at the endowed point had $-(dI_1^j/dI_0) < 1$, for all j, redistribution would be from the single rich person to small gains by each of the many poor persons.

I showed in the previous section a public project that changed incomes in the neighborhood of a political equilibrium with no dead weight loss would raise political utility if, and only if, it raised aggregate income, regardless of the effect on the distribution of income. A project that changed incomes in the neighborhood of an equilibrium with a positive dead weight loss, say in the neighborhood of point e^* in Figure 4.6, obviously would also raise political utility if all incomes were raised: point e_1 is on a higher indifference curve than point e^*.

However, an increase in aggregate income is no longer sufficient because equation 6 shows that changes in the incomes of persons subsidized—necessarily poor persons in a democracy—are weighted more heavily in calculating political utility than are changes in the incomes of those taxed. A project that "worsened" the distribution of income could lower political utility even if aggregate income were raised; for example, aggregate income is larger at point e_2 than at point e^*, but e_2

is on a lower indifference curve because the income of the poorer person j is significantly lower. Similarly, a project that lowered aggregate income could raise political utility if it sufficiently "improved" the distribution of income. Political utility is higher at point e_3 than at e^* in Figure 4.6 even though aggregate income is lower because the income of j is sufficiently higher.

Therefore, whether a public project raises political utility when there is dead weight loss depends not only on its effect on efficiency but also on its effect on equity. Fortunately, both efficiency and equity can be combined into a simple necessary and sufficient condition: a project with "small" effects on income raises political utility if, and only if, a weighted sum of the income changes is positive, where the weight is larger for persons subsidized. Equation 6 shows why they should receive a higher weight, for if political utility is unchanged when 6 holds, it must increase or decrease as

$$dP = dI_i + \frac{1}{1-w}dI_j \gtreqless 0, \tag{12}$$

where i is taxed and j is subsidized. More generally, political utility would increase, remain constant, or decrease as $dP \gtreqless 0$, that is, as

$$\sum\nolimits_{all\ i \in t} dI_i + \frac{1}{1-w}\sum\nolimits_{all\ j \in s} dI_j + \sum\nolimits_{all\ p \in 0} \frac{1}{1-\alpha_p w}dI_p \gtreqless 0,^{11} \tag{13}$$

with $0 \le \alpha_p \le 1$, where ΣdI_i and ΣdI_j are the total changes in the incomes of persons taxed and subsidized, respectively, and dI_p is the change in income of a person neither taxed nor subsidized.

When redistribution has a dead weight loss, efficiency and equity cannot be separated, with public projects evaluated solely by efficiency and with equity separately handled through the tax system. The dead weight loss implies that "full" equity cannot be achieved through the tax system alone because redistribution lowers efficiency. Consequently, a project may be undertaken even when aggregate income is reduced if it is a more "efficient" redistributor of income than the tax system; similarly, it may not be undertaken even when aggregate income is raised if it has perverse effects on equity.

The weights in equation 13 are in the same spirit as the "distributional" weights suggested for evaluating public projects (see the discussion and criticisms in Harberger 1978). A major difference, however, is that the weights in 13 are not based on ad hoc notions of equity, but are derived from a positive analysis of political behavior that also indicates how they can be determined from information on the tax system. For example, given a true tax system of the kind graphed in Figure 4.5, and assuming that the political preference function is Cobb-Douglas, then all persons taxed would receive a weight of unity, all those subsidized would receive a larger weight equal to $(1/b)(\bar{I}/\underline{I}) > 1$, where $\bar{I}$ is the minimum income taxed and $\underline{I}$ is the maximum income subsidized, and $b > 1$ is a measure of the deviation from a full democracy (see equation 11), and persons neither taxed nor subsidized with an income I_p would receive a weight equal to 1 $< (I_p/\underline{I})(1/b_p) < (\bar{I}/\underline{I})(1/b)$ because $\underline{I} < I_p \, / \, b_p < \bar{I}/b$.

A public project could both raise political utility and lower the incomes of many persons; in Figure 4.6 utility is higher at e_3 than at e^* although i's income is lower. However, if all incomes were superior "goods" in the political preference function, an optimal redistribution of income after a project is undertaken would raise the incomes of all persons taxed or subsidized above their initial levels because the rate of exchange between the incomes of these persons would be unchanged. The new redistributive equilibrium after a project changes incomes from point e^* to e_3 in Figure 4.6 is at e_4, where the disposable incomes of both i and j are larger than at point e^*. Since their disposable incomes would be larger, all the "poor" persons subsidized and all the "rich" persons taxed would *unanimously* approve of a project that raised political utility. The same reasoning shows that they would *unanimously* oppose a project that lowered political utility.

Members of the "middle class," on the other hand, would not be unanimous in their evaluation of different projects. If a project that raised political utility lowered the income of a person initially neither taxed nor subsidized, even an optimal redistribution of income would not affect his income if he continued to remain at a "corner." Similarly, even an optimal redistribution of income after a project that raised his income but lowered political utility would not reduce his income. Therefore, some members of this middle class would tend to be political opponents of the rich and poor, preferring projects that they oppose unanimously and opposing projects that they prefer unanimously.

Equation 12 gives a necessary and sufficient condition for large as well as small projects to raise political utility if income is always optimally redistributed. Moreover, all rich and poor persons—those taxed or subsidized—would benefit from large projects that raised political utility and would form a political "coalition" against members of the middle class harmed by these projects. However, if income were not further redistributed after a project were undertaken, equation 12 would not be sufficient when the project is large, for the inequality in 12 could be positive and yet political utility could be reduced. For example, point e_5 in Figure 4.6 is on a higher redistributive line than point e^*, signifying that the inequality in 12 is positive, and yet e_5 is on a lower political indifference curve.

When income is optimally redistributed, the selfish private interest of each rich and poor person is identical to the public "interest" because each would only want to take actions that raised political utility and would refrain from actions that lowered it. Consider, for example, a rich person who could raise his own income while lowering the incomes of many others so that political utility would also be lowered. Since his disposable income rises and falls as political utility rises and falls, his own selfish interest would induce him to refrain from these actions, in effect, to internalize all the external effects of his actions. His disposable income goes down when political utility goes down because the increase in his taxes would exceed the increase in his endowed income: his effective marginal tax rate would actually *exceed* 100 percent. Not only does he consider the "external" effects on everyone else, but he even assigns a greater weight to the changes in their endowed incomes than to the change in his own endowed income because political utility is more affected by changes in the endowed incomes of persons not taxed than by changes in the incomes of persons taxed (see equation 12).

The same argument shows that persons subsidized, poor persons, also fully internalize all externalities, and act as if they are trying to raise political utility, even when their own *endowed* (not disposable) incomes fall. The middle class again is different: they would not internalize the external effects of their actions because there is a conflict between their own and the public interest. Since by assumption they pay no taxes and receive no subsidies, they are not affected by redistributions of income and hence have no incentive to refrain from actions that raise their endowed incomes, no matter what the adverse effects on others. Stated differently, the rich and the poor would appear to be more concerned about the whole society, to be more publicly altruistic, than the middle class, even when everyone is fully selfish, because the disposable incomes of the rich and poor are closely related to the level of political utility, whereas those of the middle class are largely independent of political utility.

C. RISING DEAD WEIGHT LOSS

A constant rate of dead weight loss from taxes and subsidies is a more realistic assumption than lump-sum taxes and subsidies, but a still more realistic assumption permits the loss to vary with the amount taxed or subsidized. A small tax levied on an undistorted position of full equilibrium would have little effect because all points in a small neighbor-

hood around an undistorted equilibrium are equally efficient. As the
tax rate continues to increase, however, further increases would cause
positive and generally increasing rates of dead weight loss because additional taxes are imposed on equilibrium positions that are increasingly
distorted.

The money value of the decline in utility as the tax-subsidy rate increases is a measure of the marginal rate of dead weight loss. If the tax
rate in the jth market increased, this measure of the marginal loss can
be approximated by

$$V \cong \sum_i T_i \frac{\Delta X_i}{\Delta T_j} + \frac{1}{2}\Delta T_j \frac{\Delta X_j}{\Delta T_j}, \tag{14}$$

where T_i is the tax or subsidy (or other distortion) in the ith market, and
ΔX_i is the induced change in output in this market.[12] If $T_i = 0$, all i, and
if ΔT_j is small, the dead weight loss would be approximately zero. The
marginal loss would tend to rise as the T_i increased unless the effect of
tax increases on the allocation of resources, the $\Delta X_i / \Delta T_j$, decreased sufficiently. A constant marginal dead weight loss requires that the $\Delta X_i / \Delta T_j$
decrease sufficiently to offset exactly the effect of the increase in the T_i.

This section makes what is probably a more reasonable assumption
that the marginal loss increases as more is taxed away. Then the boundary of the redistribution set would not be a straight line, but a concave
curve through the point representing endowed incomes. If these incomes
formed an undistorted equilibrium position, the slope of this boundary
would equal −1 at the endowed point, and would decrease in absolute
value as incomes were redistributed; see the boundary AE_0B in Figure 4.7.
Income is assumed to be redistributed in the most efficient manner in
the sense of minimizing the dead weight loss of any given amount redistributed. Since the public sector maximizes political utility, it would
impose an "optimal" set of taxes that minimized the dead weight loss.[13]
Therefore, rising marginal dead weight loss and the other properties of
the boundary of the redistribution set do not presume inefficient taxation and other public mistakes or irrationalities.

Disposable incomes are given by the point of tangency between the
concave redistribution boundary and a political indifference curve, or at
point e^* in Figure 4.7, where

$$-\frac{dI_j}{dI_i} = 1 - w\left(R_{ij}, I_i^0, I_j^0\right)$$

with

$$\frac{dw}{dR_{ij}} > 0, \text{and presumably} \frac{\partial w}{\partial I_k^0} < 0, k = i,j, \tag{15}$$

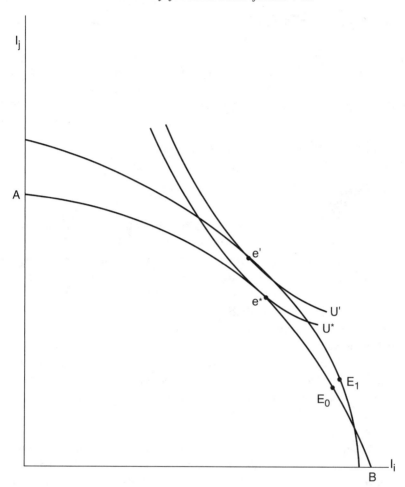

Figure 4.7

where w is the margina l dead weight loss when R_{ij} has been taxed away
from i. If $w = 0$ when $R_{ij} = 0$, a democratic society would redistribute
income away from persons like i with higher endowed incomes, but it
would not equalize disposable income because the dead weight loss rises
as the amount redistributed increases. Since the redistribution boundary
is concave, it could be tangent to a concave section of a political indifference curve, or a section where a more equal distribution of a given
aggregate income lowers political utility. However, the concavity of the
indifference curve at the equilibrium position must be less than that
of the boundary, and hence could not be substantial unless the marginal dead weight loss rose rapidly as more was redistributed. There-

fore, I continue to simplify the discussion by assuming that political indifference curves are convex, at least in a neighborhood of equilibrium positions.

I also simplify by assuming for much of the discussion that the dead weight loss does not depend on scale, that equal percentage changes in R_{ij}, I_i^0 and I_j^0 do not affect w. Therefore,

$$
\left.
\begin{aligned}
w(R_{ij}, I_i^0, I_j^0) &= g\left(\frac{I_i^0}{R_{ij}}, \frac{I_j^0}{R_{ij}}\right) = f\left(\frac{R_{ij}}{I_i^0}, \frac{R_{ij}}{I_j^0}\right), \text{with} \\[2mm]
\frac{\partial w}{\partial(R_{ij}/I_i^0)} &> 0 \text{ and } \frac{\partial w}{\partial(R_{ij}/I_j^0)} > 0.
\end{aligned}
\right\}
\tag{16}
$$

The marginal dead weight loss would increase with an increase in either the fraction of i's income that is taxed or j's income that is subsidized.

A public project that has a "small" effect on incomes raises political utility if, and only if, the change in i's income plus the change in j's income weighted by $1/1 - w$ is positive.[14] The same necessary and sufficient condition applies when the dead weight loss is constant, except that the marginal and average losses are then equal (see the discussion in the previous section). If incomes were optimally redistributed after as well as before a project was undertaken, a political income effect would raise the incomes of both i and j (and, more generally, of anyone taxed or subsidized) above their initial levels. This income effect, however, in turn induces a change in the marginal loss, which increases the cost of raising the incomes of persons hurt by the project.

Consider, for example, a desirable project that lowers the income of i and raises that of j. Income would be redistributed toward i by reducing his taxes. Since the marginal dead weight loss is reduced when taxes are reduced, a substitution effect away from i is induced by the redistribution toward i. As a result, i's equilibrium disposable income could be reduced by the project, even though political utility has been raised (compare points e^* and e' in Figure 4.7). Therefore, the surprising conclusion of the previous section that all persons taxed or subsidized unanimously support or oppose different public projects does not necessarily hold when the marginal dead weight loss is not constant but depends on the amount redistributed.

The previous section also concluded that each selfish person taxed or subsidized internalizes all the external effects of his private actions and only takes actions that raise political utility. This paradoxical conclusion is virtually eliminated when the marginal dead weight loss depends on the amount redistributed. Suppose that i could lower his own income by an action that raised j's income and political utility. We have just shown that the decrease in the marginal loss induced by a reduction in the amount taxed from i could sufficiently discourage redistribution toward i so that his equilibrium disposable income would be lower. If so, a selfish i who correctly anticipates the public response to his action would not take the action. Similarly, he might take an action that lowered political utility if it sufficiently raised his own income because of the limited redistribution away from him.

Therefore, the external effects of private actions are not necessarily internalized when the marginal dead weight loss depends on the amount taxed. Indeed, since the effect of any one person's actions on aggregate political utility is almost always minuscule, the political substitution effect induced by his actions would dominate the political income effect, and selfish persons would have little political incentive to consider the external effects of their private actions.

If the political preference function were homothetic, an increase in all endowed incomes by the same percentage, so that the endowed inequality was unchanged, would increase all taxes and all disposable incomes by the same percentage because the marginal dead weight losses (see equation 16) and the slope of the political indifference curve would then both be unchanged. Hence the opportunity set would be tangent to an indifference curve at the same amount of relative inequality. Therefore, the equilibrium inequality in disposable incomes would be independent of aggregate income, and the political definition of "poverty" would be some constant proportion of average income.

An increase in endowed inequality would increase the redistribution toward poorer persons and also the marginal dead weight loss since that positively depends on the amount redistributed. If the preference function were homothetic and if the marginal loss were given by equation 16, the inequality in disposable incomes must increase when the inequality in endowed incomes did in order to reduce the slope of the indifference curve along with one minus the marginal loss ($1 - w$ in equation 15). Not surprisingly, the political definition of "poverty" depends on the cost of reducing "poverty." Note that the equilibrium weight assigned to changes in the incomes of poorer persons would also increase when the inequality in endowed and disposable incomes increased because the political rate of exchange between the incomes of poorer and richer persons would be shifted in favor of poorer persons.

An increase in the political power of poorer persons that changed the political preference function in their favor would increase the redistribution toward them and thereby would reduce the inequality in disposable incomes. Since an increase in redistribution also increases the marginal loss, changes in the incomes of poorer persons would be weighted more heavily in political evaluations of public projects. Therefore, an increase in the political power of poorer persons increases the attention to equity in public projects and other political decisions at the same time that redistribution increases and income inequality decreases. Does this describe what has been happening in the Western world during the twentieth century?

Assume that the political preference function is symmetric in the incomes of different persons (a full democracy) and that many persons are taxed and subsidized. Assume further that the marginal dead weight loss from increasing taxes is the same for all persons when the fraction of their income paid in taxes is the same; similarly, the marginal loss from increasing subsidies is assumed to be the same for all persons when the fraction received in subsidies is the same. Then the politically optimal tax structure would be progressive: the marginal tax rate would be between −1 and +1 and would rise with income.

To prove this assume the contrary, that the fraction paid in taxes does not depend on income. The marginal dead weight loss would be the same for each person taxed but the marginal rate of substitution between their incomes in the political preference function would favor persons with lower incomes. Therefore, political utility could be increased by raising the tax rates on persons with higher incomes and lowering the rates on persons with lower incomes until

$$-\frac{dI_g}{dI_i} = \frac{1-w_i}{1-w_g}.$$ (17)

The term on the left is the marginal rate of substitution between I_g and I_i in the political preference function, and is < 1 in a democracy if $I_g < I_i$, while the term on the right depends on the marginal losses from additional taxes on i and g, respectively. In equilibrium, therefore, the marginal loss from taxing i must exceed that from g, which implies, given our assumption about the marginal loss function, that the fraction of income paid in taxes by i exceeds the fraction paid by g, or that the tax structure is progressive. The same argument shows that the fraction of income received in subsidies is larger for persons with lower endowed incomes.

However, the loss functions for persons with different incomes may not be the same because they tend to differ in ability, occupation, expenditures, children, marital status, and in other ways that influence their reaction to different taxes. Moreover, the marginal loss from taxing (or subsidizing) a particular person may depend on who is being subsidized (or taxed) because some taxes and subsidies are more naturally complementary; for example, a tax on gasoline implies a "subsidy" to subway and bus employees, or a subsidy to public schools is also a "tax" on employees of private schools.

These considerations imply that even a full democracy might maximize its political utility with an optimal tax and subsidy system that is only weakly and not uniformly progressive (see also Atkinson and Stiglitz 1976) and that quite differently affects persons with the same total income. An optimal system might also have multi-lateral "trade": lower income j could be taxed to subsidize higher income g who is taxed to subsidize still higher income i who is taxed to subsidize j. The net effect could be a substantial redistribution from both g and i to lower income j, but particular taxes or subsidies would be "regressive." Consequently, the net effect of the tax and subsidy *system* could not be inferred from particular taxes or subsidies alone: for example, state subsidies to higher education that redistribute income from poorer to richer persons (see)[15] may be part of a system that is highly progressive (as is the tax and subsidy system in the United States; see Reynolds and Smolensky 1977). The redistribution in higher education cannot be evaluated, therefore, without understanding its contribution to the overall system.

Bibliography[16]

Arrow, Kenneth J. 1951. *Social Choice and Individual Values*. New York: Wiley. Cowles Commission for Research in Economics, monograph no. 12.

Atkinson, Anthony, and Joseph Stiglitz. 1976. "The Design of Tax Structure: Direct versus Indirect Taxation." *Journal of Public Economics* 6, nos. 1–2: 55–75.

Becker, Gary S. 1967. "Human Capital and the Personal Distribution of Income: An Analytical Approach." Ann Arbor: Institute of Public Administration, University of Michigan. (Reprinted in Becker 1975, 94–144).

———. 1974. "A Theory of Social Interactions," *Journal of Political Economy*, November/December.

———. 1975. *Human Capital: A Theoretical and Empirical Analysis, with Special Reference to Education*. 2nd ed. National Bureau of Economic Research.

———. 1976a. "Comment." *Journal of Law and Economics* 19, no. 2 (August): 245–48. [Comment on Peltzman 1976.]

———. 1976b. *The Economic Approach to Human Behavior*. Chicago: University of Chicago Press.

———. 1981. *A Treatise on the Family*. National Bureau of Economic Research. Cambridge: Harvard University Press.

Becker, Gary S., and Nigel Tomes. 1976. "Child Endowments and the Quantity and Quality of Children." *Journal of Political Economy*, special supplement. August.

Bergson, A. 1938. "A Reformulation of Certain Aspects of Welfare Economics." *Quarterly Journal of Economics* 52: 310–34.

Blinder, Alan S. 1976. "Inequality and Mobility in the Distribution of Wealth." *Kyklos* 29, no. 4: 607–38.

Filer, John E. 1977. "An Economic Theory of Voter Turnout." PhD dissertation, University of Chicago.

Harberger, Arnold C. 1971. "Three Basic Postulates for Applied Welfare Economics: An Interpretive Essay." *Journal of Economic Literature* 9, no. 3 (September): 785–97.

———. 1978. "On the Use of Distributional Weights in Social Cost-Benefit Analysis." *Journal of Political Economy* 86, no. 2, part 2 (April): S87–S120.

Keynes, John Maynard. 1936. *The General Theory of Employment, Interest, and Money*. New York: Harcourt, Brace.

Loury, Glenn C. 1981. "Intergenerational Transfers and the Distribution of Earnings." *Econometrica* 49, no. 4: 843–67.

Moore, Thomas Gale. 1972. *Flight Transportation Regulation: Surface Freight and the Interstate Commerce Commission*. Washington, DC: American Enterprise Institute of Public Policy Research.

Peltzman, Sam. 1976. "Towards a More General Theory of Regulation." *Journal of Law and Economics* 19, no. 2 (August): 211–40.

Rawls, John. 1971. *A Theory of Justice*. Cambridge, MA: Belknap Press of Harvard University Press.

Reynolds, Morgan, and Eugene Smolensky. 1977. *Public Expenditures, Taxes, and the Distribution of Income*. New York: Academic Press.

Samuelson, Paul A. 1947. *Foundations of Economic Analysis*. Cambridge, MA: Harvard University Press.

Sandmo, Agnar. 1976. "Optimal Taxation: An Introduction to the Literature." *Journal of Public Economics* 6, nos. 1–2: 37–54.

Stigler, George J. 1975. *The Citizen and the State*. Chicago: University of Chicago Press.

Tobin.[17]

US Bureau of the Census. 1976. *Current Population Reports*. Series P-60, No. 101, "Money Income in 1974 of Families and Persons in the United States," Washington, DC: US Government Printing Office.

A Note on Optimal First Best Taxation and the Optimal Distribution of Utilities

Unpublished Manuscript, Department of Economics, University of Chicago, 1982

GARY S. BECKER

The optimal tax literature has generally avoided lump-sum taxation because of the assumed imperfect knowledge about the characteristics of individuals that generate different wage rates and other differences in welfare. As a result, a paradoxical implication of lump-sum or first best taxation apparently has gone unnoticed. The paradoxical implication is that optimal lump-sum taxation will *reverse* the ranking of different individuals by utility level.

To show this, assume an additive social welfare function, that the utility functions of different individuals are identical, and that they depend positively on leisure and an aggregate consumer good. Consider individual a who has higher wage rate than individual b, where both wage rates are simply given as a result perhaps of differences in the abilities of a and b. Also assume diminishing marginal utility of income for both a and b.

Since the wage rate of a is higher than that of b, the equilibrium utility level of a prior to taxation must also be higher than that of b. The assumption of diminishing marginal utility of income can be shown to imply that the marginal utility of income must be less to a than to b. Therefore, given also our assumption of an additive social welfare function, the optimal lump-sum tax would take income from a and give it to b until the marginal utilities of income of both a and b are equal. The issue now simply becomes: how do the utility levels of a and b compare when their marginal utilities of income are equal?

The issue is decided by the effect of an increase in wage rates on the marginal utility of income when the level of utility is held constant. The sign of this effect is easily determined from the expenditure function; that is, from the equilibrium cost of obtaining a given level of utility. This cost depends positively on the wage rate. Using the basic result on expenditure functions, we can write

$\partial C(w) \,/\, \partial w = l,$

where l is the equilibrium level of leisure. By differentiating this equation with respect to the level of utility, we get

$\partial^2 C \,/\, \partial w \partial u = \partial l \,/\, \partial u > 0$

if leisure is a superior good. But we can rewrite this cross derivative by reversing the order of differentiation:

$\partial^2 C \,/\, \partial w \partial u = \partial^2 C \,/\, \partial u \partial w = \partial \lambda^* \,/\, \partial w > 0,$

where λ^* is the inverse of the marginal utility of income. Hence an increase in the wage rate lowers the marginal utility of income at a given level of utility.

Therefore, optimal lump-sum taxes must lower the utilities of those with higher wages below the utilities of those with lower wages in order to equalize the marginal utilities of income of different persons. Put differently, optimal lump-sum taxes must completely reverse the utility rankings of different individuals! The rank correlation between the utilities before and after such optimal taxation would equal -1.

The intuitive explanation for this finding is straightforward. Individuals with lower wages are more efficient consumers of leisure than are individuals with higher wages because earnings foregone by leisure are less when wages are lower. Hence society can improve efficiency of the total allocation of time between the market and leisure sectors by inducing low-wage individuals to spend relatively large amounts of their time at leisure, and high wage individuals to spend relatively large amounts of their time at work. Redistributing income away from high wage individuals raises their market activity and lowers the market activity of low wage individuals.

This conclusion holds for any type of tax based upon wage rates on full incomes. Although income taxation is usually justified by the inability to distinguish wage rates from hours of work, it does not seem unfeasible. Many surveys now do distinguish hours of work from income, and the accuracy of this distinction could be improved with further effort.

This analysis is automatically generalized to n different goods, with given relative prices, as long as these relative prices are unaffected by lump-sum redistributions. For then Hicks's Composite Good Theorem implies that we can aggregate all these goods into a single good, and the preceding analysis then applies automatically. We can also generalize the analysis to differences in ability that produce not only differences in wage rates, but also differences in the effective prices paid for different goods by different individuals. Perhaps some individuals are more efficient searchers than others, or have more efficient household production functions. Individuals who are more efficient at producing a particular good, and therefore experience a lower effective price for that good, would have a higher level of utility initially than less efficient individuals. As long as the good has a positive income elasticity, then the marginal utility of income would be lower to the more efficient individuals when the level of utility is the same for all individuals. Consequently, a lump-sum tax would also reduce the utility level of more efficient individuals below that of the less efficient individuals in this case as well.

We can give the following interpretation of the main result. Suppose that wage rates are partly the result of different realizations of luck in a lottery. This lottery might be with regard to the distribution of abilities, or with regard to the distribution of health that affects market wages. Let us now interpret government redistribution as government insurance of individuals against the uncertainty due to this lottery. The above argument implies that the optimal insurance purchase ex ante by each individual would be such that their utility level would be higher in states of the world where they experience bad luck—that is, lower wage rates— than in states of the world where they experience good luck. Of course, ex post, individuals experiencing good luck would wish they had not entered into such an insurance arrangement since they will end up with lower utility than individuals experiencing bad luck. But this difference between ex ante and ex post attitudes is the same for all kinds of insurance arrangements.

Some may want to interpret welfare programs that make recipients better off than productive individuals as an application of this theorem. However, the subsequent "impossibility theorem" makes such an interpretation of actual redistribution implausible.

Suppose that it is impossible to use lump-sum transfers, and that only income taxes and commodity excise taxes are available. Let these taxes be as nonlinear and as complicated as possible. The only restriction is that individuals with the same income or with the same consumption must pay the same income or consumption tax.

The question I want to ask is: could a complicated system of income and consumption taxes—that is, a complicated system of "second-best" taxes—reproduce the first best results? Each consumption or income tax would introduce distortions, but the distortions introduced by one tax might offset the distortions introduced by another, so that the combined set would have no distortions, like first best taxation. It is well known that in simple general equilibrium models, monopoly in all industries could be as efficient as competition in all industries, even though any single monopoly introduces a distortion. Perhaps a tax on a good whose consumption is complementary with leisure could exactly offset the effect of income taxes on the consumption of leisure.

If all persons enter symmetrically into the social welfare function, then our basic theorem shows that even the most complicated system of taxes on incomes and consumptions could not reproduce the first best equilibrium with lump-sum taxes and subsidies. Recall that our first best equilibrium reversed the utility rankings of individuals before and after taxation. Consider now an individual with a high wage rate. High wage rate individuals could insure that they have the same income and the same consumption of all commodities as low wage rate individuals. Hence they would pay equal amounts in income and consumption taxes. But high wage individuals can have the same income as others only if they work fewer hours and consume more leisure. As long as leisure has positive marginal utility, they must end up with greater utility after taxes than lower wage individuals. Since we have already shown that the first best solution requires high wage individuals to end up with lower levels of utility than low wage individuals, income and commodity taxes cannot reproduce the first best results.

5

FAMILY ECONOMICS

Human capital is so uncontroversial nowadays that it may be difficult to appreciate the hostility in the 1950s and 1960s toward the approach that went with the term. The very concept of human capital was alleged to be demeaning because it treated people as machines. To approach schooling as an investment rather than a cultural experience was considered unfeeling and extremely narrow.

—GARY S. BECKER, Nobel Lecture, 1992

This enlarged edition of A Treatise on the Family *is an effort to demonstrate further that the rational choice interpretation of family behavior has much to offer not only to economists, but also to researchers in the many other disciplines that study the family. The family merits the great attention it receives from both scholars and laypersons, for despite major changes over time and enormous variations across social and economic environments, it remains the most influential of all institutions.*

—GARY S. BECKER, *A Treatise on the Family* (enlarged edition), 1991

The building blocks of Becker's economics are human capital, the family and time allocation, and preference formation. In the notes presented in this part, they are combined to understand the sudden changes in the family organization in the modern economy.

The notes were for a lecture that Becker delivered at a conference on "Economic Dimensions of the Family" in Madrid in 1999. Becker began to use economic analysis to think about the family very early in his career in the late 1950s, starting with "An Economic Analysis of Fertility." This was the beginning of a long quest to understand the family organization and its interaction with market and nonmarket forces.

In the development of family economics, Becker applies the economic approach to marriage, divorce, altruism, the relations among family members, and investment by parents in children. His approach was so controversial and ambitious that it is worth recalling what economists were saying at the time. A review of his *Treatise on the Family* (1981) reads "The reader will find much that intrigues in this book, and much that annoys . . . But for all its folly it is a book that makes one think. The size and importance of its subject makes it a courageous undertaking."[1] A review in the *Economic Journal* is less optimistic about Becker's approach to the family: "While economists have happily postulated behavioural assumptions which allowed economic problems . . . to be cast in the framework of constrained maximization, the profession as a whole has never been entirely conformable with the Chicago School's enthusiastic application of a choice theoretic framework to church attendance, dating, choice of spouse, and production of children."[2]

Sherwin Rosen (1993) highlighted that Becker had "gone against the grain of establishment thinking in the economics profession, invariably choosing to work on problems that were considered beyond the boundaries of modern economics. Yet his work made close contact with many of the great economists of the past, and many of the concepts he invented and developed are now widely, if not routinely used in modern economics."[3] Becker's novel approach to the problem of the family soon evolved into a field and specialization in economics.

In the lecture notes below, Becker puts the economic approach to work to provide an understanding of the changes in the family organization and in "family values" over the second half of the past century. The emphasis is on the role of opportunities in the determination of the number of children, the choice of partner, and other fundamental decisions in people's lives. According to Becker's analysis of the family as an economic unit, even loyalty and love respond to costs and benefits, material and nonmaterial, and could adversely be affected by social welfare programs. The analysis shows the importance of integrating individual and family behavior into a market framework, where different participants interact with each other, instead of focusing on individual behavior.

Economics and the Family

Prepared for the Economic Dimensions of the Family Conference, Madrid, September 21, 1999

GARY S. BECKER

1. Introduction

The family is one of the most important institutions in all societies: it raises the young and inculcates values in the next generation, produces food, clothing, etc., helps out in emergencies, and cares for the elderly. These contributions are so fundamental, some scholars speculate that the remarkable advances apparently made by human beings thousands of years ago may have been due to the development of the father-mother-children type of family organization.

Of course, the family has not remained unchanged over the centuries. The typical family is very different today in many respects than it was several centuries ago. For a while in Europe and North America the changes were slow. But they speeded up in this century, especially during the past forty years. Indeed, the changes have been more revolutionary during the past four decades than during any comparable period in modern history. Let me give a few prominent examples.

A. BIRTH RATES

In the 19th century, even in the United States and most of Europe, the typical family had four to six births. This declined throughout the 20th century so that now fertility in many countries is too low to replace the population.

Some extremes:

Italy—had high fertility—now	1.3
Spain—had high fertility—now	1.3
Germany	1.4
Poland	1.8
United States	1.9

True in Asia as well:

Hong Kong	1.6
Korea	1.6
Taiwan	1.6

As birth rates fell, the fraction of births to *unmarried women rose.*

B. LABOR FORCE PARTICIPATION OF WOMEN

In the early 20th century, many farm women worked on the farm, and urban women sometimes worked at home for pay, but relatively few were in the labor force. Now labor force participation rates even of married women are quite high:

Sweden	80 percent
United States	65–70 percent

C. OLD AGE

The fraction of population over age 60 have been growing rapidly and will continue to grow for two reasons: low and declining fertility and declining mortality at older ages.

D. DIVORCE AND SEPARATION

Divorce and separation was unimportant in Western countries until the 1960s, although many couples stopped living together and separated even in the past. But the changes since the early 60s have constituted a revolution in family living patterns. Today almost 40% of all first marriage in the United States, Sweden, Great Britain, and Russia end in divorce, and the rate of marital breakups are high in other nations as well even when they do not divorce.

2. Why These Changes?

In order to understand why family has changed so much, and feasibility of returning to older style family structures, it is necessary to understand what determined family structure and how these determinants have changed. I will consider four or five important aspects of the family as an "economic" unit broadly defined to go beyond the material aspects of family life. Economic means providing various useful functions, whether materialistic or not.

A. CHILDREN

Parents had many children in the past for several quite practical reasons.

a. High child *death rates*—25–50 percent of births—maybe only three or four survived.

b. Children, especially on farms, could start working very early and contribute significantly to their upkeep by age 12. Adam Smith on widows with three sons. In urban areas, children sent out to work by age 12 and contributed significantly to family income. So children could be valuable assets.

c. Old Age Support: Grown children helped support elderly parents who did not accumulate much savings. Old age motive for children especially important for widows who may have had no assets and no other persons to turn to.

B. DIVISION OF LABOR BY SEX

Men and women traditionally had very different roles: women raised as well as bred children. And with so many births, raising children took much of the time of mothers for thirty years or so, or the majority of adulthood. Women also cooked, kept house, helped out on the farm or in business. Men, by contrast, did very little child rearing. They devoted time mainly to work on the farm or in the city—earning pay to cover family expenses. The main reason for the division of labor, I believe, at these times was that women were superior at caring for children and with so many children, that took most of their time.

Feminists don't like this explanation. But it does not imply that power in a family was shared equally. Often men had most of the power and a wife's life was even much more difficult than that of her husband. But distribution of power is distinct from the source of the division of labor, which had to do with efficiency at different roles.

C. INSURANCE

The family was a major force in helping people out in emergencies due to illness or economic reverses: members took care of each other, and gave or loaned money to each other in time of *need*.

D. OLD AGE

The family was the primary source of social security: older parents usually lived with sons or daughters, and typically children supported elderly parents in ill health or with few resources. Existence of many children raised likelihood that such support would be forthcoming, although many times the church helped out the elderly because children could not or would not support them.

By looking at the family as an economic unit it is possible, I believe, to explain most of the drastic changes during the past 40 years in family organization. For there were important shifts in both benefits and costs, material as well as nonmaterial, of previous decisions and arrangements. Let me take in turn some of the dramatic changes and see how we can explain them.

3. Fertility

It is not difficult to understand why parents want to have few children now. It is not that parents love their children any less than parents did in the past, but

a. There are fewer child deaths—don't need so many births to give two or three survivors.
b. Children are much less useful on the farm in modern agriculture or in industry than in the past because production is much more skill-based and less dependent on raw labor.
c. Old age support—social security taken over by government so children are less needed to help out the elderly than in the past.
d. Human capital—more important.

It is not surprising, therefore, parents now want few children. Instead, they invest much in the health, education, and training of each child so they can be better prepared for the modern economy.

4. Women's Role

At the same time, various changes in the economy helped propel more married women into the labor force while they took their children out. The decline in emphasis on strength and physical skills and the growth in services and the government sector created jobs that suited women more than the assembly jobs available in the past. The attraction of entering the labor force was reinforced by the growing education of women.

They were acquiring the training and skills that made them valuable workers in modern economies.

The forces reducing the number of children, which I just discussed, also gave them more time for work outside the home. Of course, by the same token, the increased labor force participation of women further reduced their interest in having many children because it raised the cost of children.

5. Divorce

The growing labor force participation of women and lower fertility also encouraged marital breakups, one of the more troublesome aspects of changes in modern families. Women could contemplate separating more easily because they had greater financial independence and had fewer children to care for. One result has been a large increase in the number of female-headed households. Another has been the increase in unmarried women who had children without getting married.

6. Family Insurance and Old Age Support

The contribution of the family to protecting against crisis was greatly reduced by the growth of market and government alternatives.

I will come back to the government later. But market changes were important.

Life and medical care insurance helped provide for a spouse and children in the event of death or serious illness.

More opportunities to save to have assets to use up in emergencies.

Pension plans helped provide for old age.

These all reduced the need to rely on parents, children, and other relatives.

7. Support

Children become less important as supporters of older parents. Pensions and savings give the elderly more resources to draw on. Most important is Social Security. The young support the old so the elderly are less in need of help from children.

Since family members needed each other less, members have drawn more apart. Parents tend to live separated from children and see them less. Mothers spent less time with their children. Husbands and wives had less stable relations. The result of all this is a *deterioration in the relations among family members*—less loyalty and love, less investment in "family values," less durability, and a partial "breakdown" of the family.

8. Reversal

Can these changes in the family be reversed? Especially, can the social pathology of many families be prevented? This is a challenging question of the utmost importance. But the answer is complicated.

To the extent that these changes are responses to fundamental trends in modern economies, changes in the family cannot easily be radically altered. For example, given the various forces I have mentioned, one cannot expect a reversal of the general trend toward smaller families than in the past. Parents inevitably want to have relatively few well-trained, healthy, and well-educated children. Similarly, the heavy labor force participation of married women cannot be sharply cut back because women with few children will have much time free, and educated women inevitably will want to use some of this time working in the economy that wants their skills.

The same is also true of most of the other changes I have considered. But the family has also changed because of *artificial* inducements created by the modern welfare state and these can be altered without harming modern economic and social life. Indeed, I believe various changes would have enormous benefits.

In some ways the welfare state has "nationalized the family" by making governments responsible for help in cases that were formerly the family's responsibility. Let me give a few examples:

a. The United States, Great Britain, Sweden, and many other Western nations provide income to unwed mothers. Such payment sanctions this behavior, and thereby also encourages unmarried men and women to have more children. Such a welfare system is destructive of basic family values and is also *harmful* to the children involved. It should and can be radically reformed. Has been in US by requiring work.

b. Western nations have a pay-as-you-go social security system where the young are taxed to pay for support of the old. A better system, found in Chile, Argentina, Peru, and Singapore, and a few other countries, is to have each worker save for old age in individual retirement accounts that they can spend when they are older. Since these are retirement accounts, they are *less* affected by the growing number of elderly and declining number of young persons, a demographic problem for the social security systems in effect in Western Europe.

Also the present system encourages parents to have fewer children because the elderly are supported from a fund. This effect would be eliminated under my system which makes individuals responsible for their own old age support, except for the poverty-stricken.

c. The most difficult issues relate to public policy toward child care facilities, leaves for mothers with children, and the like. On one hand, if the government subsidizes these a lot, it encourages more women to work and they spend less time caring for their own children—partly, working women will take care of other working women's children. This is not likely to be conducive to stronger family ties.

But on the other hand, if we don't have these care facilities, leaves, etc., more children may be neglected by mothers who work and provide inadequate arrangements for care of children.

I do not have an answer to this social dilemma, but the economic viewpoint helps lay out the issues more carefully.

d. Divorce—not no-fault—encourages breakups, but especially bad on women.

Marriage contract—decide if no divorce, easy come, easy go.

e. Bad public schools, especially children from poorer broken homes.

Conclusions

Family has greatly changed, been weakened.

Many changes rational responses to changing conditions. Some responses to bad _____ policies.

Despite these changes, the family is still crucial to a well-functioning economy and society. Indeed, it is no accident that Asian nations have both rapid economic growth and a vibrant and powerful family life. Examples of the responsibilities of families in modern economies include:

Parents have the main influence over population growth through their decisions about how many children to have. The negative effects on the economy of more rapid population growth have been greatly exaggerated, and the positive effects have received insufficient attention.

The family is responsible for much of the investment in their children's *human capital*, which refers to the knowledge, skills, and health of people. Since human capital is crucial to more rapid growth of modern economies, this role of families is especially important. The importance of human capital places people rather than machinery at the center of economic progress.

Families also make major contributions to the formation of the attitudes and values of a population. Attitudes toward honesty, responsibility, hard work, and self-reliance determine not only the quality of economic life, but social and political behavior as well.

Families still provide much of the support to members who become sick, unemployed, or infirm. In other words, families continue to help members insure against the many uncertainties and hazards of life.

The main reason for concern about the modern deterioration of many families is that families in disarray usually do not perform these valuable functions very well. Divorced parents, and unmarried teenagers who are mothers, have difficulty paying much attention to the training and development of their children. And frequent conflict between divorced parents over custody and financial support provides an unpleasant environment for the growth and development of children.

These are the major issues about the family that can be usefully discussed with economic analysis.

Thank you.

CHRONOLOGICAL ACADEMIC LIFE OF GARY S. BECKER

1930. Born on December 2 in Pottsville, Pennsylvania.

1935. Moves with his family to Brooklyn, New York. Natalie Becker, his sister, remembers that "we all were supposed to study hard, to focus, to plan ahead, to think independently, to not follow the crowd, to use your brains as they would say. Gary was intense about the Giants, about ping pong, stickball, handball, math problems, about strength, competition, ringolevio, not about religion, politics, art, poetry" (Heckman, 2014).

1948. Becker graduates from James Madison High School, where the neo-Keynesian economist Robert Solow (Nobel Laureate in Economics, 1987) graduated some years before.

"We had many lively discussions in the house about politics and justice. I believe this does help explain why by the time I finished high school, my interest in mathematics was beginning to compete with a desire to do something useful for society" (Becker, 1993).

1950. Elected Member of Phi Beta Kappa, Princeton University Chapter.

1951. Completes his undergraduate studies (summa cum laude) in mathematics at Princeton University. He recalls in his autobiography that he "accidentally took an economics course" and "was greatly attracted by the mathematical rigor of a subject that dealt with social organization."

He is a student of Jacob Viner and Oskar Morgenstern and contemporary with graduate students John Nash (Nobel Laureate in Economics, 1994), Lloyd Shapley (Nobel Laureate in Economics, 2012) and Martin Shubik. The famous mathematician John Milnor (Fields Medal, 1962) is his room-mate at Princeton. His senior thesis is on international trade (1952).[1] He also writes a paper on monetary theory with William Baumol (1952). On his letter of recommendation to Chicago, Jacob Viner writes, "Becker is the best student I ever had."

He begins his doctoral studies at the University of Chicago. He takes Milton Friedman's (Nobel Laureate in Economics, 1976) famous two-quarter graduate course sequence on price theory. Becker recalls that "he developed the theory in a clear, systematic, logically consistent fashion. He also gave numerous illustrations and applications . . . These applications helped students absorb Friedman's vision of economics as a tool for understanding the real world, not as a game played by clever academics" (Becker, 1991). During his first period in Chicago Becker meets and inter-acts with Gregg Lewis, T. W. Schultz (Nobel Laureate in Economics, 1979), Aaron Director, and Jimmie Savage.

In a letter supporting Becker for an Earhart Foundation Fellowship in 1953, Milton Friedman describes him as a student: "Becker has a brilliant, analytical mind; great originality; knowledge of the history of economic thought and respect for its importance; a real feeling for the interrela-tionships between economic and political issues; and a profound under-standing of both the operation of a price system and its importance as a protection of individual liberty" (Heckman, 2014).

1955. Becker completes the PhD in economics at the University of Chicago. His dissertation is on "The Economics of Racial Discrimination." His the-sis committee is Greg Lewis (Chair), Jacob Marschak, D. Gale Johnson, and William Bradbury (sociologist).

Gary Becker remembers the first steps of his dissertation at the memo-rial for Milton Friedman in 2007: "I sent a draft of a first five or six pages to him (Milton Friedman was visiting Cambridge, England) . . . stickle while over a month before I got an answer . . . finally I saw this envelope from Milton Friedman, so I ripped open and then my dismay just grew, it was ripping me from one end to the other . . . I was thinking I have to look for another topic, finally in the very end he said 'but there are a couple of good ideas in here and I think it is worth developing as a thesis.'"[2]

"Becker's discipline-changing insight was to frame race discrimination within a market context, using the framework to analyze and identify reasons for the black-white wage differential. In this way, he was able to illustrate standard features of economics while applying them to the questions of why wage differentials exist and persist between races" (Murphy, 2015).

A year before graduating, in 1954, he is appointed assistant professor in the Department of Economics at the University of Chicago.

1957. Becker moves to the Department of Economics of Columbia University and also joins the Center for Economic Analysis of Human Behavior and Social Institutions of the National Bureau of Economic Research as an associate researcher. "I felt that I would become intellectually more independent if I left the nest and had to make it on my own" (Becker, 1993).

The first edition of his book *The Economics of Discrimination* is published. In a review of the book, Armen A. Alchian (1958) claims that "To say that this is the best book on the manifestation of discrimination would be no great compliment, since so little has been done elsewhere. But praise is due Becker for having written so superb an analysis in a relatively unexplored but important field. The reader will gain a richer understanding of discrimination. Furthermore, many preconceptions and errors will be removed—to judge by this reviewer's experience."

During his period at Columbia University, Becker produces major work on family fertility, human capital, the theory of allocation of time and household production, irrational behavior, and the economics of "crime and punishment." His thinking about the economics of crime begins with his decision to park illegally on the street outside Columbia University because the expected parking penalty is low, and it is valuable to arrive on time for his student's examination.

At Columbia, Becker teaches "Price Theory" and "Human Capital," which cover his still unpublished manuscript on that subject. About Becker's price theory course, William Landes recalls: "Having been a member of a law school faculty for over twenty years, I am still struck by the difference between Becker's teaching style (unusual even in economics departments) and that of the typical law school professor. Like law classes, Becker called on students who did not volunteer. But Becker would work with the student for a few minutes until (hopefully) he came up with the right answer . . . For three or four months before the oral exams I was part of a small group of students (we called ourselves 'Becker Bombers') who met regularly to review questions from Becker's prior exams and problems from Milton Friedman's soft cover textbook. Working through this material made it clear to me the difference between knowing economics and thinking like an economist. The former comes from mastering the language and formal principles of economics that are found in graduate textbooks and articles in professional journals. The latter from applying these tools with varying degrees of sophistication to solving problems" (Landes, 1997).

Isaac Ehrlich recalls: "Participating in his price theory course, both as a student and later as a teaching assistant (TA), was the most intense intellectual experience I have had as a student. The text was still Milton Friedman's *Price Theory: A Provisional Text*, but the content was vintage Becker. We were kept alert at all times, partly because of the inspiring materials he weaved into it, based on his 'Irrational Behavior and Economic Theory' (1962), his theory of the allocation of time, and his work on investment in human capital—these were not in the text—but also because of his practice of surprising students by calling on them in the middle of the lecture to answer questions about the material he was teaching—a technique he may have acquired as a student in Chicago" (Ehrlich, 2018).

1958. Becker publishes "Competition and Democracy" in the inaugural issue of the *Journal of Law and Economics*. Although Becker regretted that editor Aaron Director neglected to send the page proofs for his review, the publication began a lifelong interest in the application of the economic approach to politics. He returns to this in his 1976 comment on Sam Peltzman's article and, especially, in his pressure-group models in the 1980s.

In the late '50s, Becker presents his early paper on fertility, "An Economic Analysis of Fertility," at the NBER conference "Demographic and Economic Change in Developed Countries." James S. Duesenberry (1960) from Harvard starts his comment to the paper saying, "For many years economists have taken variations in rates of population growth, and in family size, as data which help to explain various economic phenomena but which cannot themselves be explained in terms of economic theory. Becker has done us a real service in bringing economic analysis to bear on the problem once more." Then Duesenberry makes some objections that were addressed by Becker many years after: "In his work with Lewis, his solo work on social interactions and his work with Barro, he refined and adapted the research on fertility. And in later joint work with Murphy, rephrased, made rigorous, and responded to Duesenberry some 40–50 years after. Culminated in a work with Kevin Murphy ('Social Economics,' 2000)" (Heckman, 2014).

1960. Jacob Mincer, another of the pioneers in the development of modern labor economics and the area of human capital, returns to Columbia as an associate professor.

> Although we did not write much together, the intellectual collaboration and interaction was continuous, so it is hard to know what was his [Mincer's] contribution and what was mine. We were engaged

CHRONOLOGICAL ACADEMIC LIFE OF GARY S. BECKER : 141

together in an exploration, an intellectual venture, that took us to a number of areas. We accomplished an enormous amount together, and that was far more important than what we might have written together.

This intellectual co-operation led to a great workshop—the labor economics workshop at Columbia. Several factors contributed to its success. First of all, it had a continuing input of first-class students. Ultimately, the quality of the students determines the success of a workshop, and I would give our students number one credit for the accomplishments of the workshop. They were hard-working, able, extremely interested in the subject, and they were ready to take criticisms of their work.

. . . The workshop consisted mainly of student presentations of their research in progress—we always tried to give first priority to our students. The temptation often is to invite known faculty speakers from elsewhere because they attract a larger audience. However, the purpose of a workshop is to train students. (Becker, 2006).

1964. The first edition of the book *Human Capital* is published. In the preface, Becker points out that "the origin of this study can be traced both to the finding that a substantial growth in income in the United States remains after the growth in physical capital and labor has been accounted for and to the emphasis of some economists on the importance of education in promoting economic development." The book receives the prestigious Woytinsky Prize.

In his book review, Robert Solow (1965) begins by saying, "The heart of this book is an estimate of the internal rate of return to college and high-school education regarded as investments. This is an 'in' question these days; but it is also a real and important question, whose significance will outlive the fad. Professor Becker has spent a lot of skill and ingenuity on finding an answer. It is hard to believe that anyone else could squeeze much more or anything very different from the data now available. If a better answer can be found, it will probably have to come from new information."

About *Human Capital*, Sherwin Rosen (1993) said: "Though not always known by this name, the concept of human capital has had a long intellectual history in economics, having been discussed by such great economists of the past as Smith and Marshall; as well as by distinguished economists of the modern era, such as Milton Friedman and T. W. Schultz. However, no one other than Becker has developed these ideas into such a coherent and empirically fruitful theory. His article on human capital [1962], elaborated further in his book [1964] and lectures [1967], constructs the foundations of what has proven to be a very useful and far-ranging theory. This work has spawned a huge volume of research and has influenced the work of others to a remarkable extent."

1965. Founding Member and Vice President of the National Academy of Education. Named Fellow of the American Statistical Association.

Publishes "A Theory of the Allocation of Time." In the introduction Becker says, "In the last few years a group of us at Columbia University have been occupied, perhaps initially independently but then increasingly less so, with introducing the cost of time systematically into decisions about non-work activities. J. Mincer has shown with several empirical examples how estimates of the income elasticity of demand for different commodities are biased when the cost of time is ignored; J. Owen has analyzed how the demand for leisure can be affected; E. Dean has considered the allocation of time between subsistence work and market participation in some African economies; while, as already mentioned, I have been concerned with the use of time in education, training and other kinds of human capital. Here I attempt to develop a general treatment of the allocation of time in all other non-work activities. Although under my name alone, much of any credit it merits belongs to the stimulus received from Mincer, Owen, Dean and other past and present participants in the Labor Workshop at Columbia."

1967. The John Bates Clark Medal is awarded to Becker by the American Economic Association. The award quote reads: "Gary Becker's versatility and imagination have enlarged the scope and power of our science. In his skillful hands, economic analysis illuminates basic aspects of the behavior of human beings in society: the importance of investment to augment their productive capacity, the allocation of their time, the growth of their members, their crimes and punishments, their racial prejudices. Throughout his work he displays a rare combination of rigor and relevance. With anticipation no less than gratitude, the Association awards Gary Becker the John Bates Clark medal."[3] He is elected Fellow of the Econometric Society.

1968. Becker is named Arthur Lehman Professor of Economics at Columbia University.

1968–71. Serves as a member of the Board of Editors of the *American Economic Review*.

During the 1970s, he devotes most of his research to the development of the theory of marriage and the economics of the family. Sherwin Rosen and Gary Becker lead together the Applications of Economics Workshop. Becker directs and organizes the workshop until his last day. In the first workshop after Becker's death, Robert Barro of Harvard presents "Protection of the Environment, Unusual Disasters and Discount Rates."

1969–70. Becker is a Ford Foundation Visiting Professor of Economics at the University of Chicago before joining the Department of Economics as University Professor there on July 1, 1970.[4] Later, in 1983, he also joins the Department of Sociology and the Graduate Business School.

Becker receives the Professional Achievement Award of the University of Chicago Alumni Association, recognizing those alumni whose achievements in their vocational field has brought distinction to themselves, credit to the university, and real benefit to their fellow citizens.

1971. His *Economic Theory* book is published, based on his price theory course at Columbia. The book is based on a transcription of recorded tapes of his classes at Columbia by his students Michael Grossman and Robert Michael. The textbook includes his famous "Why?" in class questions. "The most efficient way to learn economic theory is to solve many problems that test one's understanding. To this end I encourage discussion during the lectures, including discussion of queries that I put to the class. Many of these queries are included, usually in the form of Why? after a sentence, and students should try seriously to answer them before passing on to new materials" (Becker, 1971). When a student would try to avoid the question by saying "I don't know," Becker would say "I will help you."

Becker serves as a member of the Board of Publications of the University of Chicago Press from 1971 to 1975.

1972. Named Fellow of the American Academy of Arts and Sciences.

1973. Becker joins the Domestic Advisory Board at the Hoover Institution. Milton Friedman, George Stigler (Nobel Laureate in Economics, 1982), and James Buchanan (Nobel Laureate in Economics, 1986) are also members of the board.

Receives a University Professorship in Economics at the University of Chicago.

Gives a Woodward Court Lecture, "An Economist Looks at Crime and Punishment."[5] The lecture series were held at Woodward Court, a student residence complex, and were sponsored by then resident master Izaak Wirszup, a mathematician in the College.

1974. Publishes with William Landes an edited volume, *Essays in the Economics of Crime and Punishment.*

Sociologist James S. Coleman (1993) explains that "when [Becker] asks, in his 'Crime and Punishment: An Economic Approach', 'how many offenses should be permitted and how many offenses should go unpunished?' he is asking an entirely new question for criminology. Until that time, the terms 'should' for criminologists (as for sociologists more generally) was typically answered in moral terms. From that normative view, no offenses should in principle be permitted, and all offenders should in principle be punished. But Becker asked the question wholly from the perspective of positive social science, a perspective with which any economist would be familiar: what is the expenditure of resources in law enforcement that minimizes the social losses resulting from crime? These losses include, in Becker's formulation, not only the damages from offenses, but also the costs of apprehending and convicting offenders, and the social costs of punishment."

Becker is elected vice president of the American Economic Association, with Walter W. Heller from Minnesota as president.

1975. Becker and Gilbert Ghez publish their book *The Allocation of Time and Goods Over the Life Cycle.* He is also elected member of the National Academy of Sciences of the United States and publishes the second edition of *Human Capital.*

1976. Becker publishes *The Economic Approach to Human Behavior.* The book is Becker's manifesto of the economic approach illustrated with his controversial and pioneer applications of the economic approach to discrimination, crime, politics, time and household production, irrational behavior, marriage, fertility, the family, and social interactions.

He also edits "Essays in Labor Economics in Honor of H. Gregg Lewis," which is published as a special supplement to the *Journal of Political Economy.*

1977. Faculty from the economics department, the law school, and the business school establish the Center for the Study of the Economy and the State (now the Stigler Center), an interdisciplinary research institution to study the long-term effects of public regulations on the economy. George Stigler is the director of the center, and other members include Gary Becker and Milton Friedman of the economics department, Sam Peltzman and Peter Pashigian from the business school, and William Landes, Richard Posner, and Kenneth Dam of the law school.

1980. Becker becomes a research associate at the Economics Research Center, NORC.

In the early 1980s, in his "Price Theory" graduate course at Chicago, Becker meets Kevin M. Murphy (Clark Medal, 1997) as a student. It starts a prolific intellectual friendship and collaboration that lasts many years. Together, Becker and Murphy produce important work on addiction, advertising, the formation of social capital and its effects on the behavior of the market, the relation between the rate of fertility, investment in human capital, and economic development, the economics of illegal goods, and other problems, mostly unexplored by economists. These projects reflect their important update of price theory that looks more carefully at the economics of complementarities.

In "Gary Becker as a Teacher," Murphy (2015) explains:

> To be a good teacher, it is necessary to understand a subject and all of its subtleties. Gary Becker was a superb teacher because he understood economics as well as anyone in the world. I taught with Gary Becker for over 15 years. We taught the introductory course in Price Theory for PhD students at the University of Chicago and, along with Edward (Ted) Snyder, we taught a public policy course for MBA students for roughly a decade. Teaching with Gary was great fun. He loved economics and enjoyed passing that love for the subject on to his students. Gary would teach economics to anyone who would listen and he would even try to teach those who refused to listen. Students in his class had no choice but to listen—they lived in constant fear that they would hear their name next in the dreaded phrase "Mr. Smith or Mrs. Jones or Mr. Murphy, what do you think?"
>
>   Becker's courses were rich in content and style, but one stand-out was on his views and discussions of the role of preferences. In many ways Gary had a love-hate relationship with preferences. On the one hand, preferences played a central role in much of his work. In Gary's world, preferences are complicated; people care about many things. They love, hate, become jealous, and want status. They want to associate with some individuals and not associate with others. They get addicted. They try to break bad habits and struggle to avoid their shortcomings. Expanding what people cared about was a big part of what Gary did in carrying out the campaign of economic imperialism that he is famous for.

1981. Becker publishes *A Treatise on the Family.* "Writing A Treatise on the Family is the most difficult sustained intellectual effort I have undertaken . . . Trying to cover this broad subject required a degree of mental commitment over more than six years, during many nighttime as well as daytime hours, that left me intellectually and emotionally exhausted. In his autobiography, Bertrand Russell says that writing the Principia Mathematica used up so much of his mental powers that he was never again fit for really hard intellectual work. It took about two years after finishing the Treatise to regain my intellectual zest" (Becker, 1993).

A review by sociologist Arthur L. Stinchcombe (1983) begins, "Sociologists will have to get into a special mood to read this book, because, by sociological standards, its style of reasoning is outrageous. Since I believe many of the ideas in A Treatise on the Family will prove valuable in family sociology, I will try to harden the prospective sociological reader who would otherwise be driven up the wall."

1982. Elected member of the International Union for the Scientific Study of Population.

George Stigler wins the Nobel Prize in Economics. "George's main contribution has been to the field of industrial organization. His contribution to this field was to bring to bear a combination of careful theorizing and empirical testing of the implications of his theory. Two major contributions have been to pioneer the economic analysis of the role of information in decision-making and the evaluation of the causes and consequences of public policy. George is a dominant person in the field of industrial organization and has influenced the research of almost every economist in his field,"[6] says Gary Becker on the occasion.

1983. The sociology department at Chicago offers him a joint appointment, which he accepts. "Its invitation to me gave a signal to the sociology profession that the rational choice approach was a respectable theoretical paradigm" (Becker, 1993). Becker and sociology professor James Coleman create the University of Chicago Seminar on Rational Choice, which Judge Richard Posner later joins as co-organizer. The seminar engages scholars from the disciplines of economics, philosophy, law, sociology, psychology—anything connected with the insights and limits of applying theories of rational choice to social, economic, and political issues.

1984–85. Becker is chair of the Department of Economics at the University of Chicago.

1985. Becker begins a monthly column for *Businessweek* magazine that extends until 2004. The columns discuss how to improve the quality of education and the opportunities of low-income families through vouchers for schools, the economic approach to the reduction of crime, the benefits of the legalization of drugs, among other issues. Many of the columns are published in 1996 in the book *The Economics of Life: From Baseball to Affirmative Action*, published in collaboration with his wife, the historian Guity Nashat. The first part of the book is titled "From the Ivory Tower to a Columnist."

Becker receives the Frank E. Seidman Distinguished Award in Political Economy, and the titles of Doctor Philosophiae Honoris Causa from the Hebrew University of Jerusalem and Doctor of Laws from Knox College, Galesburg, Illinois.

1986. Becker chairs the program committee of the annual meeting of the American Economic Association. Of the sixty sessions organized, ten are dedicated to the topic of the relationship of economics with other fields, such as law, politics, family, and discrimination. Judge Richard Posner (1987) delivers the Ely Lecture on the Law and Economics Movement. Posner begins the conference by noting, "In the last thirty years, the scope of economics has expanded dramatically beyond its traditional domain of explicit market transactions. Today there is an economic theory of property rights, of corporate and other organizations, of government and politics, of education, of the family, of crime and punishment, of anthropology, of history, of information, of racial and sexual discrimination . . . Some economists oppose this expansion, in whole or (more commonly) in part."

Becker receives the Merit Award from the National Institutes of Health, for the first time granted to someone from the social sciences. He is elected a member of the American Philosophical Society.

1987. Becker is appointed president of the American Economic Association. His presidential address, delivered at the hundredth meeting of the American Economic Association in Chicago, deals with family economics and macro behavior. Becker points out, "Although family behavior presumably has only a small part in the generation of ordinary business cycles, it is likely to be crucial to long cycles in economic activity" (Becker, 1988).

1988. Becker receives the title of Doctor of Arts from the University of Illinois at Chicago and is elected a Distinguished Fellow of the American Economic Association.

1990. Becker is president of the Mont Pelerin Society until 1992. He is elected Rose-Marie and Jack R. Anderson Senior Fellow of the Hoover Institution and receives the title of doctor of science from the State University of New York at Stony Brook.

1991. Becker publishes an enlarged edition of *A Treatise on the Family*, where he incorporates the analysis of the effects of the composition and structure of families on inequality and economic growth. He receives the title of Doctor of Humane Letters from Princeton University.

1992. He is awarded the Nobel Prize in Economics "for having extended the domain of microeconomic analysis to a wide range of human behaviour and interaction, including nonmarket behavior."

In the banquet speech, Becker says: "this Prize gives recognition in the most influential way possible to all economists who endured many obstacles, criticisms, and even ridicule to study and analyze broader aspects of behavior than is traditional in economics . . . Economics surely does not provide a romantic vision of life. But the widespread poverty, misery, and crises in many parts of the world, much of it unnecessary, are strong reminders that understanding economic and social laws can make an enormous contribution to the welfare of people" (Frängsmyr, 1993).

The *University of Chicago Magazine* reports in the December 1992 issue on what Becker intends to do with the $1.2 million that came with the prize. "'The answer to that is a simple lesson in economics,' he said with a shy grin. 'Wants always expand to take advantage of new opportunities.'"

As part of the celebration of the Centennial of the University of Chicago organized by the Alumni Association, Becker, together with Provost Gerhard Gasper, is a speaker at the Centennial Forum on the topic "What's Happened to the Welfare State?" held in Seattle and Philadelphia.

1993. The third edition of *Human Capital* is published, in which Becker adds the Ryerson Lecture that offers an excellent summary for the general public of the field of human capital study and some applications of the theory of human capital to the understanding of inequality and economic growth. He receives the titles of Doctor Honoris Causa from the University of Palermo, Argentina, and Doctor of Humane Letters from Columbia University. He is named a fellow of the National Association of Business Economists.

In the symposia in celebration of the inauguration of Hugo F. Sonnenschein as eleventh president of the University of Chicago, Becker participates in a panel, "Altruism and Egotism." The panel explores to what extent an assumption of rational, individual self-interest best explains human social behavior and is moderated by professor of law Richard Epstein. In the panel, Becker argues that both self-interest and altruism are consistent with rational behavior when "rational" is defined as goal directed.[7]

The University of Michigan–Flint produces a set of trading cards called

"Economist Greats." The set includes Gary Becker and Milton Friedman. Each card's back holds stats on the twenty-nine scholastic greats, including recommended readings. The Flint department creates the cards ($5 a set) to fund a field trip to the Chicago Federal Reserve Bank.

1994. James Coleman receives the social sciences division's first Phoenix Award. Becker comments on the occasion that Coleman's main contribution to the social sciences "has been his creativity . . . Jim has always come up with new ideas and new perspectives and then tried to see how well they work with the data."[8]

1995. Becker is honored with Doctoris Honoris Causa Scientiarum Oeconomicarum, Warsaw School of Economics; Doctoris Honoris Causa, University of Economics, Prague; Doctor of Business Administration, University of Miami; Doctor of Science, University of Rochester.

50 Great Americans, Marquis Who's Who, 1995.

Lord Foundation Award, 1995.

The Hoover Institution publishes *The Essence of Becker*, edited by Ramon Febrero and Pedro S. Schwartz. Becker joins Friedman, Hayek, and Stigler in the Hoover Essence series.

1996. Publishes *Accounting for Tastes*, which includes his essay with George Stigler "De Gustibus Non Est Disputandum," his work on rational addiction and advertising with Kevin M. Murphy, and his work on the formation of habits, social norms, and fads.

Receives the Harold Lasswell Award of the Policy Studies Organization for outstanding scholarship contributing to our understanding of the substance and the process of public policy.

He is also appointed honorary member of Gente Nueva, Mexico City.

1997. Becker is appointed member of the Pontifical Academy of Sciences of the Vatican. The academic summary of the academy reads: "A detailed specialist, he has also sought a wide audience for his discipline and his thought. Prof. Becker is a prominent 'savant,' recognized and appreciated with universally high respect by the members of the world's communities of economists and experts in public policy."

He receives the Irene B. Taeuber Award in Excellence in Demographic Research of the Population Association of America. The award cites Becker for research that "conclusively demonstrated the relevance of economic theory to demography."

He is also named Doctor of Humane Letters, Hofstra University.

President of the Western Economic Association.

Kevin M. Murphy Wins the Clark Medal. Murphy has "made major contributions not only to the study of income inequality, but in his analysis of economic growth, the economic theory of addiction, industrial organization and other fields," says Gary Becker on the occasion.

1999. Becker is named Doctor of Humane Letters, University of Aix–Marseilles.

2000. Becker and Kevin M. Murphy publish *Social Economics: Market Behavior in a Social Environment.* In his review, David Throsby highlights that "[Becker and Murphy] are pioneers in the quest to extend the boundaries of rational choice theory in economics . . . They depict human beings not as isolated individuals but as members of society, shaped by social and cultural forces . . . This book marks another step in bringing economic theory closer to social reality."

During the 2000s, Becker works with Kevin M. Murphy on the markets for illegal goods; evolution, habits, and happiness; education and consumption at home; the distribution of income and the market by status; and the value of health. He also works on the economic analysis of the markets of organs for transplants.

US President Bill Clinton awards the National Medal of Science to Becker for "pioneering the economic analysis of racial discrimination, inventing the economics of human resources, producing the major modern innovations in economic demography and in economic criminology, and leading recent developments in how social forces shape individual economic behavior."

Becker is named Corresponding Member, National Academy of Sciences of Buenos Aires.

2001. The American Academy of Achievement awards Becker its Golden Plate Award. Becker is honored by the University of Chicago's Division of Social Sciences with its rare Phoenix Prize. "Gary Becker is the greatest social scientist who has lived and worked in the last half century," Milton Friedman declares when he introduces Becker at the award ceremony.

2002. Doctor Honoris Causa, University of Athens, and the Heartland Prize.

2003. Doctor of Laws, Harvard University, and the Hayek Award.

Becker is selected for the National Institute of Child Health and Human Development's Hall of Honor "for pioneering the application of microeconomic theory and analysis to marriage, fertility, education, and the formation of human capital."

2004. Becker and Jacob Mincer receive the inaugural "Career Achievement Award for Lifetime Contributions to the Field of Labor Economics" (known as Jacob Mincer Award). Becker also receives the Medal of the Italian Presidency and the John von Neumann Award of the Rajk László College for Advanced Studies, Budapest, given annually "to an outstanding scholar in economics and other social sciences, whose works have had substantial influence over a long period of time on the studies and intellectual activity of the students of the college."

Richard O. Ryan (MBA '66 of the Booth School of Business of the University of Chicago) founds the Initiative on Chicago Price Theory research center at the University of Chicago, "for the purpose to sustain and strengthen the University's leading role in price theory—economic research that combines theory and data to analyze the fundamental role of markets and incentives in explaining virtually all aspects of modern life." Steven Levitt is appointed its director. Levitt, Becker, and Kevin Murphy are the founding members of the Initiative. In 2006, the research center is renamed the Becker Center on Chicago Price Theory.

Becker publishes his last *Businessweek* column. "Gary S. Becker is writing his last Economic Viewpoint column this week. We will sorely miss him. Becker is one of the most original economists of our time, and his thoughtful, conservative voice stands out in an era of shouting, partisan ideologues. The 1992 Nobel prize winner and University of Chicago professor is always the gentleman—but one willing to brave criticism from all quarters by taking unpopular positions" (Stephen B. Shepard, Editor of *Businessweek*).

Becker and Judge Richard Posner together begin their online "Becker-Posner Blog." Most of the posts are published in 2009 in the book *Uncommon Sense: Economic Insights, from Marriage to Terrorism*.

2005. Doctor Honoris Causa, Hitotsubashi University.

2006. Becker's article "The Quantity and Quality of Life and the Evolution of World Inequality," written in collaboration with Tomas Philipson and Rodrigo Soares, receives the Arrow Award for Best Article in Health Economics published in 2005. He delivers the Hicks Lecture at Oxford University, "Health as Human Capital: Synthesis and Extensions."

Becker receives the Provost's Teaching Award from the University of Chicago.

The Initiative on Chicago Price Theory founded by Richard O. Ryan is renamed the Becker Center on Chicago Price Theory. For the occasion, Kevin Murphy, George J. Stigler Distinguished Service Professor of Economics, presents Becker with a first-edition copy of Adam Smith's *Theory of Moral Sentiments* in a wood book holder created by Murphy himself.

The Becker Center launches the Price Theory Scholars program, inspired by Jesse Shapiro's (Inaugural Becker Fellow) experience as a visiting student at the University of Chicago during 2002. The Price Theory Scholars program allows PhD students in economics at other institutions to experience and learn to apply price theory in the Chicago tradition. Students selected as scholars spend the fall academic quarter in residence at the University of Chicago enrolled in the first quarter of the Price Theory sequence currently taught by Kevin M. Murphy. This program is made possible through the generous support of the Searle Freedom Trust.

2007. President George W. Bush awards Becker the Presidential Medal of Freedom, remarking that

> Professor Gary Becker once said, 'Many intellectuals, many economists, use obscure language when they write. Sometimes it's a way of disguising that they are not saying a heck of a lot.' This economist, however, is different. Gary Becker's many books and articles, and his 19 years as a weekly columnist, have proved him to be a thinker of originality and clarity.
>
> Professor Becker has shown that economic principles do not just exist in theory. Instead, they help to explain human behavior in fields well beyond economics. He has shown that by applying these principles to public policy, we can make great strides in promoting enterprise and public safety, protecting the environment, improving public schools, and strengthening the family. Professor Becker has explained, as well, the real value of investing in human capital—he knows full well that an educated and well-trained workforce adds to the vigor of our economy and helps raise the standard of living for all of us.

The Becker Center creates the Price Theory Summer Camp. Currently led by Kevin Murphy, the Camp is an intensive one-week program where PhD students from other universities hear lectures from University of Chicago price theory faculty and experience a series of "Chicago-style" seminars where faculty present their research in progress.

2008. Becker receives the Bradley Prize. "The Bradley Foundation selected Dr. Becker for his original research in the fields of economics and sociology. Dr. Becker's pioneering work in the fields of economics and human behavior has revolutionized those fields of study and inspired a generation of economists" (Michael W. Grebe, President and Chief Executive Officer of the Bradley Foundation).

The *Princeton Alumni Weekly* includes him among the 25 most influential Princetonians of all time.

Named, with President Robert J. Zimmer of the University of Chicago, to the committee that recommends individuals to receive the National Medal of Science.

2010. Receives the Alumni Medal, the highest honor the Alumni Association of the University of Chicago can bestow.

Named to the Center in Beijing, University of Chicago, steering committee. The steering committee helps shape the center's intellectual direction and programming.

John Cassidy of the *New Yorker* runs a round of interviews with Chicago economists (Posner, Fama, Cochrane, Heckman, Becker, Murphy, Thaler, Rajan), "After the Blowup." In his reflection about Chicago Economics and the Great Recession, Becker says, "I think the last twelve months have shown that free markets sometimes don't do a very good job . . . What I have always learned to be the Chicago view, and taught to be the Chicago view, is that free markets do a good job. They are not perfect, but governments do a worse job. Again, in some cases we need government. It is not an anarchistic position. But in general governments do a worse job. I haven't seen any reason to change that other than, yes, we've seen another example where free markets didn't do a good job: they did a bad job. But to me there is no evidence the government did a good job either, leading up to or during the process."

The Lectures on Human Capital (Econ 343) by Gary Becker are recorded during the spring of 2010. The nineteen lectures, filmed by Joey Brown, are posted at youtube.com, with lecture summaries by Jorge L. Garcia and lectures notes by Salvador Navarro Lozano. "Over the years, thousands of graduate students in Economics, Sociology, Public Policy, and other fields have benefited from the teachings of Gary Becker in his Human Capital class. We hope that by providing these lecture videos and notes that people around the world can increase their own human capital and enjoy studying this fascinating subject of human capital as taught by Gary Becker."

2011. The Becker Friedman Institute is established at the University of Chicago. The Institute combines the three-year-old Friedman Institute and the Becker Center on Chicago Price Theory. The center builds on the tradition of Chicago economics: "For decades, UChicago economists have questioned the conventional wisdom, examined evidence, and produced bold, even revolutionary ideas. Rooted in theory and tested with data, these ideas gathered force and fundamentally changed economic thinking around the world. The Becker Friedman Institute builds on this tradition, supporting innovative research and activities designed to inspire a future of powerful new ideas." Becker serves as chairman of the new institute, and Lars Peter Hansen, founding director of the Friedman Institute, serves as research director.

"Honoring Gary S. Becker: A Conference," organized by Ed Lazear and Kevin M. Murphy and hosted by the Milton Friedman Institute, celebrates the eightieth birthday of Gary Becker. Friends and colleagues gather at the Law School for a conference that highlights his contributions to the field of economics. "In his intellectual fearlessness, which he has demonstrated time and time again, he is an exemplar of the aspirations of the University of Chicago," says President Robert J. Zimmer in his opening remarks. James Heckman closes the conference with a deep lecture (Private Notes on Gary Becker, 2014) that puts Becker's intellectual contributions in a historical context and highlights other leading economists he has worked with and influenced over his career.

A 2011 survey of economics professors conducted by Davis et al. (2011) names Becker their favorite living economist over the age of sixty.

2014. Becker dies on May 3 in the city of Chicago. His latest articles in the media deal with the benefits of marijuana legalization, the lifting of the embargo on Cuba, and the introduction of monetary incentives for the donation of organs for transplants.

"If there is one economist who can legitimately be called a giant of the discipline upon whose shoulders future generations will stand, Becker, with his trailblazing application of economics to aspects of everyday life, is a candidate for that title. He changed the nature of economics and made it relevant to entirely new spheres of human life and interaction. It shows his impact that his methods of economic analysis—derided when he introduced them—have now become the tools used by the very best researchers across criminology, sociology and other social sciences" (*The Guardian*, May 15, 2014).

"As a scholar, Professor Becker was fearless, brilliant and intellectually honest. He saw value in economic theory, but kept it in close communication with the data. He was motivated by the belief that economics, taken seriously, could improve the human condition. He founded so many new fields of inquiry that the Nobel committee was forced to veer from the policy of awarding the prize for a specific piece of work, lauding him instead for 'having extended the domain of microeconomic analysis to a wide range of human behavior and interaction, including nonmarket behavior'" (Justin Wolfers, *New York Times*, May 5, 2014).

"Gary had a reputation for being extremely tough. He absolutely terrified people. But not once in twenty years did I hear him raise his voice, or even appear openly angry. People feared him because he could see the truth. At his core, though, he had a deep humanity" (Steven Levitt, Freakonomics Blog, May 5, 2014).

"Becker's contributions are only partially in print under his own name. His introductory 'Price Theory' course (that's 'microeconomics' to those outside of Chicago) was a core intellectual experience in the life of most Chicago PhD students. It was in mine. No one could equal him in seminars, where it sometimes felt as if the intellectual river of the Scottish Enlightenment ran through his veins. He was unfailingly generous with his students and has remained an inspiration for my entire life. Every day I write or teach, I hope to be worthy of having been Becker's student" (Edward Glaeser, *New Republic*, May 5, 2014).

"For those of us who knew him, he was the most creative thinker we ever encountered. It was his astounding imagination that made many of his early critics think of him as a heretic. They were correct: he was a heretic much like Luther, Copernicus, and Galileo, who transformed their worlds, just as he transformed economics. He brought a rigorous and insightful approach to issues that were viewed as inherently noneconomic. Eventually, he won over the economics profession, detractors and all, who eventually became converts" (Heckman, Lazear and Murphy, 2018).

In 2018, the *Journal of Political Economy* and the *Journal of Human Capital* publish special issues honoring Gary Becker.

References

Alchian, Armen A. 1958. Review of The Economics of Discrimination, by G. Becker. *Journal of the American Statistical Association* 53, no. 284: 1047–48.
Becker, Gary S. 1952. "A Note on Multi-country Trade." *American Economic Review* 42, no. 4, 558–68.
———. 1971. *Economic Theory*. 2nd ed. 2007. New York: Alfred A. Knopf.
———. 1976. "Comment on Peltzman." *Journal of Law and Economics* 19: 245–48.
———. 1988. "Family Economics and Macro Behavior." *American Economic Review* 78, no. 1, 1–13.
———. 1991. "Milton Friedman." In *Remembering the University of Chicago: Teachers, Scientists, and Scholars*, ed. Edward Shils. University of Chicago Press.
———. 1993. Nobel Lecture: The Economic Way of Looking at Behavior. *Journal of Political Economy* 101, no. 3, 385–409.

———. 2006. Working with Jacob Mincer: Reminiscences of Columbia's Labor Workshop. In *Jacob Mincer: A Pioneer of Modern Labor Economics*, ed. S. Grossbard. Boston: Springer.

Becker, Gary S., and William Baumol. 1952. "The Classical Monetary Theory: The Outcome of the Discussion." *Economica* 19, no. 76, 355–76.

Coleman, James S. 1993. "The Impact of Gary Becker's Work on Sociology." *Acta Sociologica* 36, no. 3: 169–78.

Davis, William L., Bob G. Figgins, David Hedengren, and Daniel B. Klein. 2011. "Economics Professors' Favorite Economic Thinkers, Journals, and Blogs (along with Party and Policy Views)." *Econ Journal Watch* 8, no. 2 (May): 126–46.

Duesenberry, James S. 1960. "Comment on 'An Economic Analysis of Fertility' by Gary S. Becker." NBER, Demographic and Economic Change in Developed Countries.

Ehrlich, Isaac. 2018. "Celebrating the Life and Work of Gary Becker." *Journal of Human Capital* 12, no. 2: 173–81.

Frängsmyr, Tore, ed. 1993. *Les Prix Nobel. The Nobel Prizes 1992*, [Nobel Foundation], Stockholm.

Heckman, James. 2014. Private Notes on Gary Becker. No 8200, IZA Discussion Papers, Institute of Labor Economics (IZA).

Heckman, James J., Edward P. Lazear, and Kevin M. Murphy. 2018. "Gary Becker Remembered." *Journal of Political Economy* 126: 1–6.

Landes, William M. 1997. "The Art of Law and Economics: An Autobiographical Essay." *The American Economist* 41, no. 1: 31–42.

Murphy, Kevin M. 2015a. "Gary Becker as Teacher." *American Economic Review* 105, no. 5: 71–73.

———. 2015b. "How Gary Becker Saw the Scourge of Discrimination." *Chicago Booth Review*, June 15.

Posner, Richard A. 1987. "The Law and Economics Movement." *American Economic Review* 77, no. 2: 1–13.

Rosen, Sherwin. 1993. "Risks and Rewards: Gary Becker's Contributions to Economics." *Scandinavian Journal of Economics* 95, no. 1, 25–36.

Solow, Robert M. 1965. Book Reviews: *Human Capital*. By Gary S. Becker. *Journal of Political Economy* 73, no. 5: 552–53.

Stinchcombe, Arthur L. 1983. Review of *A Treatise on the Family*, by G. S. Becker. *American Journal of Sociology* 89, no. 2: 468–70.

Selected Writings about Gary S. Becker

Boskin, Michael J. 2014. "The Courage of His Intuition: A Scholar Whose Penetrating Questions Led Economists and Social Scientists Where Many Had Feared to Tread." *Hoover Digest*, no. 3, summer.

Cassidy, John. January 14, 2010. Interview with Gary Becker. *New Yorker*.

Clement, Douglas. 2002. Interview with Gary Becker. *The Region*, June issue, 16–25.

Coleman, James S. 1993. "The Impact of Gary Becker's Work on Sociology." *Acta Sociologica* 36, no. 3: 169–78.

Ehrlich, Isaac. 2018. "Celebrating the Life and Work of Gary Becker." *Journal of Human Capital* 12, no. 2: 173–81.

Febrero, R., and P. Schwartz, eds., 1995. *The Essence of Becker*. Stanford, CA: Hoover Institution Press.

Fuchs, Victor R. 1994. "Nobel Laureate: Gary S. Becker: Ideas About Facts." *Journal of Economic Perspectives* 8, no. 2: 183–92.

Heckman, James. 2014. Private Notes on Gary Becker. No 8200, IZA Discussion Papers, Institute of Labor Economics (IZA).

———. 2015a. "Gary Becker: Model Economic Scientist." *American Economic Review* 105 (5): 74–79.

———. 2015b. Gary Becker: Model Economic Scientist. Discussion paper series, Institute for the Study of Labor (IZA).

Heckman, James J., Edward P. Lazear, and Kevin M. Murphy. 2018. "Gary Becker Remembered." *Journal of Political Economy* 126: 1–6.

Lazear, Edward Paul. 2014. "Numbers to Live By. To Gary Becker, the Invisible Hand Was Inescapably Human." *Hoover Digest*, no. 3, summer.

———. 2015. "Gary Becker's Impact on Economics and Policy." *American Economic Review* 105 (5): 80–84.

MacRae, Duncan. 1978. "The Sociological Economics of Gary S. Becker." *American Journal of Sociology* 83, no. 5: 1244–58.

Mulligan, Casey B. 2008. "Becker, Gary S. (born 1930)." In *The New Palgrave Dictionary of Economics*, 2nd ed., ed. Steven N. Durlauf and Lawrence E. Blume. Basingstoke, UK: Palgrave Macmillan.

Murphy, Kevin M. 2015a. "Gary Becker as Teacher." *American Economic Review* 105 (5): 71–73.

———. 2015b. "How Gary Becker Saw the Scourge of Discrimination." *Chicago Booth Review*. June 15.

Posner, Richard A. 1993. "Gary Becker's Contributions to Law and Economics." *Journal of Legal Studies* 22, no. 2: 211–15.

Roberts, Russell. 2014. "A Professor's Professor: In His Classroom, Rigor Was Its Own Reward." *Hoover Digest*, no. 3, summer.

Robinson, Peter. 2014. "Markets Are Hard to Appreciate." *Hoover Digest*, no. 3, summer.

Rosen, Sherwin. 1993. "Risks and Rewards: Gary Becker's Contributions to Economics." *Scandinavian Journal of Economics* 95, no. 1, 25–36.

Soares, R. 2015. "Gary Becker's Contributions in Health Economics." *Journal of Demographic Economics* 81, no. 1, 51–57. doi:10.1017/dem.2014.10.

Taylor, John B. 2014. "An Economic Trailblazer. The Late Hoover Fellow Gary Becker Followed the Data to 'Amazing Ideas and Predictions.'" *Hoover Digest*, no. 3, summer.

Bibliography of Gary S. Becker

Monographs

1957 (2nd ed. 1971). *The Economics of Discrimination*. University of Chicago Press.

1964 (2nd ed. 1975, 3rd edition 1993). *Human Capital*. Columbia University Press for the NBER.

1967. *Human Capital and the Personal Distribution of Income: An Analytical Approach*. University of Michigan Press, 1967.

1971 (2nd ed. 2007). *Economic Theory*. Alfred A. Knopf.

1974. *Essays in the Economics of Crime and Punishment*. Edited with William M. Landes. Columbia University Press for the National Bureau of Economic Research.

1975. *The Allocation of Time and Goods Over the Life Cycle*. With Gilbert Ghez. Columbia University Press for the National Bureau of Economic Research.

1976. *The Economic Approach to Human Behavior*. University of Chicago Press.

1976. *Essays in Labor Economics in Honor of H. Gregg Lewis*. Edited. Special Supplement to the *Journal of Political Economy* 84, no. 2, part 2, August.

1981 (enlarged edition 1991). *A Treatise on the Family*. Harvard University Press.

1996. *Accounting for Tastes*. Harvard University Press.

1996. *The Economics of Life*. With Guity Nashat Becker. McGraw-Hill.

2000. *Social Economics*. With Kevin M. Murphy. Harvard University Press.

2009. *Uncommon Sense: Economic Insights, from Marriage to Terrorism*. With Richard A. Posner. University of Chicago Press.

Selected Articles

1952. A Note on Multi-country Trade. *American Economic Review* 42, 558–68.

1952. (With William Baumol) The Classical Monetary Theory: The Outcome of the Discussion. *Economica* 19, no. 76, 355–76.

1957. "The Case Against Conscription." Working paper number D-4514, RAND Corporation, August. Published with an introduction by Becker as "The Case Against the Draft," *Hoover Digest*, no. 3, 2007.

1957. (With Milton Friedman) A Statistical Illusion in Judging Keynesian Models. *Journal of Political Economy* 65, no. 1, 64–75.

1958. Competition and Democracy. *Journal of Law and Economics* 1, 105–9.

1958. (With Milton Friedman) The Friedman-Becker Illusion: Reply. *Journal of Political Economy* 66, no. 6, 545–57.

1958. (With Milton Friedman) Reply to Kuh and Johnston. *Review of Economics and Statistics* 40, no. 3, 298.

1959. Union Restrictions on Entry. In *The Public Stake in Union Power*, ed. Philip D. Bradley. Charlottesville: University of Virginia Press.

1960. An Economic Analysis of Fertility. In *Demographic and Economic Change in Developed Countries*, Conference of the Universities-National Bureau of Economic Research. Princeton, NJ: Princeton University Press, 209–40.

1960. (With William Baumol) The Classical Monetary Theory: The Outcome of the Discussion. Revised and published in *Essays in Economic Thought*, ed. J. Spengler and W. Allen. Chicago: Rand McNally.

1962. Irrational Behavior and Economic Theory. *Journal of Political Economy* 70, no. 1, 1–13.

1962. Discrimination and the Occupational Progress of Negroes: A Comment. *Review of Economics and Statistics* 44, no. 2, May.

1962. Investment in Human Capital: A Theoretical Analysis. *Journal of Political Economy* 70, no. 5, part 2, 9–49, October.

1962. Underinvestment in College Education? In E. Phelps, ed., *Problems of Economic Growth*. New York: W. W. Norton. Originally published, *American Economic Review* 50, no. 2, 346–54, 1960.

1963. Rational Action and Economic Theory: A Reply to I. Kirzner. *Journal of Political Economy* 71 (no. 1): 82–83, February.

1965. A Theory of the Allocation of Time. *Economic Journal* 75, 493–508.

1966. (With Barry Chiswick) Education and the Distribution of Earnings. *American Economic Review* 56 (no. 2): 358–69, May.

1966. Human Capital and the Personal Distribution of Income: An Analytic Approach. Dept. of Economics and Institution of Public Administration, University of Michigan, Ann Arbor.

1968. Crime and Punishment: An Economic Approach. *Journal of Political Economy* 76, 169–217.

1972. Schooling and Inequality from Generation to Generation: Comment. *Journal of Political Economy* 80, no. 3, pt. 2, May–June.

1972. (With Isaac Ehrlich) Market Insurance, Self-Insurance, and Self-Protection. *Journal of Political Economy* 80, no. 4, 623–48.

1973. (With H. Gregg Lewis) On the Interaction between the Quantity and Quality of Children. *Journal of Political Economy* 81, part II, S279–S288.

1973. A Theory of Marriage: Part I. *Journal of Political Economy* 81, no. 4, 813–46.

1973. (With Robert T. Michael) On the New Theory of Consumer Behavior. *Swedish Journal of Economics* 75, 378–96.

1974. A Theory of Social Interactions. *Journal of Political Economy* 82, 1063–93.

1974. A Theory of Marriage: Part II. *Journal of Political Economy* 82, no. 2, 1974, S11–S26.

1974. On the Relevance of the New Economics of the Family. *American Economic Review* 64 (no. 2): 317–19.

1974. (With George J. Stigler) Law Enforcement, Malfeasance, and Compensation of Enforcers. *Journal of Legal Studies* 3, no. 1, 1–18.

1976. Comment on Peltzman. *Journal of Law and Economics* 19, 245–48.

1976. Altruism, Egoism, and Genetic Fitness: Economics and Sociobiology. *Journal of Economic Literature* 14, no. 3, 817–26.

1976. Toward a More General Theory of Regulation: Comment. *Journal of Law and Economics* 19, no. 2, 245–48.

1976. (With Nigel Tomes) Child Endowments and the Quantity and Quality of Children. In *Essays in Labor Economics in Honor of H. Gregg Lewis*, ed. G. S. Becker. *Journal of Political Economy* 84, no. 4, part 2, S143–62.

1977. Economic Analysis and Human Behavior. In *Sociological Economics*, ed. L. Levy-Garboua. Beverly Hills, CA: Sage.

1977. Altruism, Egoism, and Genetic Fitness: Economics and Sociobiology: Reply. *Journal of Economic Literature* 15, no. 2, 506–7.

1977. Reply to Hirshleifer and Tullock. *Journal of Economic Literature* 15, no. 2, 506–7.

1977. (With Elisabeth M. Landes and Robert T. Michael) An Economic Analysis of Marital Instability. *Journal of Political Economy* 85, no. 6, 1153–89.

1977. (With George J. Stigler) De Gustibus Non Est Disputandum. *American Economic Review* 67, no. 2, 76–90.

1979. (With Nigel Tomes.) An Equilibrium Theory of the Distribution of Income and Intergenerational Mobility. *Journal of Political Economy* 87, 1153–89.

1980. Privacy and Malfeasance: A Comment. *Journal of Legal Studies* 9, no. 4, 823–26.

1981. Altruism in the Family and Selfishness in the Market Place. *Economica* 48, 1–15.

1983. A Theory of Competition among Pressure Groups for Political Influence. *Quarterly Journal of Economics* 98, 371–400.

1985. Public Policies, Pressure Groups, and Deadweight Costs. *Journal of Public Economics* 28, 329–47.

1985. Human Capital, Effort, and the Sexual Division of Labor. *Journal of Labor Economics* 3, no. 1, 1985, S33–S58.

1985. Special Interests and Public Policies. Acceptance Paper, Frank E. Seidman Distinguished Award in Political Economy, Rhodes College.

1985. Pressure Groups and Political Behavior. In *Capitalism and Democracy: Schumpeter Revisited*, ed. R. D. Coe and C. K. Wilbur. Notre Dame, IN: University of Notre Dame Press, 1985.

1985. An Economic Analysis of the Family. Seventeenth Geary Lecture. Economic and Social Research Institute, Dublin, Ireland.

1986. (With Robert J. Barro) Altruism and the Economic Theory of Fertility. *Population and Development Review* 12, 69–76.

1986. (With Nigel Tomes) Human Capital and the Rise and Fall of Families. *Journal of Labor Economics* 4, S1–S39.

1988. Family Economics and Macro Behavior. *American Economic Review* 78, no. 1, 1–13.

1988. (With Robert J. Barro) A Reformulation of the Economic Theory of Fertility. *Quarterly Journal of Economics* 103, 1–25.

1988. (With Kevin M. Murphy) A Theory of Rational Addiction. *Journal of Political Economy* 96, 675–700.

1988. (With Kevin M. Murphy.) The Family and the State. *Journal of Law and Economics* 31, 1–18.

1989. On the Economics of the Family: Reply to a Skeptic. *American Economic Review* 79, 514–18.

1989. (With Robert J. Barro.) Fertility Choice in a Model of Economic Growth. *Econometrica* 57, 481–501.

1990. (With Kevin M. Murphy and Robert F. Tamura) Human Capital, Fertility, and Economic Growth. *Journal of Political Economy* 98, no. 5, pt. 2, S12–S70.

1991. A Note on Restaurant Pricing and Other Examples of Social Influences on Price. *Journal of Political Economy* 99, no. 5, 1991, 1109–16.

1991. Milton Friedman. In *Remembering the University of Chicago: Teachers, Scientists, and Scholars*, ed. Edward Shils. University of Chicago Press, 1991.

1991. (With Michael Grossman and Kevin M. Murphy) Rational Addiction and the Effect of Price on Consumption. *American Economic Review* 81, 237–41.

1992. George Joseph Stigler. *Journal des Economistes et des Etudes Humaines* 3, no. 1, 5–9.

1992. Human Capital and the Economy. *Proceedings of the American Philosophical Society* 136, no. 1, 85–92.

1992. On the New Institutional Economics: Comments. *Contract Economics*, ed. Lars Werin, and Hans Wijkander. Cambridge, MA: Blackwell, 66–71.

1992. Education, Labor Force Quality and the Economy. *Business Economics* 27, no. 1, 7–12.

1992. Habits, Addictions, and Traditions. *Kyklos* 45, 327–45.

1992. Fertility and the Economy. *Journal of Population Economics* 5, no. 3, 185–201.

1992. (With Kevin M. Murphy) The Division of Labor, Coordination Costs, and Knowledge. *Quarterly Journal of Economics* 107, no. 4, 1137–1160.

1993. Nobel Lecture: The Economic Way of Looking at Behavior. *Journal of Political Economy* 101, no. 3, 385–409.

1993. Gary S. Becker—Autobiography. In *Les Prix Nobel. The Nobel Prizes 1992*, ed. Tore Frängsmyr. [Nobel Foundation], Stockholm.

1993. Government, Human Capital, and Economic Growth. Presidential Address to the Mont Pelerin Society, Vancouver General Meeting, September 1992. *Industry of Free China* 79, no. 6, 47–56.

1993. U.S. and Canadian Maintenance Programs: Comments. *Journal of Labor Economics* 11, no. 1, S326–29.

1993. George Joseph Stigler: January 17, 1911–December 1, 1991. *Journal of Political Economy* 101, no. 5, 761–67.

1993. (With Kevin M. Murphy) A Simple Theory of Advertising as a Good or Bad. *Quarterly Journal of Economics* 108, no. 4, 941–64.

1993. (With Richard A. Posner) Cross-Cultural Differences in Family and Sexual Life: An Economic Analysis. *Rationality and Society* 5, no. 4, 421–31.

1994. (With Michael Grossman and Kevin M. Murphy) An Empirical Analysis of Cigarette Addiction. *American Economic Review* 84, 396–418.

1995. Human Capital and Economic Growth. *Prague Economic Papers*, 4(3), 223–28.

1995. The Economics of Crime. *Cross Sections*, Federal Reserve Bank of Richmond, 8–15.

1995. Human Capital and Economic Growth. *Prague Economic Papers*, 4(3), 223–28.

1997. (With Casey B. Mulligan) The Endogenous Determination of Time Preference. *Quarterly Journal of Economics* 112, 729–58.

1998. (With Tomas J. Philipson) Old-Age Longevity and Mortality-Contingent Claims. *Journal of Political Economy* 106, no. 3, 551–73.

1999. Milton Friedman: 1921. In *The Legacy of Milton Friedman as Teacher*, ed. J. D. Hammond, 30–37. Cheltenham, UK: Elgar.

1999. (With Edward L. Glaeser and Kevin M. Murphy) Population and Economic Growth. *American Economic Review* 89, no. 2, 145–49.

2000. Competition. In *Leadership for America*, ed. Edwin J. Feulner Jr. Dallas, TX: Spence Publishing, 2000, 275–89.

2000. A Comment on the Conference on Cost-Benefit Analysis. *Journal of Legal Studies* 29, no. 2, 1149–52.

2002. The Age of Human Capital. In *Education in the Twenty-First Century*, ed. E. P. Lazear, 3–8. Palo Alto: Hoover Institution Press.

2003. (With Casey B. Mulligan) Deadweight Costs and the Size of Government. *Journal of Law and Economics* 46, 293–340.

2005. The Economics of Immigration: Foreword. In *The Economics of Immigration: Selected Papers of Barry R Chiswick*. Cheltenham, UK: Elgar, 2005, vii.

2005. (With Kevin M. Murphy and Ivan Werning) The Equilibrium Distribution of Income and the Market for Status. *Journal of Political Economy* 113, no. 2: 282–310.

2005. (With Tomas J. Philipson and Rodrigo R. Soares) The Quality and Quantity of Life and the Evolution of World Inequality. *American Economic Review* 95, 277–91.

2006. Health and Human Capital: The Inaugural T.W. Schultz Lecture. *Review of Agricultural Economics* 28, no. 3, 323–25.

2006. Working with Jacob Mincer: Reminiscences of Columbia's Labor Workshop. In *Jacob Mincer: A Pioneer of Modern Labor Economics*, ed. S. Grossbard. Boston: Springer.

2006. On the Economics of Capital Punishment. *The Economists' Voice*, 3, no. 3.

2006. (With K. Murphy and M. Grossman) The Market for Illegal Goods: The Case of Drugs. *Journal of Political Economy* 114, 38–60.

2006. (With Martin C. McGuire) Reversal of Misfortune When Providing for Adversity. *Defense and Peace Economics* 17, no. 6, 619–43.

2006 (With Luis Rayo) Peer Comparisons and Consumer Debt. *University of Chicago Law Review* 73, no. 1, 231–48.

2007. Health as Human Capital: Synthesis and Extensions. *Oxford Economic Papers* 59, 379–410.

2007. (With Julio J. Elias) Introducing Incentives in the Market for Live and Cadaveric Organ Donations. *Journal of Economic Perspectives* 21, 3–24.

2007. (With Kevin M. Murphy) Education and Consumption: The Effects of Education in the Household Compared to the Marketplace. *Journal of Human Capital* 1, no. 1, 9–35.

2007. (With Kevin M. Murphy) The Upside of Income Inequality. *American: A Magazine of Ideas* 1, no. 4, 20–23.

2007. (With Luis Rayo) Evolutionary Efficiency and Happiness. *Journal of Political Economy* 115, 302–37.

2007. (With Luis Rayo) Habits, Peers, and Happiness: An Evolutionary Perspective. *American Economic Review* 97, no. 2, 487–91.

2008. (With Luis Rayo) Economic Growth and Subjective Well-Being: Reassessing the Easterlin Paradox. Comments and Discussion. Brookings Papers on Economic Activity 2008 (2008): 88–102.

2010. (With William H. J. Hubbard and Kevin M. Murphy) Explaining the Worldwide Boom in Higher Education of Women. *Journal of Human Capital* 4, 203–41.

2010. (With Dennis W. Carlton and Hal S. Sider) Net Neutrality and Consumer Welfare. *Journal of Competition Law and Economics*, Oxford University Press, 6, no. 3, 497–519.

2010. (With William H. J. Hubbard and Kevin M. Murphy) The Market for College Graduates and the Worldwide Boom in Higher Education of Women. *American Economic Review* 100, no. 2, 229–33.

2011. (With Kevin M. Murphy and Robert H. Topel) On the Economics of Climate Policy. *B. E. Journal of Economic Analysis & Policy*, De Gruyter, 10, no. 2, 1–27.

2012. Growing Human Capital Investment in China Compared to Falling Investment in the United States. *Journal of Policy Modeling*, Elsevier, 34, no. 4, 517–24.

2014. (With Richard A. Posner) The Future of Law and Economics. *Review of Law & Economics*, De Gruyter, 10, no. 3, 1–6.

2016. (With Kevin M. Murphy and Jörg L. Spenkuch) The Manipulation of Children's Preferences, Old-Age Support, and Investment in Children's Human Capital. *Journal of Labor Economics* 34(S2), 3–30.

2017. (With Casey B. Mulligan) Is Voting Rational or Instrumental? In *Explorations in Public Sector Economics*, ed. Joshua Hall. Springer Cham, 1–11.

2018. (With Scott Duke Kominers, Kevin M. Murphy, and Jörg L. Spenkuch) A Theory of Intergenerational Mobility. *Journal of Political Economy* 126, S1, S7–S25.

2022. (With Julio J. Elias and Karen J. Ye) The Shortage of Kidneys for Transplant: Altruism, Exchanges, Opt In vs. Opt Out, and the Market for Kidneys. *Journal of Economic Behavior & Organization* 202, 211–226.

Dissertations Chaired by Gary S. Becker at Columbia University and the University of Chicago[1]

Columbia University

1966   William Landes. An Economic Analysis of Fair Employment Practice Laws.

1967   Barry Chiswick. Human Capital and Distribution of Personal Income.

Reuben Gronau. The Effect of Traveling Time on the Demand for Passenger Airline Transportation.

1968   Anthony Clinton Fisher. The Supply of Enlisted Volunteers for Military Service.

1969   Robert Michael. The Effect of Education on Efficiency in Consumption.

1970   June O'Neill (née Cohn). The Effect of Income and Education on Inter-Regional Migration.

Gilbert Ghez. A Theory of Life Cycle Consumption.

Isaac Ehrlich. Participation in Illegitimate Activities: An Economic Analysis.

Michael Grossman. The Demand for Health: A Theoretical and Empirical Investigation.

1971   Haim Ofek. Allocation of Goods and Time in a Family Context.

The University of Chicago

Gary Becker was a member of 228 dissertation committees at the Department of Economics of the University of Chicago, of which he chaired 79.

1971   Edi Karni. The Value of Time and the Demand for Money.

1972   Alan Freiden. A Model of Marriage and Fertility.

1973   Neil Komesar. Economic Analysis of Criminal Victimization.

1974   Michael Keeley. A Model of Marital Formation: The Determinants of the Optimal Age at First Marriage.

1976   James Adams. A Theory of Intergenerational Transfers.

Lawrence Olson. The Allocation of Time to Vocational School Training.

Rodney Smith. The Legal and Illegal Markets for Taxed Goods and Taxation Policy: Pure Theory and an Application to State Government Taxation of Distilled Spirits.

Walter Wessels. The Theory of Search in Heterogenous Markets: The Case of Marital Search.

1977   Itzhak Goldberg. Enforcement of Work Discipline: An Economic Analysis.

Christopher Robinson. Allocation of Time across the Day: An Analysis of the Demand and Supply of Shiftworkers.

1978   Shoshana Grossbard-Shechtman. The Economics of Polygamy.

Nigel Tomes. A Model of Child Endowments, and the Quality and Quantity of Children.

1979   Peter Lewin. The Economics of Apartheid.

1980   James Brown. Employee Risk Aversion, Income Uncertainty, and Optimal Labor Contracts.

Stephen Layson. Homicide and Deterrence: A Re-Examination of the U.S. Time Series Evidence.

1981   Russell Roberts. A Positive Analysis of the Design of Government Transfer Programs.

Yuechim Wong. Earnings Distribution in Hong Kong.

1982   Frederick Miller. Wages and Establishment Size.

1983   Elizabeth Peters. The Impact of Regulation of Marriage, Divorce, and Property Settlements in a Private Contracting Framework.

1984   Matthew Goldberg. Compensation and Retention in the U.S. Navy.

Daniel Gros. Increasing Returns and Human Capital in International Trade.

Laurence Iannaccone. Consumption Capital and Habit Formation with an Application to Religious Participation.

Seyed Mirani. Collective Political Violence and the Redistribution of Political Income.

1985   Christopher Flinn. Behavioral Models of Wage Growth and Job Change over the Life Cycle.

Jenny Wahl. Fertility in America: Historical Patterns and Wealth Effects on the Quantity and Quality of Children.

1987   Siu Fai Leung. A Theoretical and Empirical Analysis of the Effects of Parental Sex Preferences on Fertility.

Avi Weiss. Firm-Specific Physical Capital: An Empirical Analysis of Vertical Mergers.

1988   Robert Tamura. Fertility, Human Capital, and the "Wealth of Nations."

1989   Indermit Gill. Technological Change, Education and Obsolescence of Human Capital: Some Evidence for the U.S.

Kristian Palda. Electoral Spending.

Martin Zelder. Children as Public Goods and the Effect of Divorce Law upon the Divorce Rate.

1991   Carlos Seiglie. Determinants of Military Expenditures.

Dean Lillard. The Effects of Neighborhood Characteristics on Investment in Human Capital: A Theoretical and Empirical Investigation.

Grace Tsiang. Married Female Labor Supply in Malaysia: Implications of Flexible Employment Arrangements.

1992   David Meltzer. Mortality Decline, the Demographic Transition, and Economic Growth.

1993   Kermit Daniel. Does Marriage Make Workers More Productive?

Ian Parry. Policy Analysis of Global Warming Uncertainties.

1994   Mary Kilburn. Minority Representation in the U.S. Military.

Jinyoung Kim. Knowledge Creation, Human Capital Investment, and Economic Growth.

1995   Avner Ahituv. Fertility Choices and Optimum Growth: A Theoretical and Empirical Investigation.

Kathryn Ierulli. Time Allocation and Wage Growth.

1996   Hideo Akabayashi. On the Role of Incentives in the Formation of Human Capital in the Family.

James Miller. Three Essays in the Economics of Litigation.

1999   John Cawley. Rational Addiction, the Consumption of Calories, and Body Weight.

Scott Drewianka. Social Effects in Marriage Markets: Theory, Existence, Magnitude, and Nature.

Jeanne-Mey Sun. Interjurisdictional Competition with an Application to International Equity Markets.

2000   Darius Lakdawalla. The Declining Quality of Teachers.

Thomas Miles. Three Empirical Essays in the Economics of Crime.

Chen Song. The Nature of Social Security and Its Impact on Family.

2002   Frederick Chen. Bargaining and Search in Marriage Markets.

Rodrigo Garcia-Verdu. Evaluation of Conditional Income Support Programs: The Case of Mexico's Progresa.

Masako Oyama. Fertility Decline and Female Labor Force Participation in Japan.

Rodrigo Soares. Life Expectancy, Educational Attainment, and Fertility Choice: The Economic Impacts of Mortality Reductions.

2003   Rodrigo Cerda. Drugs, Population, and Market Size.

Damien De Walque. How Does Education Affect Health Decisions? The Cases of HIV/AIDS and Smoking.

Audrius Girnius. Market Share vs. Market Size Effect of Advertising: Analysis of Market Structure.

Todd Kendall. General Human Capital and Specialization in Academia.

Edward Morrison. Bankruptcy Decision-Making: An Empirical Study of Small Business Bankruptcies.

2004   Patricia Pierotti. Sons versus Daughters: Evidence from Educational Achievement Outcomes in Brazil.

2005   Erica Benton. Female Occupational Choice and Family Mobility.

Julio Elias. The Effects of Ability and Family Background on Nonmonetary Returns to Education.

Valentin Rios. Liberals, Conservatives, and Your Tax Returns: Partisan Politics and the Enforcement Activities of the IRS.

John Pfaff. The Continued Vitality of Structured Sentencing Following Blakely: The Effectiveness of Voluntary Guidelines.

2006   Fernando Wilson. Explaining the Growth of Child Obesity in the US.

Samantha Taam. Optimal Water Use: A Matter of Giving the Right Incentives.

Sebastien Gay. The Impact of Default Rules on Economic Behavior with Primary Attention to Organ Donations.

2007   Alexander Popov. Financial Markets Development, Allocation of Capital to Ideas, and Firm-Sponsored Training.

Atonu Rabbani. Essays in Health and Labor Economics: Market Size and Supply of Doctors with Implication for Mortality.

Salavat Gabdrakhamanov. Essays on Innovation and Dissemination of Ideas.

2008   Young-Il Albert Kim. Impact of Birth Studies on Fertility: Empirical Study of Allowance for Newborn Children, A Pronatal Policy.

2010   Lee Lockwood. The Importance of Bequest Motives for Saving and Insurance Decisions in Old Age.

Matias Tapia Gonzalez. Competition, Incentives, and the Distribution of Investments in Private School Markets.

2011   Yuri Sanchez Gonzalez. The Longevity Gains of Education.

Francisco Parro Greco. Economic Growth and the Gender Gap in Education.

William Hubbard. The Problem of Measuring Legal Change, with Application to *Bell Atlantic v. Twombly*.

2012   Jonathan Hall. Pareto Improvements from Lexus Lanes: The Case for Value Pricing on Heavily Congested Highways.

Rui Colaco e Silva. Internal Labor Markets and Investment Behavior of Conglomerates.

2013   Hays Golden. Childhood Autism and Assortative Mating.

2015   Hanzhe Zhang. Essays in Matching, Auctions, and Evolution.

Acknowledgments

We are very grateful to Guity Becker for her continuing encouragement and support during the whole project. This project benefited from the financial support of Marr Gwen and Stuart Townsend. Virginia Bova contributed essential secretarial services. Chad Zimmerman of the University of Chicago Press was an outstanding editor and Susan Tarcov did outstanding editing work. Arjun Kilari provided excellent research assistance, especially with the elaboration of the list of dissertations chaired by Gary Becker. We thank Angela M. Raid from the Department of Economics at Columbia University, Colleen Mullarkey from the Dissertation Office of Regenstein Library of the University of Chicago, and Amy Schulz, administrator of graduate student affairs in the Department of Economics of the University of Chicago, for help with the elaboration of the list of dissertations chaired by Gary Becker. We thank RAND Corporation for giving permission to publish the material from the RAND paper D-4508 and Tim Perri for calling to our attention and sending us a copy of the paper. Five anonymous reviewers provided comments and suggestions. We also thank Alejandro Rodriguez for his valuable comments on the book.

Notes

Just the Beginning

1. J. Heckman, "Gary Becker: Model Economic Scientist," Discussion paper series, Institute of the Study of Labor (IZA), 2015, p. 2.

2. Gary S. Becker, *The Economic Approach to Human Behavior* (Chicago: University of Chicago Press, 1976), 8.

3. George J. Stigler, *Memoirs of an Unregulated Economist* (New York: Basic Books), 199.

4. Gary S. Becker, *Economics Theory* (New York: A. Knopf, 1971), viii.

5. Clement Douglas, Interview with Gary Becker, *The Region*, June 2002, 16–25.

Accounting for Tastes

1. Gary S. Becker, *Accounting for Tastes* (Cambridge, MA: Harvard University Press, 1996), 4.

2. Gary S. Becker, "Nobel Lecture: The Economic Way of Looking at Behavior," *Journal of Political Economy* 101, no. 3 (1993): 400.

3. Gary S. Becker, Kevin M. Murphy, and Jörg L. Spenkuch, "The Manipulation of Children's Preferences, Old-Age Support, and Investment in Children's Human Capital," *Journal of Labor Economics* 34(S2) (2016): 3–30.

4. Becker, *Accounting for Tastes*, 226.

5. See Gary S. Becker and Kevin M. Murphy, *Social Economics* (Cambridge, MA: Harvard University Press, 2000).

6. Becker, *Accounting for Tastes*, 400.

7. Becker and Murphy, *Social Economics*.

8. https://www.becker-posner-blog.com/2014/02/why-marijuana-should-be-decriminalized-becker.html.

9. Becker, *Accounting for Tastes*, 12.

Household Production and Human Capital

1. We are grateful to Tim Perri for calling to our attention and sending us a copy of this paper. Michael Gibbs and Tim Perri discuss the history of the paper

in "Dodging a Draft: Gary Becker's Lost Paper on Conscription," IZA Discussion Papers, no. 14284, Institute of Labor Economics (IZA), Bonn (2021).

2. "Should the Military Pay for Training of Skilled Personnel?," RAND Document, D-4508, 15 August 1957, in this volume, p. 61.

3. *Human Capital: A Theoretical and Empirical Analysis with Special Reference to Education* (NBER, 1964), 22.

4. Gary S. Becker, "A Theory of the Allocation of Time," *Economic Journal* 75, no. 299 (1965): 493.

5. Becker, "Theory of the Allocation of Time," 493–94.

6. Mark Aguiar, Mark Bils, Kerwin Kofi Charles, and Erik Hurst, "Leisure Luxuries and the Labor Supply of Young Men," *Journal of Political Economy*, vol 129, no. (2) (2021): 337–82.

7. 125th Anniversary Special Issue, *Economic Journal* 125, no. 583 (March 2015).

8. J. J. Heckman, "Introduction to *A Theory of the Allocation of Time* by Gary Becker," *Economic Journal* 125 (2015): 406.

9. P.-A. Chiappori and A. Lewbel, "Gary Becker's *A Theory of the Allocation of Time*," *Economic Journal* 125 (2015): 416.

10. Isaac Ehrlich and Gary S. Becker, "Market Insurance, Self-Insurance, and Self-Protection," *Journal of Political Economy* 80, no. 4 (1972): 623–48.

11. Council of Economic Advisers (CEA), "Chapter 6: Jobs and Income: Today and Tomorrow," Economic Report of the President, 2012.

Should the Military Pay for Training of Skilled Personnel?

1. I am indebted for helpful comments to A. Alchian, A. Enthoven, W. Gorham, M. Hoag, J. Kershaw, B. Klein, and especially R. McKean.

2. See *The Economics of Navy Pay*, P-1051, and *Supply and Demand for Soldiers*, P-1037.

3. Let p represent the present value of the future income stream received by any member of this occupation in the civilian sector, t the average per capita training cost, and t_m the per capita training costs borne by the military. Then the per capita cost borne by individuals in this occupation is $t_i = t - t_m$, the net return to them is $p - t_i = p - (t - t_m)$, and the total cost to the military is $p + t_m$. If $S(p - t_i)$, $D_m(p + t_m)$, and $D_c(p)$ represent, respectively, the supply function of, and military and civilian demand functions of members in this occupation, equilibrium requires:

$$S(p - t_i) = D_m(p + t_m) + D_c(p) \tag{1'}$$

Then:

$$\frac{\partial S}{\partial p} dp + \frac{\partial S}{\partial t_i} dt_i = \frac{\partial D_m}{\partial p} dp + \frac{\partial D_m}{\partial t_m} dt_m + \frac{\partial D_c}{\partial p} dp \tag{2'}$$

We know that

$$\frac{\partial S}{\partial t_i} = -\frac{\partial S}{\partial p}, \text{ and } \frac{\partial D_m}{\partial t_m} = \frac{\partial D_m}{\partial p} \tag{3'}$$

By reducing their expenditures on training, the military shifts them to individuals entering this occupation; hence

$$dt_i = -dt_m \qquad\qquad (4')$$

After substituting equations 3' and 4' into 2', one has

$$\frac{\partial S}{\partial p}dp + \frac{\partial S}{\partial p}dt_m = \frac{\partial D_m}{\partial p}dp + \frac{\partial D_m}{\partial p}dt_m + \frac{\partial D_c}{\partial p}dp \qquad\qquad (5')$$

On dividing through by dt_m and rearranging terms:

$$\left[\frac{\partial S}{\partial p} - \left(\frac{\partial D_m}{\partial p} + \frac{\partial D_c}{\partial p}\right)\right]\frac{dp}{dt_m} = \frac{\partial D_m}{\partial p} - \frac{\partial S}{\partial p} \qquad\qquad (6')$$

or:

$$\frac{dp}{dt_m} = \frac{\dfrac{\partial D_m}{\partial p} - \dfrac{\partial S}{\partial p}}{\dfrac{\partial S}{\partial p} - \left(\dfrac{\partial D_m}{\partial p} + \dfrac{\partial D_c}{\partial p}\right)} \qquad\qquad (7')$$

If we want the change in military costs from hiring a given number of persons, we must set $\partial D_m / \partial p = 0$. Let E_{sp} and E_{d_cp} be the elasticity of supply and civilian demand, respectively, with respect to price. After converting the slopes in 7' into elasticities and dividing through by S and p, we get

$$\frac{dp}{dt_m} = \frac{-E_{sp}}{E_{sp} - \dfrac{D_c}{S}E_{d_cp}} \qquad\qquad (8')$$

Hence, $|dp|$ always $\leq |dt_m|$; $dp / dt_m = 0$ whenever $E_{sp} = 0$ or $E_{d_cp} = -\infty$; $dp = dt_m$ whenever $D_c = 0$ or $E_{d_cp} = 0$; and dp / dt_m is smaller (in absolute value), the smaller E_{sp}, and the larger D_c / S and $-E_{d_cp}$.

4. The draft is analyzed in detail in another memorandum. [The memorandum, dated August 19, 1957, was entitled "The Case Against Conscription." It was published fifty years later with an introductory note by Gary Becker. Gary S. Becker, "The Case Against the Draft," *Hoover Digest*, no. 3 (2007).]

The Insurance of Market and Nonmarket Human Capital

1. [Blank space in the original.]
2. [Rosen 1981 in the reference list. The Rosen paper was not published yet when Becker wrote this draft.]

Derivation of Relation Between Schooling of Parents and Children and Inequality

1. $[H_c = f_y(y^*, H_p)]$
2. [Council of Economic Advisers (CEA), 2012, "Chapter 6: Jobs and Income: Today and Tomorrow," *Economic Report of the President*.]

3. [The figures were not available. We decided not to add them since the analysis does not rely much on them.]

Income Inequality and the Public Sector

1. Gary S. Becker, "The Case Against the Draft," *Hoover Digest*, no. 3 (2007).

2. Gary S. Becker, and Julio J. Elias, "Cash for Kidneys: The Case for a Market for Organs," *Wall Street Journal*, January 18, 2014.

A Positive Theory of the Redistribution of Income

1. This comment was heavily influenced by Peltzman (1976) and Stigler (1975).

2. In particular, there are no "[m]admen in authority, who hear voices in the air" (Keynes, 1936, p. 383).

3. Therefore, this theory is immune to Tobin's objection to theories that assume that the government sector is less rational or efficient than the private sector (Tobin   ) [blank in original draft].

4. [Blank in original draft.]

5. For example, Samuelson defined the social welfare function as: "Without inquiring into its origins, we take as a starting point for our discussion a function of all the economic magnitudes of a system which is supposed to characterize *some ethical belief*. . . We only require that the belief be such as to admit of an unequivocal answer as to whether one configuration of the economic system is 'better' or 'worse' than any other or 'indifferent,' and that these relationships are transitive" (1947, p. 221, my italics). Also see the statements by Bergson (1938), Arrow (1951), and many others.

6. That is, if i is selfish and j is envious of i in the sense that $U_i = U_i(I_i)$ and $U_j = U_j(I_j, I_i)$, with $\partial U_j / \partial I_i < 0$, then selfishness has more political influence than envy if

$$\frac{\partial P}{\partial I_i} = \frac{\partial P}{\partial U_i}\frac{dU_i}{dI_i} + \frac{\partial P}{\partial U_j}\frac{\partial U_j}{\partial I_i} \geq 0,$$

or if

$$\frac{\partial P}{\partial U_i}\frac{dU_i}{dI_i} \geq \frac{\partial P}{\partial U_j}\left(-\frac{\partial U_j}{\partial I_i}\right).$$

7. This conclusion is simply a direct application to public redistributions of the "rotten kid theorem" developed for redistributions within a family (see Becker 1976b and Becker 1981, chapter VI).

8. More generally, a full democracy would have $\underline{I} / \bar{I} = (1 - w)^\sigma$, where σ is the constant elasticity of substitution between different incomes in the political preference function.

9. That is,

$$-\frac{\partial P}{\partial I_i} \bigg/ \frac{\partial P}{\partial I_j} = -\frac{dI_j}{dI_i} > 1 \text{ when } I_i = I_j \text{ if } I_i^0 > I_j^0,$$

where I_i^0 and I_j^0 are the endowed incomes of i and j, respectively.

10. If $w = 0$, equilibrium requires $-dI_j / dI_i = 1$. However, if $-dI_j / dI_i > 1$ when $I_i = I_j$, convexity of the indifference curves implies that $-dI_j / dI_i = 1$ only when $I_i > I_j$.

11. The change in political utility equals

$$dP = \sum_{k=1}^{n} \frac{\partial P}{\partial I_k} dI_k = \frac{\partial P}{\partial I_i} \sum \left(\frac{\partial P}{\partial I_k} \bigg/ \frac{\partial P}{\partial I_i} \right) dI_k.$$

If i is taxed, in a political equilibrium $(\partial P / \partial I_k \,/\, \partial P / \partial I_i)$ equals 1 for all persons taxed, $1/1-w$ for all persons subsidized, and is between 1 and $1/1-w$ for persons neither taxed nor subsidized (see equations 8 and 9 and the discussion at that point). Hence

$$dP \gtreqless 0, \text{ as } \sum_{\text{all } i \in t} dI_i + \frac{1}{1-w} \sum_{\text{all } j \in s} dI_j + \sum_{\text{all } p \in 0} \frac{1}{1-\alpha_p w} dI_p \gtreqless 0, \text{ where } 0 \leq \alpha_p \leq 1.$$

12. For a lucid derivation of this formula, with various qualifications and extensions, se Harberger 1971, especially equation 5″ and footnote 5.

13. For a survey of the literature on optimal taxation, see Sandmo 1976.

14. $dP = MP_i\, dI_i + MP_j\, dI_j$

$$= MP_i \left(dI_i + \frac{MP_j}{MP_i} dI_j \right)$$

$$= MP_i \left(dI_i + \frac{1}{1-w} dI_j \right)$$

(see equation 12). Hence $dP \gtreqless 0$ as $dI_i + (1/1 - w)\, dI_j \gtreqless 0$.

15. [Blank in original draft.]

16. [Completed by the editors.]

17. [Blank in original draft.]

Family Economics

1. W. Brian Arthur, Review Work: *A Treatise on the Family* by Gary S. Becker. *Population and Development Review* 8, no. 2 (Jun. 1982): 393–97.

2. Jane Humphries, Review Work: *A Treatise on the Family* by Gary S. Becker, *Economic Journal* 92, no. 367 (Sep. 1982): 739–40.

3. Sherwin Rosen, "Risks and Rewards: Gary Becker's Contributions to Economics," *Scandinavian Journal of Economics* 95, no. 1 (1993): 25–36.

Chronological Academic Life of Gary S. Becker

1. In a footnote to the published paper, Becker says: "This note is taken from a larger essay originally submitted as a senior thesis in the department of economics and social institutions of Princeton University."

2. Milton Friedman Memorial Service, University of Chicago, 2007. https://www.youtube.com/watch?v=yjemk7SEfzA.

3. "The John Bates Clard Award: Citation on the Occasion of the Presentation

of the Medal to Gary S. Becker, December 29, 1967," *American Economic Review* 58, no. 2 (1968): 684–84.

4. *University of Chicago Record* 5, no. 2 (February 4, 1971).

5. *Daily Maroon*, January 5, 1973.

6. *Daily Maroon*, October 22, 1982.

7. *University of Chicago Magazine* 86, no. 2 (December 1993).

8. *University of Chicago Magazine* 86, no. 5 (June 1994).

Dissertations Chaired by Gary S. Becker

1. The list of dissertations chaired by Gary Becker at Columbia University was kindly provided from paper records by Angela Reid from the Department of Economics of Columbia University. The complete list of dissertations of the Department of Economics of the University of Chicago where Gary Becker was a committee member was provided by Amy Schulz, administrator of graduate student affairs. In order to identify the dissertations chaired by Becker, we surveyed online and physical copies of dissertations, as well as personally reaching out to authors via email. The Proquest database was also used as a source for dissertations after 1994. Both lists of dissertations chaired by Gary Becker may have omissions.

Index

The letter *f* following a page number denotes a figure.

Accounting for Tastes (Becker), 11, 149
addiction, xxiii, 4, 13, 14, 43–47
"After the Blowup" (Cassidy), 153
Aguiar, Mark, 57, 71
Alchian, Armen A., 139
Allied Social Science Associations (ASSA) Annual Meeting, 12
Allocation of Time and Goods Over the Life Cycle, The (Becker and Ghez), 144
altruism, 12, 13, 16–17, 20–22, 24, 26–30
"Altruism and Egotism" (panel), 148
Alumni Medal of the University of Chicago, 4, 8–10, 153
American Academy of Achievement, 150
American Academy of Arts and Sciences, 143
American Dilemma, An (Myrdal), xii
American Economic Association, xvi, 142, 144, 147
American Economic Review, xvii, 142
American Philosophical Society, 147
American Statistical Association, 142
Applications of Economics Workshop, 143
Arrow, Kenneth, viii–ix, x
Arrow Award, 151

Arrow's Information Paradox, ix
asymmetric information, ix
Atkinson, Anthony B., 93

Barro, Robert, 140, 143
Baumol, William, 138
Becker, Natalie, 137
Becker Center on Chicago Price Theory, 151–52, 153–54
Becker Friedman Institute, 153–54
Becker-Posner Blog, 14, 151
beliefs, xxii–xxiii
Bentham, Jeremy, 97
bequests, 17, 18, 19, 21, 23, 26, 89
Bergstrom, T., xxiii
Berman, Eli, ix
birth rates, 45, 129–30
Bowen, Francis "Fanny," xv
Bradbury, William, 138
Bradley Award/Prize, xxi, 4, 5–7, 152–53
Brown, Joey, 153
Buchanan, James, 143
budget sets, xiii
Bush, George W., 152
Businessweek, xvii, xix, xx, 146–47, 151

Capital in the Twenty-First Century (Piketty), 92
Capitalism and Freedom (Friedman), xv

Career Achievement Award for Lifetime Contributions to the Field of Labor Economics, 151

Carnap, Rudolf, 8

"Case Against Conscription, The" (Becker), 91

"Cash for Kidneys" (Becker and Elias), 92

Cassidy, John, 153

Centennial Forum, 148

Center for Economic Analysis of Human Behavior and Social Institutions, 139

Center for the Study of the Economy and the State (Stigler Center), 144

Center in Beijing, University of Chicago, steering committee, 153

Chiappori, Pierre-André, 58

Chicago Federal Reserve Bank, 149

Chicago School, viii, xi, xiv, xv, xviii, xix, 128

children: addiction and, 45; care for, 135; changes in family structure and, 131; death rates and, 131; divorce and separation and, 136; education and, 80–84, 85–89; overview of work on, xxi–xxii; parental investment in, xiii, xxv; preference formation and, 4, 12–13, 15–31, 44, 47; time allocation and, 71–72

choice sets, expansion of, xix

chronological academic life, 137–55

Clark, John Bates, viii

Clinton, Bill, 150

Cochrane, John H., 153

"coldness" of families, 22

Coleman, James S., 144, 146, 149

college earnings premium, 7

Columbia University, 139, 140–41, 142, 143, 148

commodity production, 74–77

commuting costs, xiii

competition, discrimination and, 6

"Competition and Democracy" (Becker), x, 140

competitive indoctrination, 40–41

consumer surplus, loss in, 105

consumption, over life cycle, 71

contracts, xxiv

Corak, Miles, 59

Cordiner, Ralph, 56

Cordiner Committee, 55–56, 61, 63, 67

crime and punishment, xix–xx, 6

"Crime and Punishment" (Becker), xiii, 144

Dam, Kenneth, 144

Davis, William L., 154

dead weight cost, 105–7, 108–9, 111, 112–13, 115–21

Dean, E., 142

death rates, 131

decriminalization of drugs, 14, 46–47

"De Gustibus Non Est Disputandum" (Stigler and Becker), xviii, 149

demand, law of, 11

deregulation, xix

"Derivation of Relation Between Schooling of Parents and Children and Inequality" (Becker), 85–89

Director, Aaron, 8, 138, 140

discrimination, 5–6, 9, 12, 138–39

dissertations chaired by Becker, 165–68

divorce, 44, 45, 47, 130, 133, 135, 136

Domestic Advisory Board, Hoover Institution, 143

"Don't Raise the Drinking Age, Raise Taxes" (Becker), xxi

draft, xxiii, 67–68, 91

drug policy, xxiii, 14, 46–47

Duesenberry, James S., 140

Dunbar, Frank, xv

Earhart Foundation Fellowship, 138

"Economic Analysis of Fertility, An" (Becker), xii–xiii, 128, 140

economic approach, 2, 5–7, 11, 14

Economic Approach to Human Behavior, The (Becker), ix, x, 144

"Economic Dimensions of the Family" (conference), 3, 127–28

Economic Journal, 3, 4, 58, 69, 128

economic redistribution, xxv

Economic Report of the President, 59

"Economics and the Family" (Becker), 129–36

Economics of Discrimination, The (Becker), 139

Economics of Life, The (Becker and Nashat Becker), 147

"Economics of Racial Discrimination, The" (Becker), 138–39

Economics Research Center, NORC, 145

Economic Theory (Becker), 2, 143

"Economist Looks at Crime and Punishment, An" (Becker), 143

education: addiction and, 47; Becker's, 137–38; changes in family structure and, 135; crime and, 6; earnings and, 7, 80–84, 85–89; economics of, 55; income inequality and, 60, 85–89; labor force participation and, 132–33; parental investment and, xxv; voting and, 98

efficiency wages, xviii

egalitarian principle, 93

Ehrlich, Isaac, 58, 140

electricity regulation, xvii

Ely, Richard, viii

Ely Lecture on the Law and Economics Movement, 147

Enthoven, Alain, 61, 67

Epstein, Richard, 148

erroneous beliefs, xi–xii

"Essays in Labor Economics in Honor of H. Gregg Lewis" (ed. Becker), 144

Essays in the Economics of Crime and Punishment (ed. Becker and Landes), 144

Essence of Becker, The (ed. Febrero and Schwartz), 149

expenditure function, xxv, 123–24

Fama, Eugene F., 153

family economics: lecture notes on, 129–36; overview of work on, 127–28. *See also* children; marital status; parents

Febrero, Ramon, 149

"Federal Pay" (Becker), xxi

Fermi, Enrico, 9

fertility, 132, 140

50 Great Americans, Marquis Who's Who, 149

fishing restrictions, xx–xxi

force, 37–39

Ford Foundation, 143

Foundations of Economic Analysis (Samuelson), x

Frank, Robert, 52

Frank E. Seidman Distinguished Award in Political Economy, 147

Freakonomics Blog, 155

free markets, Smith on, xiv

Free to Choose (Friedman), xv, xvi

Friedman, Milton, viii, x, xiv, xv–xx, 5, 8–9, 138–41, 143–44, 149–50

Friedman Institute, 153–54

full income, concept of, 70, 71

"Further Reflections on the Allocation of Time" (Becker), 69–72

Garcia, Jorge L., 153

"Gary Becker as a Teacher" (Murphy), 145

Gasper, Gerhard, 148

Gates Commission, 91

gender: division of labor and, 77–78, 131; education and, 84; labor force participation and, 130, 132–33

General Electric Company, 56

general equilibrium theory, viii

General Theory of Employment, Interest, and Money (Keynes), viii

Gente Nueva, Mexico City, 149

Ghez, Gilbert, 144

Giffen goods, xxvi

Glaeser, Edward, 155

Golden Plate Award, 150

gold standard, xv

government, limited, xiv–xv, xx

governments: indoctrination and, 37–38; programs of, 24–26; totalitarian/dictatorial, 37, 38

Great Gatsby Curve, xxv, 59–60, 59f
Grebe, Michael W., 153
Grossman, Michael, 45, 78, 143
Guardian, The, 154
guilt, xxii, 20–24, 26

habit formation, rational, 13–14
Hansen, Alvin, viii
Hansen, Lars Peter, 154
Harberger, Al, 8
Harold Lasswell Award, 149
Harvard University, 150
Hayek, Friedrich, 8–9, 149
Hayek Award, 150
"Health as Human Capital" (Becker), 151
health insurance, 25
Heartland Prize, 150
Hebrew University of Jerusalem, 147
Heckman, James, 1–2, 58, 153, 154, 155
Heller, Walter W., 144
Hicks Lecture, 151
Hicks's Composite Good Theorem, 124
Hitotsubashi University, 151
Hofstra University, 149
Holmström, Bengt, xviii
"Honoring Gary S. Becker: A Confer-ence," 154
Hoover Essence series, 149
Hoover Institution, 143, 147, 149
Hotelling, Harold, x–xi
household production theory, 57, 70
housing: Friedman on, xvi; Stigler on, xvii
"How to Scuttle Overfishing?" (Becker), xxi
human capital: changes in family structure and, 135; insurance and, 73–79; intergenerational mobility and, 80–84; on-the-job training and, 61–68; opposition to concept of, 127; overview of work on, xxiii–xxiv, 2, 4, 55–60; preference forma-tion and, 16, 17–19, 23; revolution in, 6–7; schooling and inequality

and, 85–89; time allocation and, 69–72
Human Capital (Becker), xii, 56, 141–42, 144, 148
Hurst, Erik, 71

Iannaccone, Laurence, ix
immigration, xx
Impossibility Theorem, ix, 125
Inada conditions, 17–18
incentives/incentive theory, xviii, xix–xx, xxi, 5, 6
income inequality, xxv, 7, 58–60, 59f, 80–84, 85–89, 91–93
indoctrination, 13, 32–42
industrial organization, xvi–xvii
inflation, Friedman on, xvi
Initiative on Chicago Price Theory, 151–52
insurance, xxiv, 4, 25, 58, 73–79, 131, 133
"Insurance of Market and Nonmarket Human Capital, The" (Becker), 73–79
interest rates, Friedman on, xvi
intergenerational earnings elasticity, 59, 59f
intergenerational mobility, 58–60, 80–84
internal promotions in military, 66–67
International Union for the Scientific Study of Population, 146
Irene B. Taeuber Award in Excellence in Demographic Research, 149
"Irrational Behavior and Economic Theory" (Becker), 11, 140

Jacob Mincer Award, 151
James Madison High School, 137
John Bates Clark Medal, 142, 150
Johnson, D. Gale, 138
John von Neumann Award, 151
Journal of Human Capital, 155
Journal of Law and Economics, 140
Journal of Political Economy, 144, 155
justice, contractual approach to, 95

Keynes, John Maynard, viii
Knox College, 147
Krueger, Alan, xxv, 59

labor force participation of women, 130, 132–33
labor market signaling, ix
Landes, William, 139, 144
Laughlin, J. Laurence, xv
"Law Enforcement, Malfeasance, and Compensation of Enforcers" (Becker and Stigler), xviii–xix
Lazear, Edward, xix, 1, 154, 155
Lectures on Human Capital, 153
Lectures on Public Economics (Atkinson and Stiglitz), 93
leisure/leisure technology, 57, 123–24, 126
Levi, Edward, 8
Levitt, Steven, ix, xix, 151, 155
Lewbel, Arthur, 58
Lewis, H. Gregg, 8, 9, 138, 140, 144
limited government, xiv–xv, xx
Lin, Justin, 9
Logic of Scientific Discovery (Popper), x
Lord Foundation Award, 149
lotteries, xxiii
Lozano, Salvador Navarro, 153
lump-sum redistribution, xxv–xxvii, 100–104

"Manipulation of Children's Preferences, Old-Age Support, and Investment in Children's Human Capital, The" (Becker, Murphy, and Spenkuch), 13
marital status: birth rates and, 130; differences related to, 77–78; divorce and separation and, 130, 133, 135, 136
Marschak, Jacob, 8, 138
Marshall, Alfred, 141
mathematics, move toward, viii
mechanism design, xviii
Medal of the Italian Presidency, 151

men, division of labor and, 77–78, 131.
    See also gender
Merit Award, 147
"Methodology of Positive Economics, The" (Friedman), x
Michael, Robert, 143
middle class family values, 26
military/military pay, 4, 56, 61–68
Milnor, John, 138
Mincer, Jacob, 55, 140–41, 142, 151
minimum wage, xvii, 92
Monetary History of the United States (Friedman and Schwartz), xvi
monopolies, 125–26
monopoly of indoctrination, 39–40
Mont Pelerin Society, x, 3, 14, 147
Morgenstern, Oskar, 138
Mulligan, Casey B., xxi
Murphy, Kevin M., 1, 12–14, 140, 145, 149–55
Myrdal, Gunnar, xii

Nash, John, 138
Nashat Becker, Guity, 5, 9–10, 147
Nash equilibrium, 30
National Academy of Education, 142
National Academy of Sciences, 144
National Academy of Sciences of Buenos Aires, 150
National Association of Business Economists, 148
National Bureau of Economic Research, 139
National Institute of Child Health and Human Development's Hall of Honor, 150
National Institutes of Health, 147
National Medal of Science, 150, 153
net utility, 32–33
New Republic, 155
New Yorker, 153
New York Times, 155
no-arbitrage equilibria, xx
Nobel Prize in Economics, 12, 148
nontransferable training, 56, 66
norms, 24–26

"Norms and the Formation of Preferences" (Becker), 13

"Note on Multi-Country Trade, A" (Becker), xv

"Note on Optimal First Best Taxation and the Optimal Distribution of Utilities, A" (Becker), 123–26

old age: changes in family structure and, 130; support in, 15–16, 20–24, 25, 39, 131, 132, 133. *See also* retirement

"On the Interaction between the Quantity and Quality of Children" (Becker), xiii

on-the-job training, 4, 56, 61–68

"On Whether Intergenerational Mobility Has Declined in US While Inequality Has Increased" (Becker), 80–84

organizational hierarchy, power and, 48–53

organs/organ donors, 56, 92

Owen, J., 142

Oxford University, 151

parents: education and, 80–84, 85–89; income of, xxv; indoctrination and, 37, 38–39; preference formation and, xxi–xxii, 4, 12–13, 15–31, 44, 47; time allocation and, 71–72

Paris School of Economics, 92

Pashigian, Peter, 144

paternalism, 27–28, 30

peer pressure, xxiii, 43–44, 45, 46

Peltzman, Sam, 140, 144

persuasion, xxii, 12, 32–42

Phelps, Edmund, ix

Phi Beta Kappa, 137

Philipson, Tomas, 151

Phillips Curve, xvi

Phoenix Award/Prize, 149, 150

Pigouvian taxes, xxi

Piketty, Thomas, 92

Policy Studies Organization, 149

political economy, xv

political equilibrium, 100

political indifference curves, 99, 100, 101, 103, 105, 119

political preference function, xxv, 96–99, 109, 111, 114, 119–20

politics/political system, x–xi, xix

Pollak, Robert A., 58

Pontifical Academy of Sciences, 149

Popper, Karl, x

Population Association of America, 149

population growth, 135. *See also* birth rates; death rates

"Positive Theory of the Redistribution of Income, A" (Becker), 95–122

Posner, Richard, 144, 146, 147, 151, 153

power: earnings and, 4, 14, 48–53; taste for, xxiii

"Preference Formation within Families" (Becker), 15–31

preferences: differences in impact of, 98; indoctrination and persuasion and, 32–42; overview of work on, 11–12; parents and, xxi–xxii, 4, 12–13, 15–31, 44, 47; power and, 14; rational habit formation and, 13–14; state-dependent, xxiv–xxv

Presidential Medal of Freedom, 152

price elasticity, addiction and, 44–45, 46

Price Theory (Friedman), 140

price theory course, vii, xv, 139–40, 143, 145

Price Theory Scholars program, 152

Price Theory Summer Camp, 152

Princeton Alumni Weekly, 153

Princeton University, 137, 148

principal-agent theory, xviii

Professional Achievement Award, University of Chicago Alumni Association, 143

"Promotion Tournaments, Power, Earnings, and Gambling" (Becker), 48–53

Provost's Teaching Award, University of Chicago, 151

public interventions, rethinking of, viii

public projects, redistribution and, 102–3, 112–14, 118

"Quantity and Quality of Life and the Evolution of World Inequality, The" (Becker, Philipson, and Soares), 151

racial discrimination, xi–xii, 5–6, 9, 138–39

Rajan, Raghuram G., 153

Rajk László College for Advanced Studies, 151

RAND Corporation, xxiv, 4, 55, 61, 91

rational indoctrination, xxii, 4

"Rational Indoctrination and Persuasion" (Becker), 32–42

Rawls, John, 95, 97

Reagan, Ronald, xix, xx

Reagan Revolution, xvi

redistribution, xxv–xxvii, 4, 92–93, 95–122, 124, 125

reenlistment rates, 56, 61–62, 67

regulation: Becker on, xx; Stigler on, xvii–xviii

religion, 24, 39, 40

resource allocation, 62

resource constraints, 11

retirement: consumption after, 71; savings for, 134–35. See also old age

"Roofs or Ceilings" (Friedman and Stigler), xvi, xvii

Rose-Marie and Jack R. Anderson Senior Fellow of the Hoover Institution, 147

Rosen, Sherwin, 49, 51, 55, 128, 141–43

Rotten Kid Theorem, xiii–xiv, 13

Rotten Parent Theorem, 13

Rousseau, Jean-Jacques, 97

Russell, Bertrand, 146

Ryan, Richard O., 151

Ryerson Lecture, 148

Samuelson, Paul, viii, ix, x, xv

Savage, Jimmie, 8, 138

scarcity of resources, 11

Schultz, T. W., 5, 8, 9, 55, 138, 141

Schwartz, Anna, xvi

Schwartz, Pedro S., 149

Scottish Enlightenment, xiv

Searle Freedom Trust, 152

segregation, xii

self-protection, 74, 76

Seminar on Rational Choice, 146

separation, divorce and, 130

Shapiro, Jesse, 152

Shapley, Lloyd, 138

Shavell, Steven, xviii

Shepard, Stephen B., 151

"Should the Military Pay for Training of Skilled Personnel?" (Becker), 56, 61–68

Shubik, Martin, 138

siblings, 29–30

skilled personnel, training for, 4, 56, 61–68

Smith, Adam, xiv–xv, xvii, 14, 131, 141, 152

Snyder, Edward (Ted), 145

Soares, Rodrigo, 151

Social Economics (Becker and Murphy), 150

socially costly redistribution, 104–15

social norms, 24–26

social pressure, 14, 43–44, 45, 46

Social Security, 4, 16, 25–26, 133

social welfare function, 97

Solow, Robert, 137, 141

"Some Notes on Drugs, Addiction, Families, and Public Policy" (Becker), 43–47

Sonnenschein, Hugo F., 148

Soviet Union, 38

Spence, Michael, ix

Spenkuch, Jörg L., 13

"Spirit of the University of Chicago, The" (Becker), 4, 8–10

Stagflation, xvi

state-dependent preferences, xxiv–xxv

State University of New York at Stony Brook, 147

statistical discrimination, ix
statistical value of life, 71
steady state inequality, 87
Stigler, George, vii–viii, xiv–xx, 2, 5, 9, 12, 143–44, 146, 149
Stiglitz, Joseph E., 93
Stinchcombe, Arthur L., 146

Taussig, Frank, xv
taxation: degree of democracy and, 109–11; excise, 95; income, 106, 124, 126; optimal, 93, 120–21, 123–26; redistribution and, 101, 104–5, 108–10, 114–15, 116–20
Thaler, Richard H., 153
"Theory of Economic Regulation, The" (Stigler), xvii
Theory of Moral Sentiments (Smith), 152
"Theory of Oligopoly, A" (Stigler), xvii
"Theory of Social Interactions, A" (Becker), 13
"Theory of the Allocation of Time, A" (Becker), 3, 56–58, 142
Theory of the Consumption Function, A (Friedman), xvi
Throsby, David, 150
time, xxiii–xxv, 56–58, 69–72, 142
totalitarian/dictatorial governments, 37, 38
tournament design, xxiii
trading cards, 148–49
training, on-the-job, 4, 56, 61–68
transferable training, 56, 66
transitivity, 97
Treatise on the Family, A (Becker), xiv, 127, 145–46, 148
"Trustbuster Who Saw the Light, A" (Becker), xvii

Uncommon Sense (Becker and Posner), 151
unemployment insurance, 25
unemployment rates, inflation and, xvi
University of Aix–Marseilles, 150

University of Athens, 150
University of Chicago, 138–39, 143, 146, 148, 150, 151, 153–54
University of Chicago Magazine, 148
University of Chicago Press, 143
University of Economics, Prague, 149
University of Illinois at Chicago, 147
University of Miami, 149
University of Michigan–Flint, 148–49
University of Palermo, Argentina, 148
University of Rochester, 149
upward mobility, xxv
USAF Training Prospectus, 64–65
utilitarianism, 93
utility: functions, xxii–xxiii, xxv–xxvii, 17, 19–20, 34, 39, 49–51, 73–75; indoctrination and, 34–37, 40
utility-maximizing approach, 11, 15, 17, 23, 85

value of life literature, 71
Veblen, Thorstein, xv
video gaming, 57
Viner, Jacob, xv, xviii, 138
voluntary army, 56, 91
voucher system, 7

wages, xxiii, xxvi. See also income inequality; redistribution
Wall Street Journal, 92
Walras's Law, xiii
"warmth" of families, 22
Warsaw School of Economics, 149
Wealth of Nations, The (Smith), 14
Welch, Finis, 55
welfare: immigration and, xx; wages and, xxvi
welfare state, 25–26, 125, 134
welfare theorems, viii
Western Economic Association, 149
"What Happens Inside Families?" (Becker), 12
"What's Happened to the Welfare State?" (Becker), 148
"Why Marijuana Should be Decriminalized" (Becker), 14

Wirszup, Izaak, 143
Wolfers, Justin, 155
women: birth rates and, 130; division
    of labor and, 77–78, 131; education
    and, 84; labor force participation
    and, 130; role of, 132–33

Wong, Richard, 9
Woodward Court Lecture, 143
Woytinsky Prize, 141
Wright, Sewall, 9

Zimmer, Robert J., 153, 154